Riders In The Sky

It's the Cowboy Way!

It's the Cowboy Way!

The Amazing True Adventures of

Riders In The Sky

DON CUSIC

THE UNIVERSITY PRESS OF KENTUCKY

Publication of this volume was made possible in part by
a grant from the National Endowment for the Humanities.

Scholarly publisher for the Commonwealth,
serving Bellarmine University, Berea College, Centre
College of Kentucky, Eastern Kentucky University,
The Filson Historical Society, Georgetown College,
Kentucky Historical Society, Kentucky State University,
Morehead State University, Murray State University,
Northern Kentucky University, Transylvania University,
University of Kentucky, University of Louisville,
and Western Kentucky University.
All rights reserved.

Editorial and Sales Offices: The University Press of Kentucky
663 South Limestone Street, Lexington, Kentucky 40508-4008
www.kentuckypress.com

The Library of Congress has cataloged the hardcover edition as follows:

Cusic, Don.
    It's the cowboy way! : the amazing true adventures of Riders In
The Sky / Don Cusic.
        p.   cm.
    Discography: p.
    ISBN 0-8131-2284-8 (hardcover : acid-free paper)
    1. Riders In The Sky. 2. Country musicians—United States—
Biography. I. Title.
    ML421.R5C87   2003
    781.642'092'2—dc21   2003007974
ISBN-13: 978-0-8131-2974-7 (pbk. : alk. paper)

 Member of the Association of
American University Presses
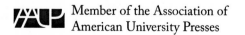

Contents

Introduction

Riders In The Sky are not superstars in country music—they've never had a gold or platinum album, never had a hit record on the radio, and never headlined a major arena tour. Yet this group is more influential than most of those with the above-mentioned achievements. Indeed, Riders In The Sky may be one of the most influential groups in the history of country music in the twentieth century.

Before the Riders were formed at the end of 1977, western music was basically dead. The Sons of the Pioneers, formed in 1932 and the guiding light and inspiration for the Riders, were still performing, but the audiences were limited. By 1977, the Sons of the Pioneers did not have a major-label recording contract and were viewed more as a nostalgia act than a current, vibrant part of the music industry.

Seminal figures in western music such as Bob Nolan, Eddie Dean, Jimmy Wakely, and Ray Whitley were living in retirement or semiretirement in California, all but forgotten. Some of the early performers—like Johnny Bond, Tex Ritter, Tim Spencer, and Lloyd Perryman—had passed away. Roy Rogers and Dale Evans were still somewhat active in the entertainment field, but Gene Autry was more involved in running a baseball team and his business empire than in being a singing cowboy.

Westerns were nearly gone from television and the movies, and the singing cowboys had been long gone for more than twenty years. There were no western festivals featuring western music, no circuit for a performer to tour, and no recognition for western music from any trade organizations. A tiny spark of western music was kept alive by the chuckwagon groups and dude ranches, who invited guests for a few days or a week or so and, during the visit, might serenade them with some western songs by a campfire.

In country music it was the period of the "outlaw"—Waylon, Willie, and the boys—whose idea of being a cowboy was that of a fiercely independent cuss doing as he pleased. There were some songs that mentioned cowboys—the most famous being "Mamas, Don't Let Your Babies Grow up to Be Cowboys" by Waylon and Willie—and Rex Allen Jr. had attempted to revive some interest in western music with recordings like "Can You Hear Those Pioneers?" but didn't make much of a mark.

The members of Riders In The Sky seemed like an unlikely source to lead a revival of western music; the three original members, Douglas Green, Fred LaBour, and Bill Collins, grew up in Michigan—far from the cactus and sage of the West. Two newer members, Woody Paul and Tommy Goldsmith, grew up in Tennessee and North Carolina, and the three core members who became Riders In The Sky were steeped heavily in folk, bluegrass, and old-time country music. Their newest member, Joey Miskulin, grew up in Chicago saturated with polka music and jazz. If you were going to bet on who would lead the revival of western music in America, it's doubtful you would have laid your money down on these guys.

And yet the convert is the strongest believer. Douglas Green came out of bluegrass to love and cherish western music with a passion. Fred LaBour, who had been only vaguely aware of the Sons of the Pioneers before he moved to Nashville, first heard a Bob Nolan song when Douglas Green performed it. Woody Paul was a fiddler whose musical tastes ran off in a number of directions—none of them toward western music—and was getting a Ph.D. in Physics while Green and LaBour were first absorbing western music. Joey Miskulin hadn't even heard of Riders In The Sky before he moved to Nashville.

You can be western by birth, by location, or by choice. Riders In The Sky weren't born in the West, have never lived in the West, but are western by choice. They might not be authentic westerners, but they are certainly authentic entertainers. They have taken the West and dressed it up in colorful costumes, put it on stage, and sung songs by, about, and for it. More than any other group in the past twenty-five years, their name has become synonymous with western music.

Pioneers don't necessarily travel by covered wagon; sometimes they travel in an old bus with some beds built in the back. Some pioneers carry muskets and gunpowder; other pioneers carry musical instruments. The story of Riders In The Sky is the story of a group of pioneers who have crossed this country a number of times as soldiers of song. Their mission is to entertain every audience with western music and offbeat humor. At the end of twenty-five years, a report from the front lines sends the message, "Mission accomplished."

This book is the story of the pioneers know as Riders In The Sky. A book could never be as entertaining as a Riders show, but hopefully this one sheds a little light on how some latter-day pioneers have brought a whole civilization of western music to the musical plains of America.

Chapter 1

There really was nothing like them when they started. The men who later became known as Riders In The Sky—but were introduced on their first night playing together simply as Doug, Fred, and Bill—had an act that was completely different from anything else that was performing nationally at the time.

Many musicians claim their music is "different than anything you've ever heard before." That's rarely true, and even if it is, it generally isn't marketable. People need a point of reference, and the totally new and unknown takes some getting used to. The key to the success of Riders In The Sky is that their music had been heard before—but it was many, many years before.

The Riders are part of the Baby Boom generation—Douglas Green was born in 1946, Fred LaBour in 1948, and Woody Paul and Joey Miskulin in 1949. This generation was too young to know the movies of Gene Autry and Roy Rogers in their heyday, but it grew up when cowboys were still popular. The recordings of Autry and Rogers weren't on the radio, but they could be heard on television. Every week you could hear Roy and Dale sing "Happy Trails," and every Christmas you were sure to hear Autry singing "Rudolph the Red-Nosed Reindeer."

The Baby Boomers are a generation that discarded the past and celebrated their youth. Their guiding beacon was the inauguration speech of President John Kennedy in January 1961—a year when the first Baby Boomers were turning fifteen. This speech, whose most famous phrase is "Ask not what your country can do for you but what you can do for your country," rang with the theme of discarding the past and turning toward youth. It was directed at closing the curtain on the Eisenhower administration, but it was a clarion call to the new youthful generation. It said that even though they were young, they mattered. It was time to discard the old in favor of the new, a time for fresh faces and fresh ideas to populate the "New Frontier."

Early Baby Boomers lived in a period of transition. The members of this generation spent their childhood in front of a TV instead of a radio. In 1956 they saw Elvis and rock 'n' roll render the music of their parents' generation obsolete and irrelevant almost overnight. It was a generation of young boys who got cowboy hats and pistol sets for Christmas and rode stick horses through their suburban neighborhoods.

Television caught on in America in the 1950s and replaced radio as the dominant mass medium. The period between 1955 and 1963—when the oldest Baby Boomers were between the ages of nine and seventeen—was the era of the TV western. Prior to 1955, several shows were on the networks—*The Lone Ranger* and *Hopalong Cassidy* debuted in 1948, *The Gene Autry Show* in 1951, *Sky King* in 1953, and *The Adventures of Rin Tin Tin* in 1954. But in 1955 TV westerns really blossomed with the addition of *Gunsmoke* and *The Life and Legend of Wyatt Earp*. In 1956, *Broken Arrow, The Adventures of Jim Bowie, My Friend Flicka,* and *Dick Powell's Zane Grey Theater* were added.

But the heyday for network television westerns in prime time began in the 1957–58 season. During that season, the overall TV ratings showed *Gunsmoke* at number one, *Tales of Wells Fargo* at three, *Have Gun, Will Travel* at four, *The Life and Legend of Wyatt Earp* at six, *The Restless Gun* at eight, *Cheyenne* at twelve, *Dick Powell's Zane Grey Theater* at twenty-one, and *Wagon Train* and *Sugarfoot* tied at number twenty-three.

During this season, *Maverick* was on Sunday nights; *Restless Gun* and *Tales of Wells Fargo* on Mondays; *Cheyenne/Sugarfoot* (they alternated), *The Life and Legend of Wyatt Earp, Broken Arrow,* and *The Californian* on Tuesday nights. On Wednesdays there were *Wagon Train* and *Tombstone Territory; Zorro* and *Sergeant Preston of the Yukon* were on Thursdays; on Friday nights there were *The Adventures of Rin Tin Tin, Adventures of Jim Bowie, Colt .45* and *Dick Powell's Zane Grey Theater*. Finishing the week on Saturday nights was *Have Gun, Will Travel,* followed by *Gunsmoke*.

The success of television westerns continued during the 1958 season, when there was a veritable feast of westerns on the tube: *Maverick, The Lawman, Colt .45, Northwest Passage* (a western in terms of the Revolutionary War), *The Texan, Restless Gun, Tales of Wells Fargo, Cheyenne/Sugarfoot, Wyatt Earp, The Rifleman, The Californians, Wagon Train, Bat Masterson, Zorro, Rough Riders, Yancy*

Derringer, Dick Powell's Zane Grey Theater, The Adventures of Rin Tin Tin, Buckskin, Wanted: Dead or Alive, Cimarron City, Have Gun, Will Travel, and *Gunsmoke.*

During the 1960–61 season and the 1961–62 season, western shows took the top three spots in the overall ratings: *Gunsmoke, Wagon Train,* and *Have Gun, Will Travel* in 1960–61 and *Wagon Train, Bonanza,* and *Rawhide* in 1961–62. The 1962–63 season marked the end of the heyday for the TV western, although one western, *Bonanza,* would consistently be rated at number one or in the top ten throughout the 1960s.

In addition to the network shows during the 1955–63 period, there were syndicated western shows such as *The Cisco Kid, Annie Oakley, Tales of the Texas Rangers, The Sheriff of Cochise, The Range Rider, Buffalo Bill Jr., The Adventures of Champion, Pony Express, Union Pacific,* and *Brave Eagle.*

A key to understanding the influence TV westerns had on the young Baby Boomers growing up in that era is to look at what appeared on Saturday morning TV. This list includes *Acrobat Ranch, Adventures of Champion, Adventures of Kit Carson, Rin Tin Tin, Annie Oakley, Broken Arrow, Buffalo Bill Jr., The Cisco Kid, Cowboy Theater* (old western movies), *Fury, The Gene Autry Show, Howdy-Doody, Hopalong Cassidy, Junior Rodeo, Lash of the West, The Lone Ranger, Red Ryder, The Rough Riders, The Roy Rogers Show, Sergeant Preston of the Yukon, Steve Donovan, Western Ranger, Tales of the Texas Rangers, Tim McCoy, Wild Bill Hickok,* and *Yancy Derringer.*

Additionally, in almost every major market there was a local "kiddie" show that featured a cowboy "star." These shows generally had a live audience of kids and a host, dressed as a cowboy, who usually sang some western songs. Some of these include Buck Barry in Grand Rapids, Michigan; Kenny Roberts in Michigan and Ohio; Bob Atcher in Chicago; Sheriff John in Los Angeles; Fred Kirby in Charlotte, North Carolina; and Pick Temple in the Washington, D.C., area. And, of course, Buffalo Bob starred on the nationally televised *Howdy Doody* show.

In the 1930s and 1940s, kids went to the theaters on Saturdays to watch a series of movies: serials, features, and "B" movies. In the 1950s kids watched television. The westerns were not the only shows on television—there were action/adventure shows as well—but the Saturday morning TV fare was actually an extension of the Saturday movie-watching habit for most Americans. The westerns that attracted these young viewers were escapist fare, so the westerns that emerged were filled with clear delineations of good versus bad guys, lots of action (horse chases, fights, and shooting), little realistic violence, and handsome (or pretty) stars who looked like heroes. In short, the Saturday morning western (indeed, the TV western of the 1955–63 period) was about heroes and role models—or, in terms of Hollywood, stars. And such stars as the Lone Ranger, Gene Autry, Wild Bill Hickok, Palladin, Red Ryder, Roy Rogers, Fury, and Rin Tin Tin became heroes to these young children.

When the shows were over, the kids went out into their yards and played "Cowboys and Indians" dressed up in their cowboy outfits, and at night they dreamed of being a hero in cowboy clothes, fighting the good fight, doing the right thing, righting wrongs—all while wearing a white cowboy hat.

The "singing-cowboy" movies ended in 1954 when Republic Pictures, the major producer of singing-cowboy movies, released *The Phantom Stallion* starring Rex Allen. Gene Autry's movie westerns lasted until 1953, and Roy Rogers lasted on the big screen until 1952. After these, the movies increasingly appealed to an adult audience, whereas TV westerns catered to children.

The 1958–62 period is characterized as a time of "realism" in westerns, when the glamor and heroes of the Old West were discarded for gritty antiheroes. Sex and violence were increasingly prevalent in westerns as the mythological Old West of the 1930s and 1940s lost its appeal and was replaced by a West in which heroes and civilization weren't what they seemed on the surface.

The years 1963–67 saw the West lose even more of its luster as the antihero became the dominant character. On television, the 1963–70 period saw a handful of westerns dominate the genre, specifically *Bonanza, Gunsmoke, The Virginian,* and *Rawhide.* But the 1967–68 season was the last one in which viewers could watch a TV western on the networks during prime time almost every night of the week.

By this time, the Baby Boomers had moved on to a counterculture. The singing cowboys and songs like "Happy Trails" gave way to "Eve of Destruction" and "Blowin' in the Wind" and to songs by the Beatles, Jimi Hendrix, the Doors, and the Rolling

Stones. This generation put away their Roy Rogers lunch boxes, double-holster sets, and cowboy hats and buried those memories in the past. Watching cowboy shows on TV every night was a distant memory. They forgot about how important and influential the local TV singing-cowboy kiddie shows had been in their lives.

Until Riders In The Sky came along.

Chapter 2

In the mid-1970s, "and western" was long gone from "country" music. Those who used the term sent a signal, a code-word that the user wasn't in the know. The term was considered outdated and out of the loop; there was no "western" in country music. The proper term was *country*, and the top artist, Kenny Rogers, presented an urbane, hip image. No cowboy boots on that singer!

Actually, there was a cowboy resurgence of sorts through the "outlaw" movement of Waylon Jennings and Willie Nelson. It was really a back-to-Texas movement in country music, but at least it made wearing cowboy hats and boots a little more acceptable. In 1978 they had their hit, "Mamas, Don't Let Your Babies Grow up to Be Cowboys," which put the word *cowboy* firmly back into American country music.

Still, it was a redefined cowboy—not western so much as an independent, freedom-loving cuss who could live anywhere and do as he pleased. The cowboy of the 1970s in Nashville was a free-thinker, an individualist, a contemporary post-hippie, post-redneck man-of-the-world dressed in cowboy clothes. He wore a black hat.

Meanwhile, in the basement of the Country Music Hall of Fame, Douglas Green was working as a researcher, collecting oral histories for their archives. He was the author of a widely respected book, *Country Roots;* an editor of an *Encyclopedia of Country Music;* and a writer of numerous articles in scholarly and consumer publications. He was also, in his heart of hearts, a musician who loved to play.

Green had been playing music since he moved to Nashville in

1968. While a graduate student at Vanderbilt University and through his jobs at Gruhn Guitars and the Country Music Foundation, he had spent many evenings around town playing with groups or as a solo act. His tastes in music—and his choice of material to play—had been evolving. By 1977 Green found he preferred playing and singing "cowboy" or "western" music and increasingly performed songs such as "Back in the Saddle" when he played at local clubs.

Patty Hall was a folk singer, married to Bill Ivey, executive director at the Country Music Foundation, the parent organization that oversaw the Country Music Hall of Fame. Douglas worked for the foundation.

Previously, Patty had worked as an intern at the Country Music Hall of Fame. "Patty was scheduled to play at a small club in Nashville, Herr Harry's Phranks 'n' Steins, on a Monday night but came down sick," said Green. "And so she called me to help. I saw this as an opportunity to try out some cowboy tunes, so I called Fred LaBour and asked if he'd like to join me. Fred said that he didn't even own a cowboy hat, so I promised to supply one. He also asked if he could play the upright bass. And I said, '*Only* if you play the upright bass!'"

Fred was playing bass for Dickey Lee and suggested that Bill Collins, who played lead guitar in Dickey Lee's band, also be invited. And so the three got together for a brief rehearsal at Green's house.

If Riders In The Sky are the Beatles of Western Music, then Windy Bill Collins is their Pete Best. The connection between Bill and Douglas Green went back to their childhoods in Michigan.

Young Bill had met Jim "Jimsonweed" Green—Douglas's younger brother—back in the fourth grade in Birmingham, Michigan, and was nicknamed "Cool Kat" Collins by the Green brothers "because I wasn't," he confessed. The boys lived about a block apart, and since the Greens had a swimming pool, Bill said they were "excellent candidates for friends." "Doug became kind of a mentor," remembers Bill. "He exposed me to, among other things, my first glimpse of *Mad Magazine*." They also watched *The Twilight Zone* together every Friday night.

"Doug was the first kid I knew who was into music," said Bill. "And, of course, being Doug, he didn't do it in half-measures.

He was an actual card-carrying member of the Conway Twitty fan club. However, if Doug was carrying a torch for cowboys singers and their music at this time, he kept it to himself."

The Greens moved after the boys had been friends for about two years, and they gradually lost touch. Bill earned a degree in English from the University of Wisconsin, then moved to New York in hopes of becoming a rock star. When that didn't pan out, he moved to Northern California, then Colorado, trying to carve out a niche as a singer/songwriter. In 1972 he landed in Nashville.

Visiting George Gruhn's guitar shop (then called GTR), where Green worked behind the counter, Bill recognized Douglas's voice, introduced himself, and reestablished their friendship. Soon they were playing music together as well as playing together on a softball team.

Bill had joined Dickey Lee's band, unofficially known as the "Dickey Birds," in 1972. In 1976, when an opening for a bass player occurred, Bill called Fred LaBour, whom he had met through Douglas.

When they got together to rehearse for the Herr Harry's gig, "it was immediately apparent that Fred had called the wrong guy," remembers Bill. "At this point I will plant my flag in the historical mud of controversy and make my claim to fame: While it is certainly (and obviously) true that Riders In The Sky get along just fine ('flourish,' if you will) without me, if I had not been there when I was, there would be no Riders. I think I was the catalyst that allowed that certain chemical reaction. Here's a telling piece of evidence: Doug and Fred had played together many, many times and had, to my knowledge, never played cowboy song one."

While this fact is not 100 percent accurate, Bill does make an interesting point. Doug and Fred were known for playing bluegrass music, and "the bluegrass oeuvre is like jazz—it's a canon, a book," states Collins. "All the players know it, and I saw occasions when Doug put together a hybrid Riders/bluegrass band to play certain gigs. They'd shout out a title and then go off and running."

The problem was that Collins wasn't a bluegrasser and "didn't know that repertoire." "I may have known every Beatles song," said Collins, "but not much bluegrass past 'Uncle Pen.' So during that first rehearsal we searched for some common ground."

At least Douglas and Bill searched, while Fred "knew everything." "What finally came up was that we had all loved the Marty Robbins cowboy-phase songs—like 'El Paso,' 'Big Iron,' 'Runnin' Gun,' and '(Ghost) Riders in the Sky'—so we ended up doing a lot of those songs, mostly by default," recounts Collins. "And then we threw in a bunch of other high-profile western songs to make it seem like we meant to do it."

Then came the night—November 11, 1977—at Herr Harry's Phranks 'n' Steins. "We needed some ambience for the stage," said Fred. "So Doug brought along a saddle and a six-foot saguaro cactus." They didn't just do cowboy songs that night, although Green remembers they played "Back in the Saddle" and some Sons of the Pioneers numbers like "Tumbling Tumbleweeds" and "Cool Water." But Fred sang "Chattanoogie Shoeshine Boy," and Bill sang "Deep River Blues."

Bill remembers that "we spent most of the night sitting around big pitchers of Harry's excellent beer and recounting old *Twilight Zone* episodes to each other. Then when we did play, much hilarity ensued."

At the end of the night, Herr Harry and his wife had rung a big bell at the end of the bar a number of times, and the eight people in attendance had managed to drink enough to enjoy themselves. And so Herr Harry gave the group twenty-five dollars for the evening. "Doug gave each of us eight dollars and then tore the last dollar into thirds," laughed Fred.

The evening was more than just music—there was a camaraderie on stage between the three—known as Deputy Doug, Windy Bill, and Fred for the evening. And the repartee between the three flew like sparks through the air, igniting snappy one-liners. The group took the music seriously but themselves lightly, joking with themselves and the audience while on stage. "We were on stage just trying to crack each other up," said Green. "We did a pretty good job of that," added Fred. "And the audience kept laughing too!"

In short, they had a blast.

The next morning Fred "woke up still laughing," he recalls, "and I called Doug and said, 'I don't know what happened back there, but America will pay to see it.'" The next night they performed western songs—as well as assorted other tunes—again at Herr Harry's Phranks 'n' Steins.

"We all had a good time," said Collins. "But it soon became apparent that Doug had a really good time, due to the fact that he did indeed love this cowboy stuff and had evidently been hankering to perform it his whole life. So he kind of charged ahead at this point, and I was more than glad to follow."

That was the official beginning of Riders In The Sky, although, like most "events," that beginning was also the end of a trail that Douglas Green and Fred LaBour had been traveling for a long time.

Ranger Doug's Story

My father is James Donald Green, who was a physician—general practitioner and then an internist—who was born in Detroit in 1921. My mother was the former Hilda Maria Peterson. She was a nurse when she met my father; after they married she stayed home and took care of the house and kids. Her family name was Moilanen, which is Finnish, but was Americanized to Peterson. She was born in Ishpeming, near Marquette in the upper peninsula of Michigan, in 1917. They were married in June 1945 in Detroit, and I was born about nine months later—on March 20, 1946—at the Great Lakes Naval Training Center in Lake County, Illinois.

We moved a lot. My dad was in the navy when I was born; after his release, he moved back to Michigan, which is where my brother and sister—Jim and Constance—were born. My dad set up a medical practice in Birmingham, a Detroit suburb. Since he didn't serve overseas in World War II, he was subject to overseas duty during the Korean War and was called back into active duty in the early fifties. We moved to Costa Mesa, California, where we stayed while he was overseas. One of my most vivid childhood memories is the day he came home after being away for a year.

After my dad was released from the navy, he returned to medical school for a year to specialize in internal medicine, so we moved to Boston around 1956. Around 1957 we returned to Michigan, and I spent my sixth grade through high school and college years there. My dad had a very successful medical practice in Birmingham and later Bloomfield Hills. We lived in three different houses during those years, but all within a five-mile radius.

My father could play piano decently, but it was mostly as a physical and intellectual exercise. My mother had the musical "soul" of the family and was always singing and humming around the house. She and her older half-brother, Arvid, and brother, Henry, apparently sang a great deal as kids, profoundly influenced by the music on the *National Barn Dance* out of Chicago. They sang folk songs like "The Spanish Cavalier" and country songs like "Worried Mind" and "Have I Told You Lately That I Love You?" Hank and Arvid both played guitar—in fact, one of my great treasures is the guitar that hung for years at "the camp," a small summer cabin on a lake in northern Michigan. It's the guitar both of my uncles played and the first guitar I ever played. Hank gave it to me a few years back. Reportedly, Arvid could yodel, although I don't remember him doing it, despite many fond memories of him.

My mother loved those old songs but at the same time was a little embarrassed by them. She played a lot of classical music on the radio and on records to make up for it, I guess. The radio was often on, and I remember hearing a lot of the popular songs of the early 1950s: "Blue Tango," "Victory at Sea," "Be My Love," "Love is a Many Splendored Thing," and a few musicals, most notably *South Pacific.* Dad, who was a natural mimic and famous for being a jokester, loved comedy albums, and we listened to a lot of Stanley Holloway, Bob Newhart, Shelley Berman, and, later, the Smothers Brothers. Early on it was Spike Jones, and I remember rolling on the floor, laughing, with my brother, Jim.

My dad could sing in tune but rarely did so except when delivering a couple of lines of parody. He could whistle quite well, though. The only line I remember him singing was "And the winner is Feedlebomb!" My mother had a beautiful voice and liked to sing a capella around the house, but was very shy about it. She sang a lot with her brothers when she was young, but as far as I know, they never made any money at it. It was just a way for youngsters to pass the time during the Depression. Although Arvid and Hank were both capable guitarists, she never learned to play.

My parents urged me to play, but I was a washout with piano lessons in California. In Boston our next-door neighbor had an old violin, which a relative had brought over to America around the turn of the century. She offered to give it to me if I'd take lessons—which I did—but that was another washout. I just hated to practice. Like every other kid, I wanted to play ball and read comics and go swimming and goof around with my brother instead. I've wished a thousand times since then that I'd learned to play that fiddle when I was a kid. But it never occurred to me to play notes off the written page on it.

My real interest in playing music occurred when we were visiting my mom's relatives in Ishpeming shortly after moving back from Massachusetts. At our summer cabin, I hauled that old guitar—a 1937 Montgomery Ward—off the wall and began banging on it, although it was missing some strings. I harangued my mother to drive into Ishpeming in our new 1958 Chevy convertible to get new strings—and the transmission blew on that trip. But I got the new strings, and once I got them on I realized I had no clue how to tune it. So I tuned it to an open chord by ear and just slid my finger up the neck to make the next chord. I spent hours with that thing and finally learned how to tune it. It was so liberating—I could play any dang note I wanted and didn't have to read it off a printed page. I could sing along with full chords— a whole band on one instrument. I'll never forget that enchanted summer I discovered the guitar.

Chapter 3

Douglas Green began playing bluegrass in high school. "A high school friend named Jim McQuaid played the banjo, and in our small school there were only a couple of guys who played guitar, so he insisted I learn to play bluegrass so he would have someone to back him up on guitar," remembers Green. By the time he entered Albion College, "I was a bluegrass maniac."

After two years at Albion, he transferred to the University of Michigan, where he played in a bluegrass group called The Big Sandy Boys. The leader of this group, Nolan Faulkner, introduced Green to the music of Bill Monroe. Douglas first saw Monroe perform at a bluegrass festival in 1966. "It was one of the two live performances which changed my life," said Green. "I was rocked by the incredible charisma and the power of Monroe's music."

As the president of the University of Michigan Folklore Society, Green arranged to book Monroe and his Bluegrass Boys for a society-sponsored concert, where he met Monroe for the first time. "In organizing the concert, I was in frequent touch with his office and his ex-wife, Carolyn, who booked him and ran the office," said Green. "So he knew who I was on April 30, 1967, when I drove down to his country music park in Bean Blossom, Indiana, with a couple of friends. Bill showed up without a guitar player and threw me on stage—I had my old Martin—and my audition was my first show. He took me on a three-week tour with him through the northwest and west while searching for a fulltime new Bluegrass Boy. The lure of the road was forever in my blood at that moment. Finally, he got Roland White to play full time, and I went back to my senior year in college a profoundly changed person.

"I don't really think I considered pursuing a career in music until I went on the road with Bill Monroe that summer," said Green. "A career in music seemed like an impossible fantasy. I didn't believe I had enough talent, for one thing, and I thought I was too shy. Plus, guys in my peer group did not become traveling singers. Doctors, lawyers, professors, executives—sure—but a singer? I might as well have thought I'd play third base for the Detroit Tigers. So I never gave it a thought, outside of a stray fantasy. But once I saw what it was like I loved it."

After graduating from the University of Michigan in the spring of 1968 and "having no particular direction except music in my life at that point," Green applied to the graduate schools at Indiana University "because of their great folklore program" and to Vanderbilt University in Nashville "because of its English department." Both accepted him, but he chose Nashville.

"I told my folks that I chose Vanderbilt for the hallowed English department, but my father saw right through it," said Green, who admits that it was the only respectable way he knew to get to Nashville and the music scene there. Green had married Mary Greenman while in college, and they would soon have a young daughter.

After he moved to Nashville, Green "played music every night with Roland White and other friends while I studied English and read books all day." For several months in 1969, he worked for Monroe again, playing bass for the Bluegrass Boys. That same year he also worked with Jimmy Martin's Sunny Mountain Boys. However, he quickly learned that "even with my wife working as a teacher, there was no way to live on that thirty-five dollars per show four or five times a month."

Since they had a second child on the way, Green began a series of jobs, starting as a historian at the Hermitage—the home of Andrew Jackson—then as an employee at Gruhn Guitars, selling vintage instruments. Still, he never quit playing.

"I was always dipping in and out of short-lived bands," he remembers, "playing everything from bluegrass to electric bass in country bands. I also played at Shakey's Pizza Parlor on Gallatin Road. I played guitar and banjo there, and it had the delightful effect of opening my ears to complicated chord changes in the vast popular repertoire. We played basically any popular song from 1920 to 1955, including 'Dixieland,' which I love. The piano player, Mac McWhirter, was a walking encyclopedia about the bands since the 1920s; and the trumpeter was Louis Brown, who was also a walking encyclopedia of popular music and for years had the most popular big band in Nashville. I was lucky enough to sing with that big band several times—pop standards like 'Prisoner of Love' and 'Among My Souvenirs.'

"My guitar playing had advanced at that point, thanks to listening to old records and to fake books. I was also helped along by two guitarists—David Sebring and Ron Hillis—so I could understand sophisticated chord changes and substitutions. While I never learned to play solos, I became passionate about the sound of the rhythm guitar and devoted myself to that muscular old-time rhythm style of Freddie Green (no relation), who played with Count Basie, and other big band guitarists."

Some of the other people and groups Green played with were Bobby Smith and the Boys from Shiloh, The Shinbone Alley All Stars, Ron Pruter, Guerry Matthews, Bob Breiske, Jim Smoak, Bobby Penn, Dana Dee, and Mickey Salter.

Green formed the Doug Green Band after recording two albums with the Buck White Family—now known as "The Whites." Fred LaBour was in the Doug Green Band, "but we only played about eight dates a year," said Green. Green also played a couple of dates with Woody Paul, then known as Paul Chrisman, backing him up on fiddle. He even put together a western trio a couple of times but couldn't find the right harmony singers for the sound he wanted. "Sometimes I made a little money and sometimes not," remembers Green about those early days.

Chapter 4

Douglas Green had known Bill Ivey since both were at the University of Michigan. Ivey taught guitar at the same little studio where Green had a job selling guitars. It was Green who told Ivey about the job opening of executive director of the Country Music Foundation, whose duties included running the Country Music Hall of Fame. Ivey, in graduate school at Indiana University's folklore program at the time, applied for the job and was hired.

In Nashville, tired and fed up with selling guitars at Gruhn's, Green quit that job but continued to do some freelance writing and played various smalltime gigs around town.

Ivey wanted to expand the staff at the foundation and wanted someone to do oral histories to preserve the heritage of early country music. Douglas Green fit the requirements of what he needed at the time, so Green took on the job of archivist, oral historian, and editor of the *Journal of Country Music* at the Country Music Foundation.

It was in his role as a historian, compiling oral histories by interviewing early country-music pioneers, that Green attended the second live performance that had a profound impact on him. In 1974 he was sent to Tulsa by the foundation to cover the first annual Western Swing Festival, organized by Guy Logsdon. After a long day of listening to western swing, the Sons of the Pioneers took the stage.

"Why they were booked on a western swing festival, I'll never know," remembers Green. "But I was blown away and sat slack-jawed as they sang all their standards." The Pioneers at that show consisted of Lloyd Perryman, Dale Warren, Rusty Richards, and Roy Lanham. After the show, Green met them backstage, "but I was so in awe I could barely think of much to say. However, Lloyd was very gracious."

When he went back to work at the Country Music Foundation, Green was "aflame with a desire to learn more" about western music. Bob Pinson, who also worked at the foundation and has an immense knowledge of early country music, western swing, and western music, helped Green in his musical education. "I dug out tons of Teleways transcriptions by the Pioneers," said Green. "Also some by Foy Willing and the Riders of the Purple Sage, who I liked—their harmony was like velvet, though I never felt they had quite the sound of the Pioneers. I learned like a sponge, both vocally and on guitar, and soon was singing oddball pieces like 'Song of the Bandit' and 'Song of the Prairie' with various bands and as a solo singing cowboy."

Douglas Green received an unofficial Ph.D. in western music during his time at the Country Music Foundation, helped immeasurably by Bob Pinson. "Bob was unbelievably generous with his knowledge and willingness to help," said Green. "And anybody who was the least bit interested in what he knew, he was happy to share. He wasn't one of those people into hiding information."

"Doug was moving towards the western music while I was moving away from it," remembers Pinson. "It was old hat to me, and I was getting interested in bluegrass—which was old hat to Doug." Pinson remembers that every afternoon they would pull out a recording from the archives—"the old-time disk of the day," as Green called it—and sit and listen to it. They often had lunch together as Douglas pumped Bob for information about western music. Since the Country Music Foundation archives hold a treasure trove of old recordings and Douglas Green was like a sponge soaking up their sounds and the knowledge about western music, he soon became a fledgling expert in western music.

That job at the Country Music Foundation was as important to the formation of Riders In The Sky as all the music Douglas Green had been playing up to that point. Not only did Green acquire an in-depth knowledge of western music and its history, he got to interview some of its pioneers, usually at western film festivals. These included Johnny Bond and Ray Whitley, who both "opened their homes to me," recalled Green. He also interviewed legendary producer Art Satherley, Jimmy Wakely, and Frankie Marvin, Gene Autry's longtime sideman.

Chapter 5

The river of western music has two main tributaries: the old folk or traditional songs of working cowboys and the songs written for the singing-cowboy movies. Many of the folk songs can be traced back to the latter half of the nineteenth century; the singing-cowboy movies began in the 1930s and by the early 1950s had run their course.

Examples of the folk songs are "Red River Valley," "Home on the Range," "I Ride an Old Paint," "The Streets of Laredo" (aka "The Dying Cowboy"), "When the Work's All Done This Fall," and "Old Chisholm Trail." Melodically, these songs can be traced back to British folks songs; lyrically, they dealt with the working cowboy of the West. Many of these songs came from poems in western magazines or from working cowboys; they were first collected and put into print by song collector Jack Tharpe and then, most significantly, John Lomax, whose book, *Cowboy Songs and Frontier Ballads*, is the first widely circulated work of cowboy and western songs.

These songs are musically simple—three or four major chords, perhaps a minor. They are easy to learn to play, and many beginning guitar players in the Baby Boom generation played these songs as they were learning guitar.

The songs for the singing-cowboy movies were written, for

the most part, by professional songwriters who had moved from Tin Pan Alley in New York to Tin Pan Alley West in Hollywood. Instead of writing for the Broadway stage, they wrote for the musical movies. Their songs were musically more complex and, melodically, reflected the pop songs of the era.

There was also an important difference in subject matter. Most of the western songs that came out of the movies—particularly those written by Bob Nolan—painted a picture of the beauty of the West, as opposed to telling a story about a working cowboy. If you compare the two types of songs to western art, the songs from groups like Sons of the Pioneers are like the huge paintings of Albert Bierstadt or Thomas Moran, showing a glorious, romantic view of the western landscape, while the working cowboy songs are like the paintings of Charlie Russell. Douglas Green was captured by the songs that painted the landscapes of the West; to him, there was a magic, a serenity, and an awesome beauty in those songs. In his heart, Douglas Green is a romantic; it is not surprising that the romance of the West roped him early and has kept him tied to the majesty of the West, rather than the dirt, grime, and sweat of the working cowboy.

A third, smaller tributary for western music is western swing, developed in Texas by band leaders like W. Lee O'Daniel, Milton Brown, and Bob Wills. During World War II, Wills moved to Southern California and, along with Spade Cooley, popularized a big-band sound that was western. It is music rooted in the jazz age, performed by musicians who generally had a rural or country background on folk instruments—fiddle, guitar, string bass— accompanied by brass and string sections. The songs are a mixture of big-band pop and jazz mixed with old-time fiddle tunes.

All of these musics came under the umbrella of what later became known as country music. But after World War II, this genre increasingly split into several different genres. Bluegrass stayed close to the sound of the string bands, which was the sound of the earliest recorded country music. Western swing died out with big bands in the 1950s, to be resurrected later in a jump band lineup. Western music also died out, although the look of country artists—wearing cowboy hats and boots—continued to reflect the western roots. However, except for some occasional songs with a western theme, western music was no longer a part of mainstream country music after the end of the singing-cowboy era in the early 1950s.

What survived as country music was a "countrypolitan" sound, which took the rough edges off of country and added orchestras and smooth-voiced singers to make it palatable to a middle-class audience. Country music, through the Country Music Association and Nashville Sound, made a conscious choice to be commercial and reach the widest number of people possible. It succeeded and became part of America's musical mainstream. But, in doing so, it left behind bluegrass, western swing, old-time string band, and western music.

The Riders reached back and resurrected this lost genre of western music.

Musically, the chief inspiration for the Riders is the Sons of the Pioneers, a group originally formed in the early 1930s by Bob Nolan, Tim Spencer, and Leonard Slye—later known as Roy Rogers. This group is known for their harmonies, and Nolan and Spencer are known for the songwriting. Nolan, in particular, was a major inspiration for Douglas Green as a western songwriter. Nolan wrote such western classics as "Cool Water," "Tumbling Tumbleweeds," and "When Payday Rolls Around," as well as numerous other songs that the Riders have recorded.

As the Sons of the Pioneers progressed, they added fiddler Hugh Farr and his brother, guitarist Karl Farr. The Sons of the Pioneers were successful recording artists as well as movie stars— they appeared in movies with Bing Crosby, Gene Autry, and Roy Rogers (who left the group in 1937). The group had a number of members through the years but always managed a distinctive sound. Although they did not record western songs exclusively, they maintained a western image in their dress, and their core repertoire—particularly "Cool Water" and "Tumbling Tumbleweeds"—was western.

The musical sound of the Sons of the Pioneers was comprised of a fiddle, rhythm guitar, and upright bass—the same lineup the Riders settled into. The fiddle featured a lot of jazzy breaks, and the guitar-playing featured a number of closed chords—as opposed to the open chord sound where the guitar "rings"—that provided a steady beat that drove the band. There were no drums—the bass and guitar provided the bottom for the band.

Many of the songs require jazz chords—sixths, minor sevenths, ninths—and the instrumental breaks in the songs are not simple "turnarounds"—a basic repeat of the melody line—but are musical phrases, take-offs of the basic melodies like jazz musicians (and western swing band members) played on their instrumental breaks.

Vocally the Pioneers sang in tight harmonies but did not sing with the usual lineup of a lead singer carrying the melody throughout a song and the harmony singers singing with him. Instead, group members stayed in their range, and the lead or melody line would switch between members. For example, if a song reached a higher note, the tenor would take the lead, then the baritone might pick up the melody when the melody moved back into his range. It is a difficult and demanding music to sing because the parts each member sings change within a song.

By reaching back musically at a time when Baby Boomers were reaching back in their lives, the Riders touched a mystic chord that resonated with their generation. This was a generation that had known the rock 'n' roll revolution firsthand, the British invasion, the turmoil of the 1960s—with Civil Rights and Vietnam—and then the 1970s crisis of Watergate and the resignation of a disgraced president. By the end of the 1970s, they were facing disco music—a music that required manic energy to dance amid strobe lights at a time when many of them just wanted to sit down, relax, and enjoy a good dose of nostalgia.

The 1950s weren't so boring anymore—they were a time of innocence and comfort. They were a time to remember the good guys in white hats in those old cowboy TV shows when the voices of the generation belonged to the Lone Ranger, Roy Rogers, and Gene Autry. But that nostalgia was tempered by the humor and music of the 1960s when the voices of the generation were Bob Dylan and the Beatles. It was an innocence intertwined with a cynicism, memories of childhood and a simple life that had grown up into a complex world. It was a naivete tempered with a hipness, both musically and in the humor that was used.

It was Riders In The Sky.

Too Slim's Story

My father's name was George LaBour Jr., and he was vice president in charge of sales for the Michigan Wheel Propeller Company, which made propellers in Grand Rapids. My mother's maiden name was Hazel Fredericka Gotch; my parents were married in Grand Rapids in 1932 or '33. I was born June 3, 1948, the fourth of four children, after a brother, Jeffy, and sisters Marcie and Chris.

We did not move during my years with the family—we were pretty stable in Grand Rapids. We lived in our house on the outskirts of town, where we had a couple of acres ourselves and about fifteen acres surrounding us that were swamp and woods. That's where I spent a large part of my time. My sister had horses, so we could ride down there.

My dad was a great gardener. It was like living in a natural park—it was a gorgeous place to grow up. It was a happy time for me. We had a swimming pool—one of the first swimming pools in Grand Rapids—orchards, grapes, every kind of vegetable. My mother was a wonderful flower gardener, and the place was really beautiful, a real showplace. It was a great house to grow up in. We lived in that house until I graduated from college, and then my mom sold the house and moved first to Montana and then out to Arizona.

There was always music in the house—we had a piano. We all took piano lessons from the nuns up at the convent, although we weren't Catholics. However, I was always wanting to play like Fats Domino, and the nuns were wanting me to play more like Chopin. So there was a problem. I remember hearing a lot of times, "Stop that pounding!" when I was trying to figure out "Blueberry Hill."

The music I heard around the house was the radio, which was omnipresent. I remember one of the first records that made an impression on me was "Somebody Bad Stole De Wedding Bell" by Eartha Kitt, which I used to go around singing when I was two or three. My family will tell you I was always singing, always cutting up. I was a class clown at an early age, always repeating what I heard on the radio around the house.

My parents took trips to New York and would buy the latest Broadway cast album, and we'd wear that out. I heard a lot of Broadway—*Guys and Dolls, Kismet, The King and I, The Sound of Music, The Music Man, Carousel, Oklahoma,* and *South Pacific.* We liked big-band stuff—my sisters had Glenn Miller, and I loved that stuff. Country music was odd for us to listen to, for people my age—nobody much listened to country. But I always loved that early fifties Nashville stuff and of course the Memphis stuff. Jerry Lee Lewis, Carl Perkins, and Johnny Cash were very important to me.

My sister Marcie had a lot to do with my early musical appreciation—she liked country-and-western music. Through Marcie, I started listening to country music and early rockabilly—the early Sun Records stuff on Johnny Cash. In terms of country music she was real important in that. I also learned to sing harmony with her. I remember driving along in her Willys jeep in about 1955, which would have made me seven, and trying to sing harmony with her to a Carl Smith or Faron Young record. I also heard a lot of Everly Brothers harmony coming from my sister Chris's bedroom. Ricky Nelson was big in our house; Elvis wasn't that big.

Music was not something you could do as a vocation—it was a hobby, part of being a well-rounded person, but you were not expected to make your living off of it. You were expected to go out and become a professional—a doctor or lawyer or something like that.

My dad loved the *Lawrence Welk Show,* but I thought it was the corniest thing on the face of the earth. Now I watch it and I love it. It tickles me because I just wish he were around to see me enjoy that show that I used to think was just the pits. We liked classical music and played it a lot. I heard the favorite performers of my parents' day—they liked Wayne King and Guy Lombardo, the sweet big-band stuff. If anything, "The Waltz You Saved for Me" would be "their" song. We liked Patti Page. My mother would bring home forty-fives from the supermarket when forty-fives started coming out—that was in '55, '56, and '57. She would bring home "O Mein Papa" by Eddie Fisher, "Blueberry Hill" by Fats

Domino, "Come On-a My House" by Rosemary Clooney. My dad
loved Teresa Brewer. We'd listen to Perry Como. We didn't listen
to Sinatra—I don't think they liked Sinatra very much. *The Ed
Sullivan Show* was a big thing.

My mother played piano, but she wasn't what you'd call a
great piano player. She was adept at playing Christmas carols,
and we'd gather around the piano and sing those at Christmas.
But I hardly remember her playing in those days. I think she had
her hands full raising four kids and keeping the house and yard
together.

Mom's singing was okay. I don't remember my dad singing
hardly at all. And they never performed professionally. But what
I got from my mom was a love of words. She was a poet and
wrote some fine poetry as a young woman. She went back to college after we'd grown up and got back into poetry, and she was
very well read—she and my dad were both very well read—and
she and my dad had a love of words and love and appreciation of
poetry, and she wrote some great stuff.

My first experience on stage that I remember was a bit part in
a class production—probably in the fifth grade. I had a part as a
butler in a little school drama, and I got this idea to come out as
Groucho Marx, so I went and got a cigar, got a mustache, got some
big glasses. No one knew I was going to do this, and the place just
erupted. I mean it was very zany, and I remember the applause
and the excitement I felt from doing something that really worked
on stage. I'm sure it was inappropriate in a drama, but it was my
idea and the idea surprised and delighted the audience. I was
kinda hooked at that point.

When I was a kid I was always selling something. Had a strawberry business, an egg route, greeting cards, donuts—everything.
The lady down the street used to see me coming up her driveway
and she'd yell, "I don't care what it is, I don't want it!" That was
the birth of Too Slim's Mercantile.

I played piano for about three years and got interested in the
guitar primarily through country music. Actually my first instrument was the ukulele, given to me by Mike DeVriendt. I used that
in school shows when I would go out and do impressions of Louis
Armstrong or Buck Barry the singing cowboy on local TV in Grand
Rapids. I bought a guitar from the girl down the street for thirty-

five dollars and played along with country records. And then the Beatles hit and I was entranced and thought, "I want to do that." So I bought an electric guitar. Borrowed the money from my mom and paid her back with three promissory notes and started making money playing.

There was a local band called the Kingtones that came to our junior high, and I vividly remember being up in the balcony and seeing these people, who were high school kids. I was just a little grade school kid. And I remember the guy saying, "Here's a song I wrote called 'The Grand Rapids Boogie,'" and I thought it was so cool that you could just stand up there and create your own music. That you could write something and do it. That was a real breakthrough moment for me. And I remember thinking, "Yeah, that's really cool! I'd like to do that someday."

The Beatles and the whole British Invasion made it very cool to play guitar and be in a band, and I was just swept up in the romance of it. The idea of being able to travel around with your friends and play music just seemed like the ultimate way to make a living. I remember telling one of my high school teachers, who asked me what I wanted to do, "Well, I'd like to travel around and play in bars." I was a naive lad. But it was just that romance aspect of it. The gypsy aspect of doing your art and getting paid for it, being on the road. I wanted to travel and see what was going on.

The first paying job I ever got was when my sister's high school friend, Mike DeVriendt, hired Rick Steketee and me to play our guitars and sing at one of their parties. I would've been in the ninth grade—thirteen or fourteen years old. We played, and they gave us each five bucks and a beer at the end of the night. Illegally, of course. But we thought that was cool. I could not believe I got money to do something that I loved doing so much, so that was a real breakthrough. After that we started a band called The Sneakers and started playing dances around Grand Rapids. It was a three-piece teenage rock 'n' roll band—a drummer and two guitarists. At that time, I didn't know what a bass was. Couldn't figure out what it did or whatever. We sang and did the rock 'n' roll hits of the day. Then we started booking dates and working every weekend on Friday, Saturday, and Sunday nights. We played at other schools as well as our school and teen clubs. We had suits that were all the same. I sort of managed the band and booked it, and we bought a sound system. We were making two hundred dollars a weekend, which was huge money in those days. We were living high and doing something we really wanted to do. Then my faith faltered—my parents suggested I concentrate more on college and treat music more as a hobby, and so consequently I did.

I went to the University of Michigan, where I received a degree in wildlife management. I was interested in the environment and ecology and thought it was a good way to save the earth. But I was out of sync with most of the other wildlife management majors there. They were into hunting and fishing, while I wanted to write poems about animals and birds and fish.

When I got out of college I thought I needed to find out if I could make a living performing, because I was going to do it anyway. I like to appear before people—I've always liked doing that. No matter how I've tried to deny it, at some point in the party I'd be up on the table with a lampshade on my head. I don't know what that gene is, but I've always liked being the center of attention, and I think that's essential to perform. You really need that "thing." I love to travel. Of course it was the girls, too—I wasn't a fantastic-looking guy, wasn't a great athlete, but I was funny. So that was sort of my niche. That was what I was good at, and the music was part of that. On class trips I always took the guitar—played all night long. Played the folk songs of the day—the Bob Dylan songbook, the Donovan songbook, the pop hits of the day that I could figure out on guitar. I played until people would say, "Please, please stop!"

Chapter 6

Douglas Green and Fred LaBour first met in the early 1970s when LaBour moved next door to Green on Wildwood Avenue in Nashville. "We shared a mutual love for softball and music," said Green. "It turned out that he'd been at the University of Michigan the same time I was there and even lived on the same street and ate at the same pizza parlor, but we never met there."

"I'd heard of Doug before I moved to Nashville but had never met him," remembers LaBour. "He was in the yard throwing the softball around, and I took my glove out and we started throwing the ball around. Started talking about the Detroit Tigers. Turned out he was a huge lifelong Tigers fan, like I was, and that he knew who number six was—Al Kaline. So I figured this guy was all right if he knew Al Kaline. He was playing bluegrass, and I was playing electric bass. I'd played in a country band in Ann Arbor when I got out of the University of Michigan—the same place Doug went to school.

"In college I started playing jazz with a group called the Continentals," continued LaBour. "That's when I first got an electric bass, and that led to me playing country music. Two friends of mine—Hershel Freeman and Lisa Silver—and I all moved to Nashville to play country music and write songs. In Nashville I discovered bluegrass music, which I'd really never heard before. The first bluegrass I played was in the Doug Green Band.

"So I was in Nashville trying to make a living playing bass," continued LaBour. "And one of my songs was recorded by Tammy Wynette. It was called 'The World's Most Broken Heart,' and I thought 'Boy, this is going to be easy.' That turned out to be the last song anybody recorded for a long time. I soon realized that I didn't want to be a Music Row songwriter—that was not me at all. I was looking for something a little different. So I played with Doug and then I played with the Larry Ballard Band—he was a country artist on Capitol—then I got a job with Dickey Lee, who had an oldies career with a song called 'Patches' and 'I Saw Linda Yesterday.' He'd also written the country classic, 'She Thinks I Still Care," which was a big hit for George Jones. Then Dickey got a whole modern country career with 'Never-ending Song of Love' and '9,999,999 Tears.' During the time I was playing with Dickey there was the gas crisis—this was '75 or '76—and petroleum prices shot up and power suddenly became an issue. And I thought, 'Boy, I'm going to have to unplug here if I want to make a living doing this. So if I get an acoustic bass, at least people will pay me in potatoes or chickens or whatever.' So the thing to do was get an acoustic bass."

The first time Fred ever saw a string bass was when he was in junior high and went to a high school show. "There was a local girl named Janice Hall who played the string bass in a trio," he said. "And I thought, 'That's really, really cool.' I was struck by the look of it, the sound of it. So I bought one from a guy named W.F. Crafton outside of Nashville—a Juzek bass—and started playing. I would emulate David Ball, who was with Uncle Walt's Band, and the bass player with Asleep at the Wheel. I also emulated Louis Vola, who was the bass player in the Hot Club of France.

"There was this loose association of acoustic musicians in Nashville who were all interested in swing and bluegrass, and we'd get together and play these shows," remembers Fred. "Doug had started showing up in a cowboy hat, and I remember him singing a tune called 'Song of the Prairie.' I was so struck by that song that after he finished I asked, 'Man, where did that song come from?' 'Cause I knew a lot of songs, but I'd never heard that one. And he said, 'That's a Bob Nolan song.' I said, 'Who?' He said 'Bob Nolan—he's the guy who wrote 'Tumbling Tumbleweeds' and 'Cool Water,' and he's one of the founders of the Sons of the Pioneers.' I said 'Man, those are such great changes and such great words,' and he said, 'Well, you know he wrote twelve hundred songs.' 'Really?' 'Yeah, there's a lot of really great ones.' I said 'Man, I'd like to hear some of that stuff.'

"I was aware of the Sons of the Pioneers back in high school," said Fred. "I recognized how beautiful and seamless the music was, but it was just part of the whole firmament of music I was hearing."

And then came the phone call that would lead to the formation of Riders In The Sky.

"Patty Hall had a gig with Herr Harry's Phranks 'n' Steins," Fred continues. "Doug called me up and said, 'Patty's canceled—she's sick. They need somebody to fill in this weekend—do you want to do it? We'll play old cowboy music.' And I said, 'Well, that's great—I can do that. Can I play the string bass?' 'Cause I wanted to make sure I could make a living on potatoes and chickens. And he said, 'Sure, that's what we need to have.' I said, 'Well I don't have a hat.' He said, 'I have a hat. I'll bring it.' And he brought me a fine, brown hat. Then I said, 'We'll get Bill Collins,' who Doug knew from the Detroit days, 'and he'll play guitar and we can have a trio to sing,' 'cause Collins was a good singer and guitar player who was working with me in Dickey Lee's band. So we went down and did the show, and we famously say there were eight drunks there. And there was a little bell at the end of the bar that Harry kept banging whenever we did something funny. From the very get-go we brought props, had a saddle. We got together and rehearsed one time, I think, over at Doug's house and probably practiced 'Tumbling Tumbleweeds.' 'Timber Trail' was one we tried to learn from the beginning. 'Back in the Saddle.' We could do 'Utah Carroll' and 'Strawberry Roan,' and then we fleshed it out with tunes like 'Chattanoogie Shoeshine Boy.' 'Deep River Blues' was one of Collins's numbers. And we had so much fun. There was practically nobody there—we were just playing for ourselves and for the sheer joy of doing it. I remember we made twenty-five bucks—we were working for the door—the first night. We split it three ways—eight dollars each, and we had a dollar left over, so we cut the dollar bill into three pieces and I carried that third with me for fifteen years. It finally disappeared—I think it finally wore into nothing. But that was the kind of all-for-one and one-for-all spirit that we had.

"That Tuesday morning I woke up in my house in Joelton, and I was still laughing—I just woke up with a smile on my face," continued Fred. "And I said to myself, 'I'm not sure what happened back there, but it was so much fun that I believe America will some day pay to see that.' So I called Doug and said, 'Let's do that again.' And he said, 'Great, let's try it.'"

The very next night they were back at Herr Harry's Phranks 'n' Steins again. About a month later—on December 16—they played at the Old Time Pickin' Parlor on Second Avenue for two nights. On January 13, 1978, they were back at the Old Time Pickin' Parlor, then played at Mississippi Whiskers on February 6 and 7. On February 20 they made their first television appearance on

Ralph Emery's morning TV show on WSM. That meant getting up at five-thirty in the morning.

That same day they played at the Knowles Senior Citizens Center. The group played for a dance every Thursday afternoon at one o'clock. "One time we were setting up," said Collins, "hadn't played a note yet. And someone came up and gave me a request: 'Please ask the band to turn it down!' I guess someone was intimidated by the size of our speakers—or more likely just the existence of our speakers!"

Collins also remembers what he called "Ranger Doug's Finest Hour." "There was some octogenarious woman who kept requesting 'San Antonio Rose,' because she had a beau she wanted to dance that song with," said Collins. "We delayed until the last set, and when we finally started to play it the woman came up and cried that her beau had left for his afternoon nap. So when we took an instrumental break, Doug put down his guitar, went over to this woman and swept her up, two-stepped her around the dance floor in a great circle route just in time to pick up his guitar at the end of the chorus and launch into singing the bridge again.

"It was an act of musical precision and gallantry that I've never seen equaled or even attempted," concluded Collins. "Ya gotta love a guy that will do that."

On March 28 they played the Exit/In, the premier listening club in Nashville; two days later they were back at the Pickin' Parlor, owned by Randy Wood, a friend of Green's.

In May they ventured outside Nashville, playing at Greenbrier Elementary School—where Douglas's ex-wife, Mary, worked as a teacher—then for the Bluegrass Manufacturing Company in Clarksville, then at Pinewood Elementary School in Fairview. It was fun as the guys developed their personas and their act. But it was tough going—the paying gigs were few and far between.

At least they had a name by this time. In December 1977, when they played at the Pickin' Parlor, they were billed as "Riders In The Sky."

"I had a pile of Sons of the Pioneers records that Doug gave me," said Fred. "We had started to learn the catechism of western music. These songs were hitting a deeper and deeper bell for me, because I was remembering trips to dude ranches when I was little and songs that my sister would sing. And I looked down and saw the Sons of the Pioneers record *Riders in the Sky*, the one that's tooled in leather, and it just jumped out at me that this is the name of the band. So I called Doug immediately and said, 'This is it, Riders In The Sky.' And he said, 'Why didn't I think of that?' So from about the third or fourth show, we were Riders In The Sky. We'd carry a big cactus with us—Doug had a live saguaro that weighed about 150 pounds in a big pot. We'd wrap it up in a sleeping bag and take it down to the shows. We always had a campfire, and we always tried to dress the part. Comedy was always a big part of the show."

"This was a very creative period for us," remembers Collins. "Doug was bringing in some great songs from groups like the Sons of the Pioneers that were quite challenging musically—at least for me and my rock 'n' roll roots. This was jazz for all intents and purposes. It had sophisticated chord progressions and harmonies. I remember having to learn to sing the sixth, above Fred and Doug. I'd know where my vocal note was on the guitar and have to quickly leap to it—'plink' it on the guitar—and get it in my ear just before the singing started.

"This is when we learned great songs like 'Timber Trail' and 'Blue Shadows on the Trail,' continued Collins. "I had this bit I used to do when I heard what I considered to be poorly played music—I'd throw back my head and howl. Well, this evolved into us doing a sequential, harmonized howl to kick off a song. Also Doug would bring in a lyric for us to learn, but part of it would just say 'yodel.' Well, you don't just 'yodel.' So Doug realized he had to start annotating the actual syllabary of the various yodels. We had to learn them phonetically—"whee—oo-wheedle—ee-dee-O—ee-O—ee—aay." And then we started yodeling in harmony, which was a whole 'nother trip! Doug would recreate his part over and over again, and having perfect pitch like he does, he made it easy for Fred and me to add a third and fifth above, or maybe a third above and a fifth below."

"I guess it all came together at the Old Time Pickin' Parlor on Second Avenue," said Collins. "We got a gig opening for Linda Hargrove, and knowing the layout of the room with that big, old staircase descending right next to the stage, we began to fantasize what it might be like to put together a little skit to intro our set. By the time we were finished it involved a fake fire, two complete saddles, and the big cactus. We would be introduced while we were at the top of the stairway—Doug and I would have a guitar in one hand and a saddle—a real, heavy western saddle—thrown over our shoulder—while Fred would have his bass. We'd come down the stairs and start a dialogue wherein we were trail cowboys looking for a place to camp. We'd decide on the spot at center stage, where we had previously left our 'campfire' composed of crumpled-up colored cellophane gels piled around a naked lightbulb. While Doug 'lit' the fire and blew on it, Fred would sneak around back of our amp and plug in the bulb. When the bulb lit up it was our first big laugh. What a rush. One time Doug blew and blew and Fred whispered that it was plugged in. Then Doug figured out he had to reach into the 'campfire' and flip the switch on the bulb socket. That was another laugh."

Chapter 7

The group continued playing through the summer of 1978, playing dates in and around Nashville. On March 30 and 31 they played the Old Time Pickin' Parlor; they played again on August 15. At one of these dates a fourth member of the group, Woody Paul, invited himself to join. At this point the group still consisted of Douglas Green, Fred LaBour, and Bill Collins.

Green had first met Woody Paul while both were at Vanderbilt—Woody as an undergraduate and Douglas as a graduate student. "I remember seeing him play," said Green. "And he was playing a Stella guitar. I was a bluegrass musician at the time, and bluegrass musicians are pretty snobby about their instruments—so playing a Stella didn't make a good impression. He was always considered quite an eccentric."

Later, after Woody had moved back to Nashville in early 1976, the two played together at various clubs around town in thrown-together groups for the evening.

Fred first met Woody in March 1976, shortly after Woody had returned from Boston. "I met Woody in the audition line at Opryland, a theme park," said LaBour. "We were both auditioning for a job in the pit band, and he was next to me in line. I'd

heard about him—people said, 'There's this guy who just graduated from M.I.T., and he's coming back to play fiddle, and you
two need to get to know each other.' Turns out we bumped into
each other in line. My audition piece was 'Dark Hollow.' I got up
and sang, 'I'd rather be in some dark hollow . . .' and played the
string bass, just by myself. I did not get the job—they were not
looking for what I could do. And Woody didn't get the job either.
But the next day he went off on tour with Loggins and Messina,
and I went back to severe unemployment."

There are three different versions of how Woody came to join
the Riders. In Woody's version, the Riders were playing at the
Pickin' Parlor. "I remember hearing them sing and play, and they
were way out of tune," he said. "I don't know why I had the idea
they were out of tune because I still can't play in tune. Don't know
when I am or not. But Willie Collins was playing the guitar with
'em, and they just sounded really bad. And after we started playing together we had a hard time staying in tune until we got a
tuner. Everybody was just starting to use tuners back then. The
first time I remember seeing a tuner, Marshall Chapman and I
were doing some demos for Harold Bradley out at the Barn, and
Harold had an electric tuner, and I thought that was the coolest
thing. He was on the road at the time playing with Danny Davis
or somebody, and he was still complaining about everybody not
being in tune."

As for the Sons of the Pioneers tradition the Riders were following at the time, Woody said, "I really didn't like that stuff. I
liked Roy Rogers movies and TV shows and stuff."

According to Fred LaBour, "Woody showed up one night while
we were playing. He listened to us and then came up to us afterward and said, 'You know, I believe I could do you boys a lot of
good.' He was playing at the Opry with Wilma Lee Cooper at the
time, and he said, 'I want to play you some songs I've written.' So
he sat down and played 'Blue Bonnet Lady' for us, which is a fine
cowboy western swing tune, and then he played 'The Cowboy
Song' and he talked about how he missed the white-hatted western heroes. Waylon and Willie and the black-hatted outlaw image
was what was sort of going on in Nashville at the time, and that
was not us. And there was not a place for us in that, and we
thought, 'Where are the Roy Rogerses? The Tex Ritters and Gene

Autrys—where are those guys that we loved when we were kids?' We were doing this music, and it was such an interesting and complex music. And you know how it is when you start looking at the music of the Pioneers—Bob Nolan and Foy Willing and Andy Parker—the deeper in the deeper it gets. And the sweeter. And you realize how complex the music is to play and how challenging it is to play and how much fun it is to play."

Finally, according to Green, "In his suave and tasteful way Woody approached us after a show and announced that we needed him in the group."

Just before Woody joined, Bill Collins quit the group. He had to choose between the Riders and Dickey Lee, and he chose the regular paycheck over starvation. Fred decided to remain with the Riders.

"I hated to leave the Riders, but it was strictly a financial decision," remembers Collins. "Doug and Fred wanted to do the cowboy thing full time, and I'm sure Doug was frustrated having to work around Dickey Lee's schedule. I had just gotten married and taken on two stepchildren and was going to buy a house. Doug and Fred had other jobs—Doug at the Hall of Fame and Fred as a puppeteer at the library. I only had music to pay my bills, and Dickey Lee paid a retainer. Even if he didn't work for a month, I knew I would have enough to make my new house payment of $286.18.

"Leaving was one of the first adult decisions I ever had to make," continued Collins. "And it broke my heart. If I'd been single I never would have considered leaving. I liked the music okay, but I considered Fred and Doug to be two of the best friends I've ever had. I think the last gig I played with them was some benefit for a school that Buddy Spicher set up."

"We needed another person, and so we put out the word," said Fred. "We auditioned a bunch of people who came over and sang with us and played with us—guitar players and fiddlers. In Nashville there are a lot of good players—it wasn't a hard problem finding somebody who could play great. It was a problem finding someone with the voice and the temperament to fit in. We got Tommy Goldsmith, who I had known and Doug had known from earlier days in Nashville. He was a fine songwriter and guitar player and a distinctive vocalist, just an all-around terrific musician and a good guy. So he became the guitar player."

Tommy Goldsmith had moved to Nashville in 1971, when he was nineteen, after a brief stint at the University of North Carolina. He moved to town with another musician, Steve Runkle, and they played in various bands. Goldsmith met Douglas Green the first year he was in town; Green was working at Gruhn's Guitars—then called GTR—and was playing bluegrass with Buck White and other bluegrassers.

Tommy soon moved to Austin, Texas, where he played with Alvin Crow, then Marcia Ball. After two years in Austin, he moved back to Nashville, where he reconnected with Green. "There was a small circle of people who did what we did—play acoustic music—so we all knew each other and played with each other," remembered Tommy. He remembers that he, Steve Runkle, and Green worked up "Tumbling Tumbleweeds" and played it several times in some small clubs.

Tommy was with a band called The Contenders, comprised of himself, Walter Hyatt, Steve Runkle, Champ Hood, and Jimbeau Walsh, which broke up in 1976. "We had tried to launch something commercially from Nashville, and it fell apart," said Tommy. "So it was quite heavy on me psychically." Hyatt, Hood, and David Ball also played in a group called Uncle Walt's Band, both before and after the break-up.

"Doug had called me a couple of times when the Riders were performing," said Tommy. "He invited me to come see them play. I think I had also transcribed some interview tapes for him at the foundation. Anyway, I went over to his house—he was living on Harvard Avenue—and the first time we practiced it was just him and me. The next time Fred and Woody were there. I'd known Woody as Woody Chrisman—he was a friend of Champ Hood. He was known as a very interesting, but unusual, different kind of guy. The four of us played together, and it really sounded good. So we put together a show.

"The Riders are very challenging musically," continued Tommy. "Nonmusicians don't understand how sophisticated the Riders are musically. It's really great stuff. Woody Paul was playing some Charlie Parker licks, and I had to learn some of those to twin with him. The western stuff isn't something you just jump on the stage and do. It's really complex—the harmonies and the music."

Woody's Story

I was born Paul Woodrow Chrisman in a hospital in Nashville on August 23, 1949. We moved around a little after I was born, but pretty much settled in our house in Triune between Arrington and Murfreesboro on Murfreesboro Road. My father had been a school teacher, but he wanted to farm. So he went with farming, and we raised tobacco, hay, cows, corn—everything but cotton.

The first time I ever played in public was at the Murfreesboro Cattle Barn when I was four years old. I sang "Home on the Range" and got a hamburger, Milky Way, and RC cola. That's when I was hooked.

I was about eleven when I started playing the fiddle. See, my father taught in a one-room school, and around 1947—before I was born—he bought a fiddle from Sears. That fiddle laid around for ten or twelve years until I was inspired by Paul Warren with Flatt and Scruggs, Jimmy Gately with Bill Anderson, Benny Martin, and some other fiddlers to pick up that fiddle and start learning. Actually, I started playing everything all at once—banjo, guitar, fiddle, harmonica—but I never did have a mandolin. My dad played the banjo. We had some guys who played with us off and on for four or five years—local guitar player–singers. Those guys were all mechanics or something.

I entertained quite frequently. I was playing the fiddle and getting to play once or twice a year in school plays in the seventh and eighth grades. In high school I was an enigmatic performer—I knew all the old-timey tunes played in an old-timey way. I got to entertain about once every three or four months.

When I was a kid I used to play a couple of local fiddle contests. They used to have one down at Ruskin Cave in Dickson, Tennessee, on Labor Day every year. And at East Cheatham High School—I used to play at that one. I played one in Smithville too. I was the Junior Champion. Me and Frasier Moss played, but Frasier beat me. That contest was filmed and became a PBS documentary.

I didn't care for rock or pop music when I was growing up. I didn't hardly ever watch Ed Sullivan on television. At that time I watched Porter Wagoner, the Wilburn Brothers, Flatt & Scruggs, Bobby Lord, and all those guys. By that time my dad and I had a gig every Saturday night in Franklin called The Williamson County Opry with some local guys.

The Beatles didn't influence me at all. I have a cousin who is identically the same age, and when we were fourteen years old she was completely sold on 'em. But they were just not me. I was a hillbilly through and through—more bluegrass than country, old-timey songs and fiddle tunes. That's me. That's what I loved to do—sing stuff like Uncle Dave Macon and Sam and Kirk McGee.

I remember the first record I got was around '63 or '64. A traveling salesman selling anything to farmers and their wives came around, and my dad got us a record player—three-speed, plastic top, cost eighteen bucks—and he told my mother to get a fiddling record for me. She was going to Nashville on Saturdays, and she bought a record at the Ernest Tubb Record Shop. It was Felix Slatkin with Gordon Terry's guest solos. And that's where I learned "Faded Love" and "Orange Blossom Special" and "Chicken Reel" and all those early tunes. He had great musical arrangements of those pieces, and I was just floored by it. I'd sit there and play with that record.

I started hanging out at the Grand Ole Opry in '64 or '65, so I knew a lot of those guys. I played with Sam McGee on the Opry and got to know all those old-timers in the mid-sixties. Roy Acuff gave me a fiddle when I graduated from high school—I've still got it. He told me not to get into this business.

After high school I went to engineering school at Vanderbilt. It was really fun after the first year. I liked all the subjects. I'm still that way. I studied engineering with physics. I was the first, last, and only student in a program of study that my faculty advisor put together because he wanted to start a visionary physics program. I went to the physics department a whole lot and took some nuclear physics courses. I wanted to be a physicist. I got married in the spring of my sophomore year; I was nineteen.

At Vanderbilt I was really playing guitar. Fiddle was really hard for me to play and still is. I played all the local clubs—played stuff by Dylan, Paul Simon, all that stuff. Lot of pop stuff too. I started to play the fiddle, but I didn't really like the fiddle—

couldn't play the fiddle very well. I couldn't play classical violin either, but I also couldn't pass English. So my teaching advisor, who had me in his own private program—I liked this guy and he liked me—said, "I see you like to play the fiddle," and I said, "Yeah." So he said, "Why don't we go over to Peabody and see if you can get into a couple of violin courses, and we'll substitute that for your English." It worked—it was a dream come true, really.

I didn't really learn the violin—I learned a little bit. I learned to kind of half-ass read music, and I learned to play the "Violin Concerto in A minor." I think I learned about three-fourths of it, but I couldn't really play it. I can't sight read now.

I met Marshall Chapman at Vanderbilt, and we were very close all the way through college. Played together. I got into the Beatles when I was at Vanderbilt—by the time their White Album came out I knew how great they were, and I loved their songs. Me and Marshall worked 'em up.

I never did listen to Jimi Hendrix a whole lot. Marshall listened to Janis Joplin a lot—she knew all of her stuff. One of the greatest moments of my life came when we were playing at The House, which was a big, old, fancy place. We went down there, and I watched Marshall negotiate, and I'm telling you she really did a good job—she could really go in and get us jobs. So we got this gig, and I'd play guitar and banjo and she would sing and I would play the fiddle—"Orange Blossom Special"—and some guy came up to me between songs and said, "You're better than Sonny James." I wasn't ever crazy about Sonny James, but he was a good fiddler.

At Vanderbilt I liked Simon and Garfunkel, and I liked Paul Simon until they put out *Bridge over Troubled Water*. I didn't like that stuff—I thought the earlier stuff was better. By the time I was a junior I was listening to classical guitar and classical violin.

I did really well my last two to three years at Vanderbilt, and they gave me a really good recommendation, so I got into graduate school at the Massachusetts Institute of Technology—M.I.T.— in the fall of 1971. Graduate school is a lot easier to get into than undergraduate school. When you go to graduate school, you generally get scholarships and you get a stipend. I borrowed some money for graduate school, but I really didn't have to pay any tuition, and I got three hundred dollars a month, which was several hundred dollars a month short of what I needed to live on.

For that, I was a research assistant, and I built some plasma machines. So I learned a lot of plasma physics.

In Boston there was a Friends of Bluegrass club run by Nancy Cunningham. If you play acoustic music, then very quickly you go out and meet all the acoustic pickers in any town you go to. Everybody gets to know everybody pretty damn fast, 'cause there ain't a lot of us. I mean there's a lot now, but in big cities there ain't that many. I met Sandy Sheenan, who ran the old-time music store in Cambridge—has a big red beard and glasses—a place called Old Joe Clark's. It's one of those big, old houses where people who stay there all pick, so I was looking at staying there. I was hoping my first wife would stay in Nashville so I could have a place to stay and play. I was hooked up with acoustic players in Boston right off, but then I was into classical guitar.

At M.I.T. I played classical guitar, almost exclusively, from November of '73 until the spring of '74. I'd already passed my doctoral qualifiers but hadn't really decided what I'd do for a dissertation yet. So I was really depressed in the spring of '75; that's when I started playing the fiddle again. Hadn't even touched it for three or four years.

I kinda lost touch with Marshall Chapman in graduate school, but she came to see me a couple of times in Boston and then she came up to visit after my first marriage ended. She lived with me from spring of 1975 until Christmas of 1975. We had played together at Vanderbilt. She liked to play rhythm and sing and tell jokes and have fun. Very charismatic. Big, old, tall girl from South Carolina. She loved me to death.

I started writing songs because of Marshall. She'd had a couple of good tunes that had been recorded. I wrote several tunes up in Boston. Wrote two or three with Marshall. I can't remember what they were. I wrote "The Cowboy Song" and then "Blue Bonnet Lady" shortly after that. I was amazed I could write those, because I'd tried to write songs before but never could do it. After Marshall came up there I was able to jump right into it. We played a lot, and then we'd just sit down and write a tune. She was better than me, though. She was way ahead of me.

She was always a wonderful, fun person to be around. But come Christmas time, a girl's got to go home. She walked through snow as deep as a windshield to get to Logan Airport to get home for Christmas. After that I didn't see her again or become close to her again for a couple or three years.

I just sat alone in my apartment in January—I wasn't depressed; I was playing a few gigs. I did a couple of really good gigs for public TV—they paid good, and that was really encouraging because I was waiting for spring to play on the streets. But then I didn't even have to do that. I'd won the New England fiddling championship in '75, so I was enjoying a little bit of renown as a fiddler.

When I got out of school the last thing I wanted to do was sit in front of a computer and solve mathematical physics problems. I was burned out. Disillusioned with the state of physics at that time, too. Still am. I wanted to know how it all operates. But I was surprised at how ignorant those guys are. I shouldn't say ignorant—but they're so proud and think they know so much that they can't see what they don't know. And a lot of the stuff is just wrong. But it has a strong tradition, and a tradition is a hard thing to break. You've got somebody teaching something wrong—like Aristotle or Plato or anybody who had theories that they knew were bad for a hundred years—they still kept teaching them. That's the way it is now—very frustrating.

I did consider going into teaching physics. Considered going to Columbia University in New York, where I had a job offer doing research and as a teaching assistant in my field, and I think it paid about eighteen thousand dollars a year. I ended up making that much with Loggins and Messina in the two months I was with them. At that time, eighteen thousand dollars wouldn't have gotten you a decent apartment in the city. So I couldn't justify it, plus it was 60 or 70 percent faculty teaching-related, 20 percent teaching, and 20 percent doing what you wanted to do. So I started playing the fiddle in earnest about that time. Marshall and I started working on the street. We'd go down to Wall Street and play.

Marshall had several really good friends in New York that she knew from South Carolina that were real upper crust. And they worked, were married, had kids and stuff in New York. So we would stay with them when we came. Then her father had a heart attack about that time, and he had open-heart surgery in New York and we went down there a whole lot to see him. That was in 1975.

By the time I left Boston I was being more influenced by those northeastern and French-Canadian fiddlers. I had just started playing fiddle again about the time Marshall left. Up till that time I was completely obsessed with playing classical guitar, and I had a really nice repertoire developed from transcriptions of my own from harpsichord suites. I wrote suites that nobody had ever put on guitar. I got a gig playing in Boston on guitar, and man, I would sit there and play my heart out, really play good. Nobody paid any attention—nobody cares anything about guitar. But if I took out my fiddle and played fiddle tunes, they threw money at me. I was listening to some Segovia—not a lot. A few John Williams things. I could figure it out by reading it, but I didn't read it. I'd listen to it—a bunch of baroque recordings on other instruments—transcribe it so I could play it on guitar.

I came back to Nashville in January 1976 and started playing a few sessions. I was in a session with Bobby Bare, and Anita Ball was there. She told me about a job playing fiddle for Loggins and Messina. I got that job, and I was on their last tour—they were coming off a lot of good hits. It was fun and exciting and a good gig. I don't think we played more than thirty-five or forty dates. That was from March until the first of October in 1976.

When I worked with Loggins and Messina, the boys that played the horns got me into jazz. I never knew anything about it until then. I started listening to Grapelli in '76, and so I figured I'd learn a tune or two of his, but I discovered I could make up melodies of my own that were just as good or better. And so I started learning jazz standards and writing songs. In one form or another you move toward jazz. I really like Ella Fitzgerald.

I got married that summer to a gal originally from Birmingham, but she was from Houston then. I met her in Boston when I was at M.I.T. I met her pretty shortly after Marshall left, and she was from Vanderbilt too. Her name was Liza Ramage.

Back in Nashville after the Loggins and Messina tour, I was farting around at the Grand Ole Opry, and Stoney Cooper died and Wilma Lee needed a fiddle player. Howdy Forrester told her that I should play with her and she should get me, so she did.

Chapter 8

"So that was the quartet," said Fred. "We started practicing together, and the first shows we did with Woody were up at the
Kentucky State Fair, which sort of marked the beginning of our
road career. It was in August of that year [1978]. Went up and
played in the hall of giant vegetables where they had giant pumpkins and giant tobacco plants and cornstalks fifteen feet high and
then there was Riders In The Sky down at the end, singing 'Ridin'
Down the Canyon' and 'Don't Fence Me In.' It was great, and it's
interesting to remember that at this time there was hardly anybody doing this music. I mean, the Pioneers were doing it, I realized that, and of course the chuck wagons were keeping it alive,
but there was nobody in the popular culture that was out in front
doing it or traveling around doing it. At least I didn't know anybody who was doing it. I knew Asleep at the Wheel was doing
western swing, and I admired them—and early on we'd talked
about having an Asleep at the Wheel–type band. But then we
thought, 'Gosh, they do it so great. Let's try something else—let's
try the cowboy music.' So that was the deal."

Along the way, they picked up some "handles." Douglas was
originally "Big Fella" or "Deputy Doug," then "Ranger Doug." "I
got that name from *The Lone Ranger* and *Sheriff John*—a kiddie TV
show I used to watch," said Green. Fred's handle, "Too Slim,"
came from a character he created at the Nashville Public Library
while working with the puppet theater—"Singing Cowboy
Slim"—and indirectly from a football player. "Ed 'Too Tall' Jones,
had played football at Tennessee State," said Fred. "And then he
joined the Dallas Cowboys, where he became a star defensive end
and was in some pickup truck commercials." Woody became
"Woody Paul, King of the Western Fiddlers." And Tommy Goldsmith became "Tumbleweed Tommy."

Chapter 9

The author of a biography should remain invisible, letting the
focus remain on the central figure—or, in this case, figures—of

the book. But I had a part in the early history of the Riders and so, in the light of truthful disclosure as well as hopefully adding some insight into those early years, I will tell my part.

I don't remember meeting Douglas Green, but I knew him back in 1975 or so when I was the country music editor at *Record World*, a trade magazine. Douglas was doing some publicity for the Country Music Hall of Fame at the time, and I probably met him through his efforts there. In 1976 Douglas convinced *Country Music Magazine* to sponsor a softball team, and we both played on it. Douglas played first base, while I pitched. In 1977 I met Fred when Douglas invited him to join the team. Fred played second base. Ballplayers are kind of funny about the numbers they wear—Green wore number six because that was the number of his boyhood hero, Al Kaline of the Detroit Tigers. I remember Fred picked number twenty-eight, and I asked him why he chose that number. "That's my age," he replied. I had worn number eleven during my baseball days but wanted a "pitcher's number" for that team, so I chose number twenty-two. It was twice number eleven.

In June 1977 I got married, and Douglas came to the wedding. At the reception, I asked him to sing some songs. I remember he did "Back in the Saddle" and a tune where he yodeled. A month or so later Doug married Cindy Jernigan. In January 1978, Dan Beck and I started a management company, New Horizon Management. Our first client was Dickey Lee—and Dan had most of the management duties there.

The Riders were playing around town, and I first saw them at the Old Time Pickin' Parlor. I loved them and felt immediately— like Fred did after that first night at Herr Harry's—that "this was something that America would pay to see." And so I became their first manager.

At that point, there was a lot of potential but no rewards. People who saw them loved them, including executives at the major labels. But these executives had absolutely no idea of what to do with them. Major labels in Nashville are geared to putting out records that get on country radio and then sell big numbers. The country music industry is part of the world of multinational corporations, who are in the game of the bottom line. They need to sell in big numbers to stay profitable—and the Riders were so different from what they were dealing with that the big label execs were all baffled about how to market them. The same with the big booking agencies. I felt that, over time, things would turn our way. But at that time we just couldn't get over that initial hump.

Adding to the frustrations of those early years was the realization that came to me that I just wasn't cut out to be a manager. Management requires contacts and business skills as well as personality. We had the contacts and we had the business skills. But I didn't have the personality. A manager must dedicate himself or herself totally to an act—putting together business deals on one hand and dealing with personal issues and problems of the act and their family members and friends on the other. It requires an attention to detail and a need to be needed. It is a job that never quits—twenty-four hours a day, seven days a week. You're always on call.

As much as I loved and believed in the Riders—who are one of the easiest groups to manage—I found that it was not my calling. The Riders are bright, intelligent, reliable, responsible, mature, hard-working people. If you can't manage the Riders, well, you can't manage anybody. They made managing as easy as possible. Still, as we moved through the fall and winter of 1978, I realized more and more that I just didn't have it in me to be a full-time manager

The problem was exacerbated by the fact that the country—and especially the music business—was in a major recession in 1978 and especially 1979. Labels and other folks in the music industry simply would not take big chances—it was a time of sticking with what you had and hoping you'd weather the storm. It wasn't a good time to start a new business, and we were victims of the national economy as well.

Having said all that, we did get the Riders a couple of fairly big breaks during that fall. When you talk with people who were involved in the early days of a successful career but didn't stick around to enjoy the big success later on, there is a tendency to hear about how significant they were to the eventual success of the career. Well, Dan Beck and I were important at the time for the Riders—we managed them for about a year—but in the long run we were insignificant. The Riders had "it" from the very beginning; we knew it and saw it. And that uniqueness is what is responsible for their success in the long run. There was always a feeling that something good was going to happen, and, of course, along the way, good things kept happening for the Riders. But that was because of their talent and the fact that they had one of the most unusual acts in America at the time and they had a great work ethic. Time would prove us all right, and that has been my greatest reward.

Perhaps the first big break they received—although in retrospect it seems rather small in comparison to a number of breaks later on—was their appearance at the Kentucky State Fair in August 1978. That came about because a friend of Green's, banjo player Jim Smoak, recommended the group to Dave Snowden, who ran Triangle Talent and booked the free stages at the Kentucky State Fair.

Green and his bluegrass group, the Doug Green Band, had worked with Snowden previously. The group had a floating set of members, one of which was Fred LaBour, and Fred remembers driving up to Louisville with Green and learning how to yodel. "We did 'Yodel Blues' by Elton Britt and Rosalie Allen," remembered Fred. "All the way up to Louisville in the car Doug worked with me until I got it."

Their first appearance at the Louisville State Fair was on August 17, and they played in Louisville for eleven straight days. It was their first road trip—they had played within a forty-mile radius of Nashville in Tennessee before this. And it was the first time Woody performed in public with them. It was also the first time I met Woody.

In Louisville the guys played every day at 10 A.M. and 4 P.M.—a musician's nightmare to get up that early—in a hall filled with vegetables and 4–H crops. They stayed at the Thrifty Dutchman and in between playing went back to their rooms and jammed. Everybody was broke—and they didn't get paid until the end of the eleven days—so there was nothing to do but either play on stage or play in their rooms.

I remember the very first appearance at the Kentucky Fair was taped by WAVE-TV in Louisville, and just before the show we all gathered for instructions about what was going to happen. The guy with the TV station and a guy with the fair stood and said something to the effect that "you guys will come out over there and take the stage, you'll play for such and such a time, etc." During this whole time, Douglas, Fred, and Tommy Goldsmith were listening closely so they'd know what to do. Woody was sitting on the floor, in the middle of this group. When the guys had finished giving instructions and we all started to move off, Woody looked up and said, "What's going on?"

That captures the essence of life on the road with Riders In The Sky.

After the dates in Louisville, there were some major conflicts that had to be dealt with. Dickey Lee—the other act we managed— was upset because the Riders were "breaking up" his band. Dates had to be worked around—Dickey couldn't take a booking if the Riders had a booking. We were making money from Dickey— and spending money on the Riders—so we had to be sensitive to Dickey's concerns. Part of that concern was solved when Bill Collins quit the Riders to remain with Dickey. But Fred elected to quit Dickey to go with the Riders—and that meant Dickey had to find another bass player. Fred was a good bass player and har- mony singer for Dickey—and he knew the material—so he would not be easy to replace.

"I was real burned out playing the same show with Dickey every night," said Fred. "And it was just time for me to move on. I'd learned a lot from the guy—he's a great songwriter and a won- derful professional musician, but it was just time for me to move on. So I went to Windy Bill and said, 'I'm gonna quit and play cowboy music,' and he said, 'I can't do that—I've got to stick with the sure paycheck.' So he did."

At the Country Music Foundation, Doug's boss, Bill Ivey, was getting increasingly frustrated with Doug's absences. Ivey ex- pected his employee to put in eight hours—nine to five—at the job he was being paid for. But Doug was increasingly leaving early and taking days off to fulfill obligations with the Riders.

Dan Beck and I were getting increasingly frustrated because we couldn't pursue opportunities full-time for the Riders because of their other obligations. And so we held a meeting at our office with Doug and Fred and laid this all out. The end result was that the guys decided to become Riders In The Sky full time and quit their other jobs. Dan and I immediately felt both relief and guilt— the guys had families and had to somehow earn money while we were pursuing opportunities for them. Fred landed a job at the public library working with Tom Tichener, the puppeteer, doing kiddie shows, while Doug cut firewood and did other odd jobs to survive. Both their wives worked to help support their families. Still, the winter of 1978–79 was a tough one for the Riders as they hoped that following their hearts would somehow, someday pay off.

Ironically, that winter did not pay off in financial terms, but would pay off handsomely in the shaping and polishing of the act, because during this winter the act now known as Riders In The Sky fully developed. This winter would provide the foundation for the rest of their career.

On August 8, the Riders had appeared for the first time at Wind in the Willows, a small club on Twenty-fourth Avenue, behind the Exit/In. They next appeared there on August 29, after they had played the Kentucky State Fair. The rest of that winter they would play there every Tuesday night in addition to the other scattered appearances they obtained.

Chapter 10

"The real formation of the group, in my mind, was every Tuesday night at a club called Wind in the Willows in Nashville," said Fred. "Tuesday night is traditionally a death night for clubs, but we took the night and really turned it into something. It became a cult kind of deal. It cost fifty cents to get in, and we soon had a regular crowd. We would play four sets—two of which we had really prepared and the rest we would just wing it. People would come down and sit in. We had a saxophone player named Jay Patten sitting in, Mark O'Connor when he was in town would sit in. A variety of girl singers came and sat in, and it just got to be this big party and it became a hip thing to do. We started doing *Riders Radio Theater* scripts there. Tommy Goldsmith wrote the first one, called 'The Cowboy Who Hated Christmas.' And we performed that as a special Christmas show. We'd stand there with a script and read our zany plays. And then I took over and started writing them. I'd crank out one a week, like 'The Riders Join

OPEC,' 'The Riders Go Hawaiian,' 'The Riders Go to Sweden,' and 'The Triple X Chainsaw Massacre.' It was all just zany stuff, so there was always, besides the music, a show going on."

Their shows were magic—so full of entertainment and so different from a run-of-the-mill club act in Nashville. So Dan Beck and I had the idea that if the Riders could play in New York that it would turn into a Big Break. And so we called Mort Cooperman with the Lone Star Cafe and talked to him about booking the Riders. It was too big a risk, he felt—paying money for an unknown, unseen act. Well, what about if they played free, we asked? He agreed to that, so on Halloween—October 31—they played the Lone Star Cafe.

But first they had a tour with some Grand Ole Opry acts that took them to Northlake, Illinois, then on to New York state, where they played in Haverstraw, Tarrytown, and Salamanca. On the tour was Ray Pillow, Bobby Wright, and Loretta Lynn's sister Peggy Sue.

"We really got that job with Ray Pillow and those guys under false pretenses," remembers Goldsmith. "They wanted a country band to back them up—and we told them we could do it. Well, we weren't really a country band. Woody did great on fiddle, of course, and Doug played the electric bass, and I played lead guitar. But we didn't have much rehearsal, and we didn't really know the songs. And Fred had, let's just say, limited ability as a drummer. I remember Bobby Wright asking him once, 'Can you not just play a simple country rim shot?!!?'

"These were police fund raisers, I believe," said Tommy. "We played in Illinois and in western New York state. Woody and Doug were in a Volkswagen van. I had my Plymouth Volare, and Fred rode with me."

"That was an unbelievable trip," remembers Fred. "Woody Paul's Volkswagen bus burnt out the engine, and he and Ranger Doug took out the engine by the side of the road, carried it over a fence down to a welding place where they rewelded it, and then they carried it back and put the whole engine back into the Volkswagen bus in about an hour and fifteen minutes, fueled by a bottle of Jack Daniels. The weld didn't hold, and the bus only lasted about fifty more miles, so they had to get a car and join us later. It was just a zoo."

Dan Beck and I had to wire them some money for them to make it into New York City.

And then they took the stage on Halloween night at the Lone Star Cafe in New York. "Everybody in New York is in costume," said Fred. "And we're wearing these cowboy outfits. There was a blues act playing that night—Otis Rush—and we opened for him. So there's a blues—not a western—crowd there. We're up on stage playing and some guy walks in, looks at us, and says, 'Where's Otis?' Then he looks us over and says, 'And what's this cowboy shit?'"

There's an element of hipness to the Riders In The Sky. Some people "get it," and some people don't; same with audiences—some "get it," and some don't. The audience in New York didn't get it. To them the Riders were something weird and out of place. New York has its own definition of hip, and the Riders didn't fit it. On the flip side, New York City never got the hip factor inherent in a performance of Riders In The Sky. It was a match made in Nashville that just didn't carry into the Big Apple.

A few days after they returned to Nashville, we organized a major showcase for them at the Exit/Inn, where we invited top executives in the Nashville music industry. We rented a cowboy movie to show before they played, and we taped the show so we'd have a recording to play for prospective labels. We felt sure that, as soon as the show was over, major label contracts and major booking deals would be offered. Alas, it would not be so.

The people at the show absolutely loved the Riders—they "got it" and thought they were terrific. But none of them had any idea of what to do with the group. The general consensus seemed to be that they were a great act to see live—free. Although one major executive confided, "A little bit of that stuff goes a long way," most of those in the audience thoroughly enjoyed themselves, then went back to their jobs. It was a great event to talk about—but no big contracts were forthcoming.

About a month later, on December 9, the Riders made their first appearance on the Grand Ole Opry. The Opry appearance came about because both Woody and Ranger Doug knew a number of folks on the Opry or connected with the show. At this time, the Grand Ole Opry was at a low point. It was no longer relevant to the country music on Music Row and the radio. It was considered a relic of the past, an antiquated show for tourists, not a vibrant, essential part of the current world of country music. The new, young acts coming to Nashville did not dream of being on the Opry—they dreamed of being on a record. The Opry didn't reach out to the new, young talent, and even if they had, they probably would have gotten their hand slapped. The movers and shakers on Music Row had declared the Opry far removed from country music. In a sense, they were right—in 1973 the Opry had moved about fifteen miles from Music Row to Opryland, leaving the downtown location at the Ryman Auditorium, which had been home to the Opry for thirty years.

The Riders didn't feel that way—Woody and Ranger Doug, especially, revered the tradition of the Grand Ole Opry and dreamed of playing there. It was not a view shared by most country acts or music business executives. Still, everyone had the feeling that the Riders were "happening" and their career was moving forward. Everyone, that is, except their bankers.

Chapter 11

"We played through that winter, sort of helter-skelter," remembers Fred. "We opened for Billy Joe Shaver, opened for other people, and we began to get a little bit of a reputation as something different and something fun in town. I got a day job at the library in Nashville in the children's room doing puppets and doing Singing Cowboy Slim. That's when I got the name Too Slim.

"I had married Peggy Young," continued LaBour. "And we had a little boy named Frank and a little girl named Lily and were trying to raise a family, so I was doing Riders In The Sky and working a day job down at the library all the rest of the time. At the library I worked from eight until five and then I might do a Riders show all night long—in those days we were playing in clubs, so we worked till one or two in the morning. Get home about three and then get up and do it again. There were stretches when that schedule went on for months and months. Ranger Doug was cutting wood to make money. But we made it through that winter."

That winter of 1978–79 would be the low point for the Riders. But that deep valley had a winding trail up a mountain they would soon start climbing.

In 1979 the Riders played 135 times—a big jump over their 72 appearances the previous year. Their first gig in 1979 was their regular Tuesday night appearance at Wind in the Willows on January 2. That would be the only place they'd play from December 19, 1978, until February 19, 1979, when they returned to Herr Harry's Phranks 'n' Steins for a Monday night. The next night they were back at Wind in the Willows, but on February 22 they began the first of four appearances in Austin, Texas, at General Sam's. The next three nights they were at 1874 Steamboat Springs.

So many of the big breaks and tremendous opportunities enjoyed by Riders In The Sky have literally fallen in their lap. It is a product of their being visible and constantly playing in public. So many times there will be someone in the audience who is "important," who will have connections and will be impressed by the Riders. For their part, the Riders usually have no idea who this person is—or their position—when they take the stage. But all of the Riders are accessible, friendly, and open to meeting and chatting with those who come to their shows. At one of their performances in Nashville, a Texan, Davis Ford, an environmental engineer with a consulting practice in Austin, was so impressed and excited he offered to get them some bookings in Austin. Ford's sister taught classics at Vanderbilt, and he had come up to visit her. So that's how the Texas booking came about.

Then, at one of those Austin appearances, Terry Likona of the public television show *Austin City Limits* came and saw them. He was impressed enough to consider booking them on *Austin City Limits* sometime in the future. It was all in a day's work for the Riders, who above all enjoy performing for an audience. Their love of playing—and the fact they do it so well—would continue to open doors throughout their career. The door that opened in Austin would be a big, wide double-door.

Douglas Green has the habits of a scholar—documenting everything about the Riders. He's also got, deep within him, the heart of a baseball statistician. And so he has kept a running count of how many times they've performed in public, how many times they have been on the Grand Ole Opry, and how many times they have appeared on television. Their one-hundredth appearance was thus recorded on April 3, 1979, when they performed at Wind in the Willows.

The first time the Riders entered a recording studio as a group was on April 9, when they sang back-up for rodeo cowboy Larry Mahan, who was in Nashville recording an album at the American Studios. That first day they sang harmonies on "Saying Goodbye to the West," then returned to the studio on the eleventh and sang back-up on "The Old Double Diamond" and "Nashville Cowboy."

On May 3 they performed on Ralph Emery's early morning television show on WSM. This was a very popular local program and got the Riders well known in Nashville. "I'd go to the cleaners or out to lunch," remembers Slim, "and people would say, 'Hey, I saw you guys on television.' It was surprising how many people watched that show in the morning—it was on from six to eight. That show really got us known in Nashville." The show also established a good relationship with Ralph Emery, which would pay big dividends in a few years when he had a national show.

The next step in the Riders' career would involve making an album. "We thought, 'We need to make a record,' and nobody in Nashville would touch it," remembers Slim. "Rounder Records and Barry Poss from Sugar Hill got in touch with us. We had known and respected Rounder for many years, and they seemed like a natural for acoustic, left-field music like we were doing. Ken Irwin—a co-owner of Rounder—came down to stay at his friend Ann Romaine's house, and he was going to come see us at a club so we could audition. There was a snowstorm and the show was canceled, so he called and said that, since he was stuck in town, 'Why don't you come over and play?' So we went over to Ann's living room and basically performed the first album for him. Went through the whole sequence of songs.

"Ranger Doug had been writing songs because from the beginning we knew that playing and performing the Pioneers songbook wasn't going to get it," continued Slim. "We had to bring something new to the table, and we wanted to not only work in the tradition but continue the tradition and add to it. We had Woody's new songs, Ranger Doug had written songs all along, but now strictly western songs for the group like 'Three on the Trail' and 'Here Comes the Santa Fe,' and he would bring the songs in and Woody would bring his in and we'd all take a hand in arranging and editing them, making them into Riders songs. We performed the songs for Ken, and he said, 'That's it, that's the album. Go make it.'"

"I'd known Ken from the bluegrass festivals since the sixties, really, and so it was logical to go to them," said Ranger Doug. "I remember we went over to Ann Romaine's house and sat down and just jammed for an hour. We had made a tape in a studio and I think he had that too, but I think it was the live thing that put us over.

"I'd spent a lot of time at the Hall of Fame," remembers Ken. "We used to go in there and do a lot of research. Doug worked there, and he wrote some liner notes for us. I believe he got in touch with us about doing that album. There was a date booked at a club, and Hazel Dickens and I came down to see them, but the day before, the date was canceled. They were scurrying around to book another date in a club. We were staying at Anne Romaine's house at 339 Valeria—Anne wasn't there—so I just said to come on over to the house.

"They came over and brought their cactus and their campfire and decked the place out in cowboy regalia," continued Ken. "And they played for us just like we were an audience. That was the very first time that had happened—a showcase just for me. I thought it was very, very cool. It was certainly different from anything we had seen before—it was a real show! Remember, I'd been used to hearing bluegrassers who just stood there and looked at their instruments while they played. It was quite a departure. We laughed a lot. I remember wondering where we'd sell it. But my usual instinct was that, if I liked it, then others would too. So we agreed to do an album. We kept the budget down, which allowed us to record a second album. Once they got a base, it made it much easier. But it was really difficult trying to explain them to people."

Things were looking up for the Riders. Then Tommy Goldsmith quit. "Tommy came to us and said 'We're just not working enough—I can't do this," said LaBour. "He said, 'I got an offer from a rock 'n' roll band and I love you guys and love playing the music but I've just got to work more.' We were struggling so hard for bookings at that time because we were weird—you have to remember how weird Riders In The Sky was at the beginning. There was no Michael Martin Murphey, there was no WestFest, there were no cowboy poetry gatherings, there was no network to plug into. We were playing for people our age—we hadn't really established a kid market yet. We were playing clubs, we were playing for a smattering of college kids and people our age, which was like thirty years old, who were just starting families and who were living La Vida Loca, as we say these days. In Nashville, people would come to hear us and say, 'That's nice.' And I remember one executive saying, 'You guys are the best band in Nashville, and you have absolutely no commercial potential,' which we took as a compliment, actually. But it was tough to make a living in that environment."

"They all had other jobs," said Tommy. "And I didn't. Fred was working at the library, and Woody was still playing sessions and playing with other people. Doug was cutting firewood, I believe. But that was the only income I had. I lived out in the country and didn't spend much money—but I needed more than I was making with Riders. So I left one weekend to play with Tim Krekel—he was a rock act, signed to Capricorn Records. He had tour support from the label, so there was some money coming in. I was offered a job with him, so I came back to Nashville and played a Tuesday night with the Riders at Wind in the Willows, and that's when I decided to quit. I remember driving all over Nashville in an ice storm—went to each guy's house—and told them I was quitting. I know Doug was really disappointed, and I hated to let him down. But I had to make more money.

"There's another part to that, though," continued Tommy. "The Riders were so good and so enthusiastic and there was such a great reaction from the crowds. I could tell the Riders were going somewhere—but it wasn't where I wanted to go. They are a terrific group of guys, great musicians—but what they were doing just wasn't what I wanted to do with my life."

"When Tommy quit, we had four pieces—we went down to three pieces, and we thought, 'We need four' for the fourth part harmony and the guitar player, the lead player," said Slim. "So we auditioned a lot of people and played with a number of people.

People came to town to play with us. This went on for about two months, endlessly looking, and finally it just occurred to us that what worked was three and that was the band. That's when the chemistry was right on stage—everybody had their moment in the spotlight, and four was just too many. It was just too diluted; three was the magic number, and that's when we decided to stick with three."

Their final electric guitarist was Jody Chalk, who lasted a few weeks.

Chapter 12

The Riders entered Audio-Media Studios on Nineteenth Avenue South in Nashville on November 26, 1979, to begin recording their first album for Rounder. The first song they recorded was "Skyball Paint," the second was "Three on the Trail," and the third was the song that gave them their name, "(Ghost) Riders in the Sky."

"Skyball Paint" is a Bob Nolan song, a fun, up-tempo number where each member of the Riders takes a verse. Ranger Doug had found the song on one of the many Sons of the Pioneers albums he owned or possibly a transcription he'd heard at the Country Music Foundation. The Riders had been performing the song in clubs.

Bob Nolan is the preeminent writer of western songs and the major influence on Ranger Doug as a songwriter. Nolan, who was born Robert Nobles in Canada on April 13, 1908, was a founding member of the Sons of the Pioneers, along with Tim Spencer and Roy Rogers. Before they were the Sons of the Pioneers, they were the O-Bar-O Cowboys. Nolan dropped out of that group—the original three members were actually Rogers (Leonard Slye), Nolan, and Bill "Slumber" Nichols—and Tim Spencer replaced Nolan. The O-Bar-O Cowboys did a tour of the southwest in 1932 that turned out to be a disaster—no money, no crowds—and when they finally made it back to Los Angeles, the group disbanded. However, Rogers and Spencer went to see Nolan, who was working as a golf caddy at the Bel Aire Country Club, and convinced him to join them in another group.

The group evolved into the Sons of the Pioneers, and Nolan's distinctive vocals and songwriting were a primary reason the group developed a western image and sang western songs. Nolan wrote a number of songs for movies and usually wrote out what he wanted to say in the song first, then worked on the lyrics, and, finally, the music.

Nolan was an integral part of the Sons of the Pioneers until he retired in 1949. In fact, during the 1940s the group was known as Bob Nolan and the Sons of the Pioneers because of his good looks, his distinctive vocals, and his immense songwriting talents. Nolan also appeared in a number of western movies, often with the Sons of the Pioneers in Roy Rogers movies. After his retirement, he came back to sing with the Sons of the Pioneers in 1955–57 when they recorded for RCA Victor. At the time the Riders recorded "Skyball Paint," Nolan was living in Studio City, California, near the old Republic Studio lot. He was frustrated and felt that he would never see his music widely accepted during his lifetime, convinced that western music was dead.

"Three on the Trail" was Ranger Doug's attempt to write a theme song for the group—an identifying number that would open each show.

> Another day, another page of life is open
> As they saddle up beneath the endless sky
> Far away in a land where they'll be loping
> Free until they die!

The story behind "(Ghost) Riders in the Sky" goes back to the D Hill Ranch, near Douglas, Arizona, where an old cowboy, Cap Watts, and a young cowpoke, Stan Jones, were working. As a storm began to develop, the moving clouds looked like figures riding through the sky, and Watts yelled "ghost riders." Later, Watts told Jones the story of "ghost riders" who tried to "catch the devil's herd" when cold air and hot air currents collide, which often results in tornadoes. Jones remembered the story and later wrote the song "(Ghost) Riders in the Sky" about that experience. In 1949, while working as a park ranger in Death Valley, Jones helped a movie company scout locations for a movie, *Three Godfathers*. One night he sang this song to the Hollywood crew by campfire, and it made an immediate impression; later that year the song became the title for a Gene Autry movie; Jones also appeared in that movie. The version by Vaughn Monroe became a major pop hit in 1949.

On December 3 the Riders returned to the studio and recorded two songs written by Ranger Doug: "Blue Montana Skies" and "Riding Alone." "Blue Montana Skies" is an attempt by Ranger Doug to follow in Bob Nolan's songwriting footsteps.

> The law of the land is to mortgage out your soul,
> But the code of the West is to be free
> Don't know where I'll roam under blue Montana skies
> But I'll be riding 'til I meet my destiny

"I got the inspiration for the key change in the release from an old Roy Rogers song, 'Rock Me to Sleep in the Saddle,'" wrote Ranger Doug in a songbook of his called *Songs of the Sage*. "I liked the song all right but not enough to learn it—but those chord changes drove me wild. The title was inspired by an old Zeke Clements tune I'd seen in a song book but never heard, called 'Blue Mexico Skies.' Come to find out some years later that 'Blue Montana Skies' was the title and the title song of a 1939 Gene Autry western."

"Riding Alone" would not be released on the Riders' first album; the group wasn't satisfied with their recording. They would re-record the song at a later date for their second album.

Two days later they recorded "Cielito Lindo," a tune in the public domain; the Cole Porter song "Don't Fence Me In"; Bob Nolan's "When Payday Rolls Around"; three songs by Woody, "So Long Saddle Pals," "The Cowboy Song," and "Blue Bonnet Lady"; and two by Ranger Doug, "That's How the Yodel Was Born" and "Here Comes the Santa Fe."

Although Cole Porter is given songwriting credit for "Don't Fence Me In" and has collected the royalties for that song, the original lyrics were written by Robert Henry Fletcher in fall 1935 after being asked by Hollywood producer Lou Brock to write some dialogue for a planned musical western, *Adios Argentina*. Fletcher was a native of Montana and had written a number of stories, poems, and songs about that area. Cole Porter was assigned to do the music for the movie, and Fletcher gave him the lyrics;

however, the movie was never done, and Porter offered Fletcher $250 for the rights to the song. Fletcher agreed but wanted recognition if the song was ever published. Cole Porter then rewrote the lyrics and music and it was sung by Roy Rogers in a movie musical, *Hollywood Canteen,* in 1944 and again the following year in his own movie titled, *Don't Fence Me In.* Hit recordings by Roy Rogers, Kate Smith, Bing Crosby, and the Andrews Sisters followed, and the song reached number-one on *Your Hit Parade.* The story of Bob Fletcher was revealed by columnist Walter Winchell twenty years after the song became a hit, and Fletcher managed to receive a financial settlement from Cole Porter's representatives.

"Cowboy Song" and "Blue Bonnet Lady" were both written by Woody Paul before he met the Riders, while living in Boston and finishing up at M.I.T.

> My daddy was a cowboy
> He rode those Texas plains
> My mother was a wandering rose
> The west wind knew her name
> I was raised on the rolling prairie
> Where the buffalo once roamed
> With the western sky and the coyote's cry
> The saddle was my home

"Blue Bonnet Lady" has proven to be one of the most durable of the Riders' songs, with other western groups also recording it. It has a strong western swing feel to it.

> Blue, blue bonnet lady
> Why are you so sad and all alone
> Blue, blue bonnet lady
> Do you need a shoulder to lean on
> I'm just a lonesome lone star cowboy
> Who's needin' someone too
> So blue blue bonnet lady
> Come with me and you won't be blue

"Woody called me up at the library one day," remembers Slim.

"He said, 'I've got our 'Happy Trails,' and he sang me 'So Long, Saddle Pals.'" "So Long, Saddle Pals" is an attempt to write a show "closer," something akin to the role the song "Happy Trails" played for Roy Rogers and Dale Evans when they sang it at the end on their weekly TV series in the 1950s. The recording begins with each of the Riders wishing listeners a fond farewell before launching into the lyrics.

> Farewell, saddle pals, our parting brings us sorrow
> But on down the line we'll find a bright tomorrow
> So keep those faces smiling around your home corral
> So until we meet again, goodbye, saddle pals

Green states that "Here Comes the Santa Fe," written while he was driving to Memphis, is "my contribution to the hoary train song tradition in western music." The song begins with the fiddle sounding like a train whistle and, like a train leaving a station, gradually picks up steam. "The tricky three-part yodel was actually Slim's idea—he learned it from his childhood local TV cowboy, Buck Barry," states Green.

> Oooh, watch her fly, here comes the Santa Fe
> She's thundering loud, she's roaring haughty and proud
> At the break of day
> Oooh, watch her fly, here comes the Santa Fe
> I'll ride her on the blinds if I can catch her on time
> Here comes the Santa Fe

The genesis for "That's How the Yodel Was Born" came from some stage repartee the Riders engaged in at the Wind in the Willows club to "explain" the yodel. In September 1979, on their way to North Carolina to play at a private party, Ranger Doug pulled the idea into a song.

> The bronco jumped up and the cowboy came down
> They met at the old saddle horn
> It made a deep impression, you could say it changed his life
> And that's how the yodel was born

Green admits that "the yodel itself was hauled directly out of Elton Britt's yodel spectacular 'Chime Bells'" and that Britt also recorded a song called "That's How the Yodel Was Born" (written by Britt and Charles Grean), but Britt's song was a blues shuffle. The song has become the most popular song the Riders do, and if there is one song that defines the group—an impossible task, for sure—it would be this one.

Although the Riders included two Bob Nolan songs—"When Payday Rolls Around" and "Skyball Paint"—and several standards—"Don't Fence Me In" and "(Ghost) Riders in the Sky"—they decided not to record the two most famous western songs of all time—"Tumbling Tumbleweeds" and "Cool Water," even though these songs were an important part of their live show.

"It would have been like a bluegrass group recording 'Rocky Top,'" said Slim. "It was just too much of a cliche." "We didn't want the first album to be a clone of the Sons of the Pioneers," added Ranger Doug. "So we wanted to do a lot of originals along with some recognizable tunes. Also—we knew we could never be the Sons of the Pioneers. They were just too good—they set the standard for western music—and we wanted to create our own identity."

The Riders added some musicians for that first album, including guitarist Paul Worley, who played the driving guitar on "(Ghost) Riders in the Sky." But cutting basic tracks was a problem. They didn't like always using a drummer and also disliked a "click track," which is a metronome that keeps a group in time. Instead, they had to struggle keeping a steady time throughout the basic tracks. Finally, "Ranger Doug got a whole lot better in keeping time," said Slim. "I'm not the strongest metronome on the block," admitted Ranger Doug.

The producer for that first album was Russ Miller, who had previously produced a western album for National Geographic.

"In retrospect, I would never have made those records like we did then," said Ranger Doug. "I had a fairly clear idea of the music we should do, but everybody else had an idea of what it should sound like. And I was certainly willing to go along with that because I didn't want to make a record that sounded like the Sons of the Pioneers. They had done it better than we could ever do it. It had to sound like us."

The group played in and around Nashville for most of 1979—including every Tuesday night at Wind in the Willows—until they returned to the Kentucky State Fair on August 8 for a twelve-day stand in Louisville. At the end of August they played in Branson, Missouri, but that town had not developed into the mecca for country music entertainment yet. At the end of September, they played in Birmingham, Alabama, and returned to Texas in October for several appearances in Stafford and Houston. At the end of October they played two dates at Eastern New Mexico University, then finished the year playing in Birmingham, Tulsa, and Tuscaloosa before returning to Nashville to play a New Year's Eve show and then one on January 1, 1980.

Things were looking up for the Riders—they were finally making a little bit of money. They were getting some out-of-town dates—a result of acquiring a new manager, David Cannon, who had connections with a number of clubs.

Of the 135 appearances the Riders made in 1979, only 37 were outside of Nashville—8 in Texas, 4 in Alabama, 3 in Missouri, 2 in New Mexico, 1 each in North Carolina and Oklahoma, and 18 in Kentucky—including 13 at the state fair. Although there were a few bright spots in their out-of-town dates, especially getting into Texas, at the end of 1979 Riders In The Sky were still primarily a local Nashville act.

Chapter 13

The Riders' first album, *Three on the Trail*, was released in early 1980. They had already gotten a big boost—psychologically, at least—before the album even came out.

Producer Snuff Garrett had recorded an album on Bob Nolan, released on Elektra Records, and Douglas Green convinced *Country Music Magazine* to let him do a story on Nolan. Fred Goodwin set up the interview, and "We ended up talking a long time, not about his record but about my admiration for him,[Nolan]" said Green. "I asked him to write the liner notes for our album and sent him a tape. And apparently, against all odds, he loved it. Ken Griffis [longtime friend and biographer of the Sons of the Pioneers] said he went over to Bob's apartment, and Bob said, 'Listen, you've got to hear these guys,' and played him the tape."

Griffis remembers that Nolan had called him and asked, "Can you spare a few minutes to drop over to listen to something?" Griffis drove over to Nolan's home, wondering what he'd be listening to—"a long-lost Nolan song or perhaps a recently conceived one?"

Inside the home, Griffis took a seat and "Nolan turned on his tape machine," said Griffis. "I was impressed with the attention the music was receiving from this unique talent. This was a bit unusual, because, during our many visits, Nolan infrequently expressed his appreciation of music, past or present. It was not an easy assignment to get him to talk about his music. But as he stood at the machine, I observed a shaking of the head, a bit of a smile; he was hearing sounds that pleased him, sounds that my untrained ear could not pick up."

After Nolan had played him a few songs he asked, "Well, what do you think?" Griffis responded, "It's good, but it's not the Pioneers." Nolan replied, "Oh, to hell with the Pioneers—that's not the only music in the world! This is a new group calling themselves Riders In The Sky. I like what they are doing."

Griffis then related that, "Properly chastised, I pushed back deeper in my chair and listened intently to the tape. When it was finished Nolan said, 'Not bad, huh?'" Griffis noted that, "If the master liked the music, I loved the music."

"Bob was very gracious," continued Green. "He had this reputation as a great loner. Antisocial, almost. But people who knew him said he could be that way but could also be a buddy—a regular good guy. Somebody good to hang out with. And I guess I caught him on one of his good days, because he was nothing but golden to me—he was wonderful.

"That marked a big moment emotionally for me when those guys, who we almost worshiped for what they'd done, really adopted us and said, 'You guys are carrying it on,'" continued Green. "They didn't say, 'You guys are threatening us' or 'You guys aren't doing it as good as we did' or 'You're trying to take over our life.' They were just the opposite. They said, 'Thanks for keeping it going—you guys are wonderful.' I can't tell you how much that meant to us. It was really a high point for me personally as well as the group. It was another positive factor that kept us going in those early days."

In January the Riders appeared at several Fair Buyers Conventions, showcasing their act, hoping for some bookings at state and county fairs. But although they performed in Topeka, Kansas; Detroit, Michigan; and St. Paul, Minnesota, for these buyers, they did not see many results for their efforts. The Fair Buyers Conventions attract a wide number of acts—everything from mud wrestlers to tractor pulls, monster trucks, and novelty acts as well as musical acts—all trying to impress the buyers and get bookings at the lucrative fair circuit. The Riders didn't really go over that well at any of their showcases that year.

Also in January they had one of their most unusual bookings. Booked to perform in Aspen, Colorado, at a ski lodge because the lodge owner had heard Waylon Jennings say how much he loved them, the owner was disappointed to find that Riders In The Sky weren't a country act with a heavy drum beat. Although the sign outside the club proclaimed "Waylon's favorite band," after their first performance the lodge owner told them he would pay them in full if they would not play. Instead, he hired a country dance band for the skiers, and the Riders lounged around Aspen for a couple of days. On January 11 they went into Aspen Sound Studios in Colorado with John McEuen, one of the founders of the Nitty Gritty Dirt Band, where they recorded a Hank Williams song, "I've Been Down That Road Before."

On February 1, 1980, they began a three-day stand in Chicago at the University of Chicago Folk Festival. "We traveled in a blue van that we called the 'Blue Hole of Death,'" said Slim. "It was Ranger Doug's van, and he was a shotputter in high school. So this was a shotputter's van; it took all your strength to roll down the window. It was a manly vehicle.

"We took out the seats and put in a nine-hundred-pound motheaten couch in the back," continued Slim. "On the trip to Chicago to the Folk Festival, Woody took out the passenger seat—the shotgun seat—and put a saddle in there and so we rode all the way up to Chicago with somebody sitting up in the saddle. Woody was yelling, 'Now we're really riders in the sky!' It was too crazy. I mean, we were committed! We took the cactus and sat in that saddle for hundreds of miles. We were having so much fun!"

On February 14 they did their first benefit for Hospital Hospitality House at the VFW Hall in Nashville. The event was organized by some fans of the Riders who had known them at the Wind in the Willows. Wanting to put together a place for out-of-town people to stay when a relative was in a Nashville hospital, they enlisted the Riders for this fund-raising event, which would become a major part of their philanthropic efforts in the years ahead. Those first benefits were really square dances—people would put their coats against the walls in the cold building and dance to keep warm.

The Riders began to get some occasional dates on the road but continued to play in and around Nashville, including a number of times on the Grand Ole Opry.

On August 20, 1980, the Riders played the Record Bar Convention in Hilton Head, South Carolina. That led to their third manager, Dave Marsden, who was hired by Record Bar to manage them. The organization wanted to move into management and felt they could do so with Riders In The Sky. Here was an act playing out a great deal and getting a lot of positive reaction to their shows. The record store chain reasoned that they would be able to stock their records and sell a good number as the Riders traveled around, performing.

Marsden "got it" with the Riders. His wife managed the Roches—three sisters who sang great harmonies and came out of the feminist folk scene in New York clubs. This led to the Riders opening for that act a few times. But the management never really worked out—the Riders played mostly in clubs and dives, paying their dues.

Another break for the Riders came when they played the Arkansas State Fair for eleven days—September 26 through October 5. Performing "next to the beekeeper's booth," the Riders noticed a guy sitting in the front row, watching intently. After their performance, Bill Fegan introduced himself to the group and offered to book them.

"Fegan had a talent agency that did arts acts," said Ranger Doug. "There are a lot of community concerts around the country, and he was a major provider of talent for them. Whether it was Chinese acrobats or an opera singer. And every so often they'd want something in the folk or popular style and we fit in there, especially in the price range of $1,200 to $1,500, which was our price range then."

Bill Fegan and Associates was based in Dallas, and they "were our first real bookers" said Slim. "We did a lot of community festivals with him. He kept us fed during those early years."

"They were terrific, and so different," said Fegan. "I had been working with Jimmy Driftwood—who wrote 'The Battle of New Orleans'—and so I knew the folkies. He's the reason I moved to Arkansas. I was also booking the Jack Daniels Silver Cornet Band and the Chinese Acrobats—who were with me for twenty-three years and my biggest client."

Fegan talked with the Riders in Arkansas, then went with them to Austin, Texas, where they received the biggest break of their career thus far: they performed on *Austin City Limits* on November 19, 1980, while the videotapes rolled. Woody Paul had a major drinking problem at the time and showed up for the date hung over, "looking like five miles of bad road," according to Slim. But they got him on stage, and the show went over well.

The Riders performed for an hour, followed by Bill Monroe and the Bluegrass Boys, who also did an hour. Then the TV production crew cut each performance down to thirty minutes and aired it in January, the following year.

On December 17, the Riders went into Creative Workshop studio and recorded the Gene Autry classic, "Back in the Saddle Again," and a song written by Woody and Slim, "Cowboy Jubilee."

Ranger Doug had been singing "Back in the Saddle Again" before the Riders were formed. The song was Gene Autry's theme song and songwriting credit is given to Autry and Ray Whitley. However, the song was actually written by Whitley, who received a call at five o'clock one morning in 1938 from a movie executive telling him they needed another song for a movie Whitley was to sing in that starred George O'Brien. Whitley had come to Hollywood as a singing cowboy, which was the rage of this period after Gene Autry created this type of western hero in 1935. Whitley had to come up with a song by 7 A.M., and as he told his wife about needing to write a song, he said, "I'm back in the saddle again." Whitley's wife said that was a good title, so he sat down and composed the song quickly. The song was first performed in the movie *Border G-Man* and later recorded by Whitley with his group, the Six Bar Cowboys, for Decca in 1938. In Gene Autry's movie *Rovin' Tumbleweeds*, Autry and Whitley rewrote the song; in 1940 Autry began using it as the theme song for his radio show *Melody Ranch.*

Autry gave Whitley six hundred dollars for cowriting credit on the song, a decision that Whitley never regretted. If he hadn't given Autry the cowriting credit—and the publishing—the song would not have been used as a theme song, and Whitley would have ended up with a hundred percent of not much instead of half of a great deal of money.

"Cowboy Jubilee," written by Woody Paul and Too Slim, was an attempt to write a theme song to replace "Three on the Trail," which had proven too difficult to sing live.

> I want to be there when they ride into town
> Can't get enough of that great western sound
> It's the best of the west, come along with me
> To the cowboy jubilee

Two days later they recorded a song by Ranger Doug, "At the End of the Rainbow Trail"; three written by Woody, "Compadres in the Old Sierra Madres," "Soon as the Roundup's Through," and "The Desperado Trail"; and Bob Nolan's "On the Rhythm Range."

"At the End of the Rainbow Trail" has "poetic visions of the glory of the West that first grabbed my attention from songs of Nolan, Spencer, and Stan Jones," states Green.

> It's a little ranch on a grassy plain
> At the end of the rainbow trail
> Oh, the hill sides blaze with the sunset's rays
> At the end of the rainbow trail

"I always see my kids, when they were small, waiting with sunny faces at the end of the rainbow trail," said Green in his songbook.

Woody's songs tell a strong story. "Compadres in the Old Sierra Madres" talks about an outlaw hideout.

> Danger rides with those who stray
> Upon this secret hideaway

Where death is sure to welcome
Anyone within the law
But if a man must run
From any lawman's gun
He'll find compadres in the old Sierra Madres

"Desperado Trail" is almost a movie in a song.

One cold night as I lay my fire
A voice behind me said
You killed my son three years ago
And now I'll see you dead
I spun and dropped my finger
But I drew to no avail
His bullet marked the ending of my desperado trail
And in his eyes I saw the face of every man I'd slain
But when the last one was his own
I knew he too must lose the game
As he turned I raised my dying gun and sent him on to hell
For vengeance never dies upon the desperado trail

"Soon As the Roundup's Through" is a love song from a cowboy to his sweetheart back home waiting.

I miss your face
I miss your tender kisses
I miss your golden hair all tied in blue
It kinda goes against my grain
But I love you Liza Jane
And I'll be ridin' home soon as the roundup's through

Two days before Christmas they returned to the studio to finish recording their second album, doing two songs written by Ranger Doug, "Ride with the Wind" and "Ridin' Alone"; a song written by Gary McMahan, "Ol' Cowpoke"; and the old classic, "Red River Valley."

"Ridin' Alone" is hauntingly beautiful with internal rhymes about a cowboy who has lost in love.

Ridin' alone
With a lobo wolf's wail
In a deep canyon's vale
Where the river's bright light
Beckons gently tonight
The song of the waters calls me
Where my heart can be free
It was once in your hand
Now it lies in the sand
Like me it lies lost and alone

On "Ride with the Wind," Ranger Doug was trying to capture "urgency, insistency, the relentless thunder of hoofbeats in flight; I was trying for a feeling more than a linear story."

Ride! Ride! Ride with the wind!
Wild hoof beats, thunder, the desert trails wander
A lightning bolt sunders a dark leaden sky

Gary McMahan is a longtime friend of both Too Slim and Ranger Doug. Slim played bass in Gary's band for a two-week stretch before Riders and heard him sing "Ol' Cowpoke." The line "I rear back in my saddle and lets my yodel go" seemed like an invitation for the Riders to add a yodel. They worked up the song and played it in a club with Gary in attendance before they recorded it. Gary listened and said, alluding to the yodel, "You put something in there that wasn't there." "I took that as a compliment," said Slim.

"Red River Valley" is a timeless classic. The first recording of this song was in 1925 by Carl T. Sprague and called "Cowboy Love Song." Jules Verne Allen, another Texas cowboy singer, recorded it in 1929, and this version was the one to achieve greatest national popularity.

Come and sit by my side if you love me
Do not hasten to bid me adieu
But remember the Red River Valley
And the cowboy who loved you so true

The last song recorded for the album, "Ojo Caliente," was written by former member Tommy Goldsmith before he left the group. The song is a mariachi-flavored song that tells of a good time in Mexico: "I went into a tavern and had the best time of my life."

By 1980 there were four types of western songs. The most popular were the contemporary country music songs where the singer proclaimed himself a cowboy because he was rebellious, individualistic, and self-assertive. He wore a cowboy hat, boots, and drove a pickup truck; this was the type of cowboy popularized by Waylon Jennings and Willie Nelson in the outlaw movement. The next-most-popular were the western songs that were really western movies set to music. "El Paso," "Big Iron," and "Running Gun" by Marty Robbins are all examples here. These songs took their stories and images from movies and television shows that featured a dramatic event in the West. By 1980 these songs had pretty much ceased being written by contemporary country artists.

The third and fourth types were part of the past: the songs of working cowboys and the songs written for singing-cowboy movies that emphasized the grandeur of the West. You had to look long and hard to find any new songs in these two fields being written. Perhaps some of the chuck wagon and dude ranch folks wrote one now and then, but mostly they sang the old, familiar songs already written. Only Riders In The Sky were carrying forth the western tradition, although they studiously avoided the outlaw-type western songs.

The two major writers in the group, Ranger Doug and Woody Paul, came to their songs from slightly different perspectives. Woody Paul leaned more to country than western in his influences, which is most obvious on his "Cowboy Song" recorded on their first album. "Blue Bonnet Lady" is another example, while "So Long, Saddle Pals" was his own version of "Happy Trails." The influence of Marty Robbins, as well as the TV westerns of the 1950s, can be heard on "The Desperado Trail" and "Compadres in the Old Sierra Madres."

Doug Green was a throwback to the 1930s and '40s with his songs that followed in the songwriting footsteps of Bob Nolan, Tim Spencer, Stan Jones, and others. Green's songs could easily have fit into any of the singing-cowboy pictures starring Gene Autry, Roy Rogers, or Tex Ritter. Green's ambition in the early days was to become a major western songwriter, and he looked at the work of the Sons of the Pioneers, especially Bob Nolan's songs, as his chief source of inspiration. Green had a clear vision of what the Riders In The Sky should be: a contemporary group who wrote and sang songs like those from the thirties and forties but with a contemporary identity and Baby Boomer sense of humor.

The year 1980 marked a turning point for the Riders, and it was easy to see them making some major progress. Still, as a group, they were struggling to survive. They had performed 198 times that year, with 118 of those being out of town. They had a new manager, a booking agent, a new album ready for release, and a national appearance on television as the year 1981 began.

Chapter 14

In early January, the Riders played in Georgia during the time when the *Austin City Limits* show was broadcast. On their way back to Nashville, the group stopped in Ringgold, Georgia, to gas up their van. Ranger Doug was dressed in cutoffs and a baseball cap, but the station attendant came out and, in a thick southern accent, asked, "Ain't you Ranger Doug?" He had seen the television show. It was their first brush with national fame, and they were ecstatic. It marked a milestone in their career and was a proof-positive sign that they were making headway.

On January 20, the Riders played at Ronald Reagan's inaugural ball in Washington. This came about because they had done their first symphony concert with the Houston Pops Orchestra, performing such songs as "Waltz Across Texas," "Blue Bonnet Lady," "Here Comes the Santa Fe," and some other western classics. After this performance, they would have the music charts to do more performances with symphonies, which gave their act some "class" and began to move them into performance halls.

The Riders were actually part of the Houston Pops for this performance and played in the Smithsonian's Air and Space Museum at one of thirteen inaugural balls. They didn't get to meet President Reagan but did get to meet Elizabeth Taylor and Robert Goulet and see Count Basie perform. "It's the only time I got to see Freddie Green play the guitar," said Ranger Doug. "But I wasn't really hip enough to his playing yet to really watch him closely. I didn't realize at the time that I was walking in the hallowed shadow of a guy who would become a major influence on me."

Woody met Vice President George Bush "and got pick-pocketed. Also, the dogs the Secret Service had there really got upset over my pot." Woody stayed high a lot in those days—either booze or pot—and the inauguration was no exception.

The Riders lean to the left in their politics and saw the event as "another gig" as they played for, in Too Slim's words, "a bunch of drunken Republicans." Their liberalism fits well with the Public Radio crowd and the anti–right wing element on college campuses, and their humor reflects this. So when the group played at the Cat's Cradle in Chapel Hill, North Carolina, a week later, they were harangued by some students "who thought we'd sold out to the Establishment," said Ranger Doug. "To us it was no political statement. It was another show—and we had to take 'em where we got 'em and move on."

"I said it was honoring the office and not the man and stuff like that," said Too Slim. "But one young lady wasn't buying it." That young lady got on stage with the Riders and stopped their show, arguing her case. "I got kind of mad at that girl on stage, and she was mad at us but she had a right to her views," said Ranger Doug. "Finally, I said, 'What is this—*Face the Nation?* We've got a job to do, lady!' But she still kept hectoring us in the club about selling out to the corporate world."

On March 4, the Riders played at No Fish Today in Baltimore, where Too Slim had a much better experience with a female in the audience. It was at this performance that he met Roberta "Bert" Samet, who would later become his wife. At the time, she and her friend were dressed in cowgirl outfits as they asked the band, "Can we get you anything?" The band replied they'd like some soup, and it was procured. This would be the beginning of a long-term, often long-distance, romance.

"I had a girlfriend who was supposed to meet me there—but

she didn't come," remembered Slim. "The club was a real dive—you couldn't stand up straight because the ceiling was so low. I had to lean the bass because I couldn't hold it straight."

The Riders had just finished an engagement at the Cat's Cradle in Chapel Hill—the scene of the January confrontation—and had driven up to Baltimore in a snowstorm. On the Washington Beltway they had a flat tire—their first road trip flat!—and Slim was suffering from bursitis. "I couldn't move my arm," he said. "We were getting three hundred dollars for the gig, and I needed some emotional support."

Roberta had first heard Riders In The Sky on the Jerry Gray Show on WAMU; her boyfriend at the time had taped the show and played it for her and some friends. Roberta is from Baltimore, so No Fish Today was in her hometown. The Riders were scheduled to play the Cellar Door, and the Baltimore date was a "pickup"—it was close, and they got some money for the Wednesday night performance.

"They were supposed to start at eight but didn't get there until ten because of the flat tire," remembers Roberta. "And when they did get there, they looked like a bunch of ragamuffins, like a folk music group. Fred's jeans had holes in them, Woody had hair down to the middle of his back, and Ranger Doug was known as 'the big guy' because at that time he had a large waist and small shoulders. About a year later, everybody started working out, and that's how Doug got a narrow waist and broad shoulders. Woody and Ranger Doug wore the shirts from the first album cover and Slim wore an attractive satin cowboy bowling shirt."

Woody's hair had been a bone of contention for some of the more conservative audiences. When he tied it in a ponytail, which he often did, Woody's hair went halfway down his back. But when he let it hang down, it fell past his shoulders and covered some of the front of his shirt. Not every audience member was pleased to see a long-haired hippie-looking fiddler performing the beloved old songs of Gene Autry, Roy Rogers, and the Sons of the Pioneers. The memories of Vietnam-era protests were not that far in the past, and some had still not accepted the fact that everyone who liked John Wayne westerns didn't automatically agree with John Wayne's right-wing political views.

A spark was kindled that night between Fred LaBour and

Roberta Samet—who discovered their mutual sense of humor that evening—that would grow into a flame.

On May 11, the Riders were in Los Angeles, where they made their first network television appearance on *The John Davidson Show* on NBC. The next night they performed at The Improv, a comedy club.

The Riders had signed with the Agency for the Performing Arts (APA) through the influence of Bill McEuen, brother of Nitty Gritty Dirt Band member John McEuen and manager of Steve Martin. "Bill McEuen was going to manage us," recounts Slim. "We were in L.A. staying at Bill's condo, and he was talking about getting us into some movies. This was a period when Woody was drinking heavily, and one evening Woody got drunk and stoned and started talking about how his kids could play him as a young boy in the movies and a lot of nonsense. He was just rapping this madness, going on and on. The next morning Bill came down and said, 'I want to thank you for last night because it reminded me why I don't want to be a manager.' That was the end of what we thought was going to be a really big break—management by a high-powered manager. But he took us to APA, introduced us, and told us, 'You don't need a manager—you need an agent.'"

"There was a move to get us in comedy clubs," remembers Slim. "But we were fish out of water. We were the wrong act for the place. That audience did not get it at all."

"The comedy clubs never really worked," added Ranger Doug. "I think we geared our act more towards comedy at those places, but our show sort of depends on that tension between a serious song setting up the comedy. To just come out and be funny—we don't grow on you in that way. We're not a stand-up comedy act in that sense."

"APA tried really hard for us," said Slim. "And they got us some big TV things. Some of what they did was almost successful."

In July the Riders performed at a folk festival in Winnipeg, Canada—their first appearance outside the United States.

"Everybody got it in the folk circuit," said Slim. "We were so new and different, and we were the hit of the festival. A lot of folks from Minneapolis came over—and that got us into the Minnesota State Fair and the Minneapolis market, which was really good for us."

"Those folk festivals were great for us, although Woody always hated them," said Ranger Doug. "He thought they were too much work and there was no money in it. They'd pay a per diem, and we'd make a few hundred bucks. But Woody would say, 'Why are we giving up a weekend?'" Also, Woody never liked to play for free, and made that point with Ranger Doug and Too Slim several times.

"We don't play in Canada much because we did those festivals, but things like that can get a buzz going," said Ranger Doug. "And I think it did help us in more subtle ways because it was part of what really got us rolling. There's a lot of communication between people in this circuit, and they really communicate with each other. So it created a good buzz."

On October 23, the Riders went into the Creative Workshop Studios in Nashville and recorded two songs, "Christmas at the Triple X Ranch," written by Woody Paul and Karen Ritter, and "Riding Home on Christmas Eve," written by Ranger Doug. This would be released as a single by Rounder for the Christmas season but never really got any air play on country radio. The genesis for the "Riding Home on Christmas Eve" song, according to Ranger Doug, was a job delivering flowers for Parmenter's Florists during Christmas seasons in high school and college. The "insistent, plodding rhythm" of "The Little Drummer Boy"—a song he came to loathe—stayed with him, and he "tried to adapt that peculiar insistence, that steady repetition, to the slow footfalls of a homebound cowpoke's horse" for this song.

> I'm riding home on Christmas Eve
> Rolling along with the tumbleweeds
> The winter wind blows cold and strong
> But still it pushes me along

The Riders pulled into radio station KCRW in Santa Monica, California, on November 14, 1981, for a radio interview. Mike Mahaney had been doing a show called *Country Liberation* since 1976, playing a wide variety of country music while avoiding the slick sounds of Nashville. Mahaney heard the Riders' first album on Rounder and called the label, wanting an interview. The Riders had a show scheduled at McCabe's that evening but turned up first for Mahaney's show.

"I was on the air for about fifteen minutes while they stood around with their instruments tuning up," said Mahaney. "I thought it was going to be a regular interview, but the next thing I know these guys ease me out of the way and take over the mike. They played for forty or fifty minutes, and the phones lit up like a Christmas tree."

On November 18 they were back in Los Angeles, where they performed at the *Twilight Theater* on NBC. "This was a television special hosted by Steve Martin," said Slim. "People often tell us they saw us on *Saturday Night Live*—but we were never on that show. We were on this one, which was hosted by Martin."

"In the period before he became a big movie star but was moving beyond *Saturday Night Live*, Steve Martin signed a contract for six TV specials," remembers Ranger Doug. "It was kind of a variety show—I think we sang one song. He was fulfilling that contract, although you almost got the feeling he wished he wasn't there. He was very pleasant to us, though." "He seemed to read *The Wall Street Journal* a lot," added Slim.

This was another opportunity provided by Bill McKuen, "who was extremely pivotal to us for a short period," said Green. "For six months he played a very significant role in our lives and career."

The Riders appeared in public 196 times in 1981; 161 of those were outside Nashville. They had gone past "mere survival," and making a living was definitely getting a whole lot easier.

Chapter 15

On January 5 and 6, 1982, the Riders were in Pittsburgh at Audio Innovators Studio to record an album's worth of songs. That album project came about because Jim Sutton, who was a fan of the Riders, wanted to have an album to sell on television. "He was going to do these infomercials, like Boxcar Willie and Slim Whitman," said Doug. "And we recorded this album of half standards and half originals that sounded like standards."

The first day they recorded two classics, "Cool Water" and "Tumbling Tumbleweeds," and two songs written by Woody, "Bound to Hit the Trail" and "West Texas Cowboy."

"Cool Water" and "Tumbling Tumbleweeds" are the two best-known western songs of all time. Both were written by Bob Nolan in the early years of the Sons of the Pioneers. Nolan had written a number of poems in his youth, and "Cool Water" was originally a poem he wrote in the mid-1920s while a student at Tucson High School. It was inspired by Nolan's fascination with the desert after he moved there from his native Canada to join his father, Harry Nobles, a veteran of World War I who had retired to Tucson, then changed his name to "Nolan" because it sounded more American. Bob was fourteen when he joined his father in Tucson, and the southwestern landscape had an immediate and profound impact on him. For the rest of his life, Nolan was captivated by the desert, and the themes of deserts and the southwestern landscape would dominate his writing.

Nolan began to seriously compose poems in Tucson, influenced by nineteenth-century poets Keats, Shelley, and Byron as well as Scottish poet Robert Burns. It was here he wrote the poem that eventually became the song "Cool Water." After college Nolan traveled a bit before moving to California, where he joined his father in 1929, who had moved there earlier. In the Los Angeles area Nolan joined a Chautauqua troupe and began to write songs and perform. This gave him the show-biz bug. He was working as a lifeguard when he read an advertisement in the newspaper for a singer who could yodel and answered it. The ad was placed by Leonard Slye—later to become Roy Rogers—and the two formed a singing duo who performed with the Rocky Mountaineers. They soon realized they needed another voice, and Nolan suggest his friend Bill "Slumber" Nichols, who joined the group. Nolan dropped out in mid-1932 and landed a job as a golf caddy at the prestigious Bel Aire Country Club. It was during this period of time, while home at his apartment one day, that he wrote "Tumbling Leaves," which later became "Tumbling Tumbleweeds."

Published in 1934, "Tumbling Tumbleweeds" was written during a rainy day in November; as Nolan stood at his window, watching the wind and rain, he was inspired to write "Tumbling Leaves." When the Sons of the Pioneers were first formed, they performed this song on the radio, but listeners thought they sang "Tumbling Weeds" so Nolan rewrote the song a bit and it became "Tumbling Tumbleweeds." Ironically, the famous opening line "I'm a roaming cowboy, riding all day long" was written by the publisher to replace Nolan's original "Days may be dreary / Still I'm not weary" opening. The song proved so popular that the first starring movie for Gene Autry in 1935 was named after it.

"Bound to Hit the Trail" by Woody could be about a traveling musician as well as a cowboy trailhand:

> For a cowboy has to ride the range
> And yodel-a-de-oddle-oo
> Listen to the dogies lowin'
> Low-oo-low-oo
> Oh I long to dream near a campfire's gleam
> And listen to the coyotes wail
> I guess I'm just a cowboy and I'm bound to hit the trail

"West Texas Cowboy" is a song of praise to Texas cowboys:

> He loves to rope and ride on his pony far and wide
> Back on those old West Texas plains
> And the prairie flowers blossom forever
> Round the steps of his home on the range
> And he strolls with his brown-eyed darling
> Down the trail of the dreams that they hold
> And if he ever has to say farewell to Texas
> He'll be saying good-bye to his soul

The next day they did two more old standards, "La Cucaracha" and "The Streets of Laredo"; three songs by Ranger Doug: "Wasteland," "That's How the Yodel Was Born," and "Singing a Song to the Sky"; and a song written by Johnny Lange and Elliot Daniel, "Pecos Bill."

The lyrics to "The Streets of Laredo," also known as "The Cowboy's Lament," were written by a cowboy, Francis Henry Maynard, in 1876 during a trail drive. This song was popular with cowboys in the West from the time it was written.

Beat the drum slowly and play the pipes lowly
And play the death march as you carry me along
I'm a young cowboy who's been shot in the chest
I know I must die because I know I've done wrong

Pecos Bill is an old folk tale from the West. According to legend, Pecos Bill fell out of a wagon his father was driving across the Pecos River; he was raised by coyotes and could ride anything—even a cyclone. He used a rattlesnake for a whip that he snapped over a mountain lion while he was riding and carved out the Grand Canyon in a week while digging for gold.

In 1948, Walt Disney filmed a movie, *Melody Time.* There were six sections to the movie; and two songwriters, Johnny Lange and Eliot Daniel, were assigned the job of writing the western section. They wrote two songs: "Pecos Bill" and "Blue Shadows on the Trail." Both were sung by Roy Rogers and the Sons of the Pioneers and were on a chart record ("Blue Shadows on the Trail" was the "A" side and did better) in 1948.

"Singing a Song to the Sky" is the story of a happy, carefree cowboy.

On the winds of the west there go I
My heart is so free it could fly
As I ride singing my song to the sky

"Wasteland" is a dark ballad about a cowboy and his horse fleeing the law with no cool, clear water in sight.

Ride: they must ride through the parched barren ground
Hide: they must hide where they'll never be found
Ride: Old Dan whinnies with fear
For the end may be near
The howling winds leer all around all around

The album didn't do particularly well on television—it was ahead of its time in terms of the resurgence of western music that occurred later in the 1980s and early 1990s—and ended up becoming the *Weeds and Water* album after Rounder purchased the masters.

The Riders also did an album for the Book of the Month Club, which was a compilation of tracks leased from Rounder. It, too, was a bit ahead of its time.

On January 27 the Riders played the legendary Los Angeles club, The Palomino. "Marty Klein, the main agent at APA, was trying to get us on the *Tonight Show*," said Slim. "He said we needed four minutes of killer stuff. So we were trying to do that—but it never really worked for us."

Ranger Doug has especially fond memories of that date because "Bill and Barbara Bowen ran the Sons of the Pioneers Fan Club, and they brought P-Nuts Nolan and Buddy Perryman—the widows of Bob Nolan and Lloyd Perryman—to the show. "That meant so much to me," remembers Green. "I can't tell you what that meant to me having them out there to see the show, because they loved it."

This was also the beginning of the top-of-the-line, high-quality western clothes. "That's when we met Manuel," said Slim. "His shop was near the Palamino, and we splurged and bought a seventy-five-dollar shirt off the sales rack. That was the beginning of the good—and expensive—clothes."

On April 5, 1982, the Riders entered Quadraphonic Studios in Nashville to begin recording their fourth album. On that first day they recorded the basic tracks for "Blue Shadows on the Trail," written by Johnny Lange and Eliot Daniel; "Cowpoke," written by Stan Jones; and the old classic, "Home on the Range."

In his book *For a Cowboy Has to Sing*, author Jim Bob Tinsley states that Johnny Lange, the lyricist for the Walt Disney movie *Melody Time*, took the script home to Palm Springs and, while sitting by his pool, was inspired to write "Blue Shadows on the Trail" by the blue shadows on the mountains as the moon illuminated the landscape. Lange, born John Logo in Philadelphia in 1909, moved to Hollywood in 1937 to write songs for the movies. Lange later wrote the lyrics for "Mule Train." Eliot Daniel, one of the two music directors on the film, was born in Boston in 1908. A graduate of Harvard University, Daniel moved to Hollywood in 1945 after serving in the coast guard during World War II. Daniel worked as composer/conductor for Walt Disney Studios; later, he wrote the music to "Lavender Blue," which received an Academy Award nomination.

"Cowpoke" begins with a carefree yodel and lyrics that begin "I'm lonesome but happy / Rich but I'm broke," which have made it a popular song to sing. The song concludes, "I'll never be branded / I'll never be broke / I'm a carefree range rider / A driftin' cowpoke."

The poem "A Home on the Range" was first recorded by folksong collector John Lomax in San Antonio, Texas, in 1908; the singer was Bill Jack McCurry, the black owner of a beer parlor in the red-light district of that city. It began to appear in sheet music form in 1925, based on McCurry's version; and in 1933 it became a top radio hit. President Roosevelt proclaimed it his favorite song.

Home, home on the range
Where the deer and the antelope play
Where seldom is heard
A discouraging word
And the skies are not cloudy all day

The next day at the studio was a long one for the Riders—they recorded basic tracks for nine songs. Three of the songs were written by Ranger Doug: "Chasing the Sun," "Old El Paso," and "Prairie Serenade." Woody Paul also wrote three: "Pretty Prairie Princess," "The Utah Trail," and "Nevada" (the last with some help from Karen Ritter). They also recorded the Deuce Spriggins song "Down the Trail to San Antone"; the old standard, "I Ride an Old Paint"; and a Tex Ritter hit from back in the forties, "Jingle Jangle Jingle."

"The slow intro to Bob Nolan's 'Trail Dreamin' 'was probably the main inspiration for 'Prairie Serenade,'" states Ranger Doug, although "I also hear a touch of Ray Whitley's 'Lonely River.'"

Prairie serenade
It's the song of a child,
It's the call of the wild
Prairie serenade
It's the longhorn's bawl,
It's the coyote's call
It's the lobo's moan to the great unknown
Prairie serenade

The song was written on the back of an interstate highway road map while traveling. "I consider it probably the epitome of my classic Pioneers-style songs," states Green.

"Old El Paso" has a mariachi feel and tells the story of the city whose "name recalls visions of daring young cowboys." It is reminiscent of Marty Robbins's classic, "El Paso."

"Chasing the Sun" is a fast-paced number about being on the move.

Racin' the wind, chasin' the sun
Headin for town, roundup is done
Boots on the fly, dead on the run
Throw my lasso round the west wind
And ride on chasin' the sun

Woody Paul's "Pretty Prairie Princess" is a beautiful, touching song about a child.

Pretty prairie princess
Daddy's little girl
Brightest flower ever
To blossom in my world
Joyous wonder fills me
As I picture you just now
Shiny laugh and deep blue eyes
Beneath your golden brow

On "Nevada," Woody got some help with the lyrics from Karen Ritter, who worked at the Nashville library at the time and wrote lyrics for Woody Paul's melody.

Nevada, silver and sage brush
Nevada, gamblin' and gold rush
The highest wildest country,
The brightest, the best
Nevada, the diamond of the west

"Down the Trail to San Antone" was a Sons of the Pioneers song that Ranger Doug learned from his record collection.

"Jingle Jangle Jingle" was written in early 1942 for the movie *The Forest Rangers*, starring Fred MacMurray and Paulette Goddard. The song was composed by Joseph J. Lilley, who was on the Paramount Pictures staff, with lyrics by Frank Loesser. Lilley, born in 1914, attended the Boston Conservatory of Music and then Juilliard.

Frank Loesser was born in New York City in 1910. In 1936 he moved to Hollywood to write for the movies; during World War II he wrote both lyrics and music to the hit, "Praise the Lord and Pass the Ammunition." After World War II he wrote a number of musicals, including *Guys and Dolls* and *How to Succeed in Business without Really Trying*. Loesser won an Academy Award in 1949 for his song "Baby, It's Cold Outside" and also wrote "Luck Be a Lady Tonight," a hit song from *Guys and Dolls*.

"Jingle Jangle Jingle" was recorded by Kay Kyser and His Orchestra and released in mid-1942; the movie wasn't released until October. The song was an immediate hit, holding down the number-one position on the charts for five weeks and selling over a million copies. Tex Ritter recorded it for the western market, and it was a country hit for him.

"I Ride an Old Paint" is remarkably similar to "Goodbye Old Paint," and both came from the oral tradition. It was learned in Santa Fe by Margaret Larkin and playwright Lynn Riggs, who popularized the song. Larkin included the song in a book published in 1931; earlier John Lomax had published both the "Old Paint" songs as "Old Paint (I)" and "Old Paint (II)." Larkin and Riggs produced the musical *Green Grow the Lilacs* in New York beginning in 1931, which starred Tex Ritter; later this play became the basis for Rodgers and Hammerstein's play *Oklahoma!*

> I ride an Old Paint and I lead an Old Dan
> I'm goin' to Montana for to throw the hoolihan
> Feed 'em in the coulees, and water in the draw
> Their tails are all matted and their backs are all raw
> Ride around little dogies, ride around them slow
> For the fiery and snuffy are a-rarin' to go

Chapter 16

During Fan Fair in Nashville that June, the Riders were inducted into the Country Music Foundation's Walkway of Stars as their name was placed in front of the building where Ranger Doug used to work. Slim remembers that "Woody wept. We were really surprised and just stared at him. But it was a very emotional experience for him. When he spoke he was very eloquent and told how much he was moved by this honor."

On June 19, 1982, Riders In The Sky achieved a lifelong dream when they were inducted into the Grand Ole Opry. By this time, the Riders had performed on the Opry twenty-six times. Ranger Doug had written a letter to Hal Durham, manager of the Opry, telling him the Riders would like to join. He noted that they had gotten a great response when they had appeared, that western music was a music that was under-represented and yet it didn't conflict with the material or performance of any other members. "It wouldn't take anybody else's light away," said Green.

Durham's major reservation was Woody. "Woody had a reputation of partying a little hard," remembered Green. "Hal Durham was concerned about Woody's erratic behavior. His reputation preceded him. But I assured him that at that point things seemed to be very much under control and have remained so. The hard-drinking days were over by then, and I assured him of that. It was something we'd all been worried about."

Woody had been drinking heavily since 1977. "I don't remember much between 1977 and 1982," he said. "I was drinking in a deathly way—I'd drink about a fifth of Jack Daniels a day, smoke a pack of weed, and toke on pot anytime I could." Indeed, it was a time that was trying for Ranger Doug and Too Slim, who had to accommodate Woody's erratic, often boorish behavior.

The turning point came in Colorado Springs, where the Riders had gone to play a small club, a booking instigated by Bill Wiley. Wiley was a longtime friend of the Sons of the Pioneers, especially Pat Brady, a former Pioneer best known as the driver of Nellybelle and sidekick of Roy Rogers on the singing cowboy's TV show. Wiley and Brady were both alcoholics and had moved to Colorado Springs. Brady died in February 1972, but Wiley remained in the area, working in real estate.

Wiley confronted Woody about his drinking and took him to an Alcoholics Anonymous meeting, which started Woody on his road to recovery. This was not the first time Woody had been confronted with his drinking, but this was the confrontation that provided positive results.

"Ranger Doug almost killed me ten or twelve times," remembered Woody. "He wanted to punch me out, but he never did. He used unbelievable restraint—I know he wanted to cream me. He did write me a letter or two. I was really screwing up at the time, worthless and useless. Playing really bad. But him and Slim stuck with me. Him and Slim are the best thing that ever happened to me."

"Slim and I told Woody several times that if he needed help, we'd help him get it," said Green. "And we had to give him an ultimatum about his drinking, but we also wanted to give the guy the benefit of the doubt. It's not like he was just a journeyman musician—Woody's brilliant, a great songwriter, and crucial to our success. Thank goodness Bill Wiley was there at the right time."

Woody's drinking threatened Ranger Doug's dream of having a top western singing group. Green always wanted to be a fulltime musician and had played bluegrass and folk in the past. As he developed a love and admiration for western music, then formed the Riders and became Ranger Doug, Green saw his dream becoming a reality. The one thing that could shatter that dream was Woody Paul's drinking—and Douglas Green, a kind-hearted, tolerant man by nature, was torn between trying to help Woody Paul overcome his addiction or booting him out of the Riders because Woody's drinking was destroying the group.

That dilemma was solved in 1982 when Woody sobered up and joined Alcoholics Anonymous. Although he is still eccentric, and "Where's Woody?" is the most-often asked question by the Riders as well as to the Riders, his drunken behavior is a thing of the past.

Durham was satisfied that Woody's wildest days were behind him, and so he invited the Riders to become official members of the Grand Ole Opry on June 19.

Getting to the Opry for their induction that evening was not an easy chore. The day before, the Riders had performed at Billy Bob's giant night club in Fort Worth. At eight o'clock on the morning of the nineteenth they performed at Fort Concho Days in San Angelo, then got a police escort to the airport. There were thunderstorms and tornadoes at the time, so the Riders barely made it in a small plane from San Angelo to the Dallas–Fort Worth Airport, where thunderstorms and tornadoes again threatened to stop their journey. However, they made it to Nashville in time to get home, change clothes, and get to the Opry.

"Ernest Tubb introduced us," remembered Slim. "He had emphysema and was breathing hard. I'm not sure he got our name quite right." Ranger Doug remembers it as a "gracious introduction," although Tubb was "very weak."

"The Opry cast was wonderful," said Slim. "They said 'Welcome to the Family.'" A photographer took a picture of the group that night, and that photo ended up on the cover of their *Weeds and Water* album.

On August 19–21, 1982, the Riders performed at the World's Fair in Knoxville. And here Too Slim got into trouble with the Society for the Prevention of Cruelty to Animals. The problem began back in Nashville while Slim was watching the news on TV one evening. There was a segment hosted by Huell Howser, who did "happy features." He would find interesting people and interview them. On this particular broadcast he interviewed a man who did the "rabbit dance," where he got down on his porch—his hands on the floor, legs straight, and feet flat—and hopped around like a rabbit. Peggy, Slim's wife at the time, said, "I'll bet you couldn't do that."

"That was like a red flag," said Slim, who proceeded to do the "rabbit dance" in his living room. On stage, Woody had always been known as the dancer—he danced while playing the fiddle and was a good clogger. But one night, without any warning to the other two, Too Slim proceeded to stop playing bass and, while Woody fiddled, did the "rabbit dance."

"Woody was looking at me like 'What in the world are you doing?'" remembered Slim. "He didn't get it at all. Plus, I was in his territory, doing a dance." This dance then evolved into the "varmint dance," "sloth dance," "armadillo dance," and various other permutations as a segment of the Riders' live act featured Too Slim abandoning his bass fiddle and doing various contortions and "dances" on the stage.

In Knoxville at the World's Fair, the Riders played on an outdoor stage, and behind them was a man-made reflecting pool. Slim had taken a live fish—a carp—from the Chinese Exhibit and put it in a bucket in the pool where the audience couldn't see it. It was a hot day, and when Slim began his "varmint dance" he went over, jumped in the pool, and pulled out the foot-and-a-half-long carp and brought it to the stage. At the microphone he "interviewed" the fish, whose mouth was moving slowly like it was talking.

It was a hoot that everyone seemed to enjoy except for an audience member who thought it was no way to treat a fish. The next day the group was contacted by the SPCA "because a lady had reported us abusing a fish." This would serve as a lesson for future events such as this.

On Thursday, August 24, the Riders began a three-night stand at "Mr. Whitekey's Fly by Night" in Anchorage, Alaska. "There was a lake outside the window—you could open the curtains and see it from the club," remembers Slim. "I had hidden a big rubber fish by the lake. I ran outside and dove in the lake and came up soaked with a big plastic fish and did the salmon dance. We ended up doing a conga line in that club." "He had to be freezing to death," reflected Ranger Doug. "It was cold, and he just dove into the lake. He was soaking wet."

The appearances at Mr. Whitekey's led to three performances at the Alaska State Fair. "It was freezing, and we were on a little covered stage outdoors," said Slim. "We were kept warm with some propane heaters. The audience consisted of about fifteen people standing in an ice-cold drizzle. It was miserable."

During the Labor Day holiday they began a series of appearances at the Minnesota State Fair that ran through September 6. During that run, they made their first appearance on the *Prairie Home Companion* on September 4.

"Garrison Keillor saw us at the fair," remembered Slim. "That's how we got on the *Prairie Home Companion*. During the radio show I remember the producer, Margaret Moos, was standing beside me backstage while Garrison was doing his monologue. And right in the middle of it she said, 'He has no idea where he's going with this.' But he kept wandering around and eventually tied it all together."

Those appearances in Minnesota were good for the Riders. "They have that public radio consciousness up there," observed Slim. "And that's what we're all about." On December 4 the Riders returned to St. Paul for another appearance on the *Prairie Home Companion.*

On September 9 the Riders went to Ann Arbor, Michigan, and played The Ark, their first performance where Douglas and Fred had both gone to college. Slim was a nervous wreck. "I was scared—stage frightened," he remembers. "It was a heavy thing for me. It was a very intimate setting—the living room in a house was the original Ark, and there were some friends there. I eventually relaxed—but I couldn't do any comedy at first."

Ranger Doug was a different story—"Ann Arbor wasn't a big emotional attachment for me," he said. "I only spent two years there because I transferred from a small college. But Slim loved college. He was, in a way that people should be, really into the college life. To me it was always passing through. I wanted to play music. I enjoyed studying English, and I was good at it, but I didn't get into college like a lot of people did. Certainly not like Slim—who spent five years there."

On Friday, Christmas Eve, the Riders performed on the Opry, then came back and performed again on Christmas night. They ended the year by celebrating New Year's Eve on the Opry as well.

That New Year's Eve performance marked their 202nd appearance that year—the most appearances they had done during a single year.

Chapter 17

In 1983 Riders In The Sky would benefit from being in the right place at the right time, connected to the right people and the right organizations. It seems appropriate that the year began with the Riders performing on the Grand Ole Opry on New Year's Day.

This would mark the beginning of a year when the Opry became extremely relevant to the music industry because it was owned by the same company that owned The Nashville Network (TNN), which would give country music daily national coverage on cable TV.

WSM, the radio station begun in 1925 that broadcasted the Grand Ole Opry, owned The Nashville Network.

The Opry has a long and storied history; it began on November, 28, 1925, a little over a month after WSM first went on the air, when program director George D. Hay, known as "The Solemn Old Judge," sat fiddler Uncle Jimmy Thompson in front of a microphone and let him play "old time" tunes. The response was overwhelming, so every Saturday evening, what was then called "old time" music or "familiar tunes" was played. In 1927 Hay named the show "The Grand Ole Opry" after it followed a broadcast from the Metropolitan Opera.

The show developed into a variety show that emphasized what would later become known as country music. In 1939 it acquired a major sponsor, Prince Albert Tobacco, and went on the NBC network. This increased its popularity, but Nashville was not the center for country music at that time. *The National Barn Dance* on WLS in Chicago was a more popular program during World War II; and the singing cowboys in Hollywood, particularly Gene Autry, as well as the western swing of bandleaders such as Bob Wills and Spade Cooley, were more popular at the end of World War II.

But Nashville had several things going for it. First, the station committed to finding the best talent available for the Opry; they were aided in this quest by their clear channel status, gained in 1934, which meant that the Opry was heard almost all over the United States because of its powerful signal. Also, the Opry was owned by an insurance company, which saw the value in terms of selling insurance. The company sold what was commonly known as "burial" or "industrial" insurance to poor people; when a salesman from the National Life and Accident Insurance Company knocked on a rural door and told them he was from "the Grand Ole Opry insurance company," they usually welcomed him in and bought a policy. Finally, their sponsor, Prince Albert Tobacco, targeted its products to the white working-class smoker, which was the audience the Opry attracted. So the sponsor re-

Ranger Doug as a child.
Photo provided by the author and Riders In The Sky.

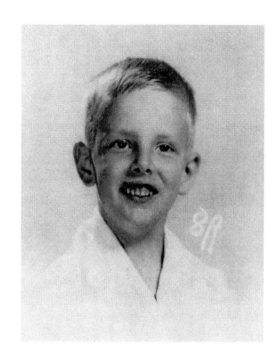

The Doug Green Band, 1974. Left to right: Bob Fowler, Too Slim, James Bryan, Bruce Nemerov, and Deputy Doug. *Photo provided by the author and Riders In The Sky.*

(*Above*) Too Slim and his mom, Hazel, February 1957 at Tanque Verde Ranch, Tucson, Arizona. *Photo provided by the author and Riders In The Sky. (Below)* (1978) First publicity photo at Exit/In. Too Slim, Ranger Doug, and Windy Bill. *Photo courtesy of New Horizon Management. Photo provided by the author and Riders In The Sky.*

Riders In The Sky, circa 1978. Fourth man is Tumbleweed Tommy Goldsmith. Photo courtesy of New Horizon Management. *Photo provided by the author and Riders In The Sky.*

(*Above*) Left to right: Woody, Ranger Doug, Terry Clark, Too Slim, and Joey as sultans on Riders Radio Theater TV. *Photo provided by the author and Riders In The Sky.* (*Below*) Signed to Rounder Records in 1980. They laid down their arms after they didn't get a bullet! Photo courtesy of Thunderbird Artists. *Photo provided by the author and Riders In The Sky.*

(Above) The Riders with Barbara Mandrell. *Photo provided by the author and Riders In The Sky. (Below)* Riders In The Sky induction into the Grand Ole Opry, June 1982. Left to right: Too Slim, Ranger Doug, Woody Paul, Opry General Manager Hal Durham, and Ernest Tubb. *Photo courtesy of the Grand Ole Opry. (WSM photo by Les Leverett.)*

Riders In The Sky with "Too Jaws," fourth or fifth smartest horse in the movies. *Photo by Alan Mayor. Photo provided by the author and Riders In The Sky.*

(*Above*) On the set of TNN's *Tumbleweed Theater* with John Hartford. *Photo provided by the author and Riders In The Sky.* (*Below*) The Riders go Hawaiian on the set of TNN's *Tumbleweed Theater, 1983-1985. Photo provided by the author and Riders In The Sky.*

Sidemeat, "The Sidekick's Sidekick" and bunkhouse cook. *Photo courtesy of MCA Records. Photo by Don Putnam. Photo provided by the author and Riders In The Sky.*

Sergeant Dudley. *Photo courtesy of MCA Records. Photo by Don Putnam. Photo provided by the author and Riders In The Sky.*

Freddie La, the Cowboy Surfer. *Photo courtesy of MCA Records. Photo by Don Putnam. Photo provided by the author and Riders In The Sky.*

(*Above*) Slocum and Charlie, Riders In The Sky's arch-enemies from Riders Radio Theater. *Photo provided by the author and Riders In The Sky.* (*Below*) Shotgun Red and Sidemeat. *Photo provided by the author and Riders In The Sky.*

(*Above*) First professional gig at Hines Veterans Hospital for Joey at eight years old. *Photo provided by the author and Riders In The Sky.* (*Below*) Early publicity photo with Joey the Cowpolka King. *Photo courtesy of New Frontier Management.*

Riders In The Sky and Roy Rogers on the set of *Hee Haw,* 1989. *Photo by Don Putnam. Photo provided by the author and Riders In The Sky.*

Postcard photo for "Livin' in a Mobile Home" 1990 "Horse Opera." "Mama" (Slim), "Dry-wall Paul" (Woody), and "Ranger Doug." *Photo provided by the author and Riders In The Sky.*

Drywall Paul. *Photo courtesy of MCA Records. Photo by Don Putnam. Photo provided by the author and Riders In The Sky.*

"It's the Cowboy Way!" marquis. *Photo provided by the author and Riders In The Sky.*

mained with the Opry until 1960, while the sponsors of other "barn dance" programs—the term generally used for live country music shows on the radio—left those shows during the late 1940s and early 1950s. In 1960 the *WLS Barn Dance* in Chicago and the *Louisiana Hayride* in Shreveport both went off the air.

The Opry emerged in the late 1940s as the premier live country music show on radio, and during the mid-1950s Nashville emerged as a major recording center, a result of excellent recording studios and a pool of available musicians who were members of the union. But in 1957, the country music industry nearly folded, a result of the success of Elvis Presley and rock 'n' roll. Almost overnight radio stations, who had lost their network shows and network sponsors to television, began playing rock 'n' roll records to attract an audience. There wasn't much demand for country music, so it wasn't getting much exposure. In 1958 the Country Music Association was formed in Nashville to help get radio airplay for country recordings and promote Nashville as the capital of country music. As part of that effort, the CMA established the Country Music Hall of Fame and elected its first members in 1961. That same year, the CMA began a fundraising campaign to construct a Country Music Hall of Fame building in Nashville. Andrew Benedict, president of First American Bank, headed the fund-raising; and the city donated some land to build on.

The Hall of Fame was opened in 1967; that same year, Nashville passed a law allowing merchants to sell mixed drinks. The Hall of Fame proved that country music could be an effective tourist attraction, while the liquor-by-the-drink law meant Nashville could become a place for conventions.

During the 1960s the Ryman Auditorium, which had been built in 1890 and had been home to the Opry since 1943, was deteriorating. There was no air-conditioning in the building, there were no dressing facilities backstage, and the bathrooms were inadequate. Further, because of the move to the suburbs by residents and the businesses that followed, downtown had become a place where the "good" citizens didn't want to go; it was dominated by adult bookstores and hotels that rented rooms by the hour.

At this point, many of the board members of the National Life and Accident Insurance Company felt the company should sell the Opry and get out of the country music business. However, in

the summer of 1967 Johnny Cash began taping his nationally televised show on ABC at the Ryman; this caused a shift in the views
of the insurance company's board members, who now felt they
should move the Opry out of the Ryman instead of selling it.

As National Life began drawing up plans for a new Opry
House, they made sure the facility included excellent television
production capabilities. They had purchased land about fifteen
miles from downtown for the Opry House, so discussions soon
followed about how to attract people out to the Opry House. From
these discussions came the idea for a theme park, Opryland, which
would also be housed on the site. The idea originated from WSM
president Irving Waugh, who had seen the Astrodome in Houston as a centerpiece for an area of parks and a hotel, as well as
Disneyland in Anaheim, which was also built along the same general model. As an afterthought, the group decided they should
also include a hotel on the site. In September 1969, the National
Life executives announced they would spend $16 million to build
Opryland U.S.A., a theme park, and a new Grand Ole Opry House
as well as a 150–room hotel, then called the Oprytowne Inn.

On July 1, 1970, ground was broken for Opryland; on May 27,
1972, the park opened, and 1.5 million people attended that first
year. Almost two million attended in 1975. On May 9, 1974, the
new Grand Ole Opry House opened, with President Richard
Nixon the special guest.

Meanwhile, construction of the hotel was delayed. Bud
Wendell, formerly an insurance salesman for National Life and
then general manager of the Grand Ole Opry, had been named to
head up the theme park and hotel. Since Wendell didn't know
anything about hotels, he hired Jack Vaughn, who had been with
Century Plaza Hotel in Los Angeles, to head up and run the
Oprytowne Inn. Vaughn recommended a convention hotel, and
the Opryland Hotel and Convention Center opened in November
1977 with six hundred rooms. The bookings were above expecta-
tions; and Opryland Hotel, which was constructed to allow for ex-
pansion, was soon a big success, benefitting from the powerful
tourist draws of the Grand Ole Opry and Opryland Theme Park.

The success of the Opry and Opryland was reflected in several ways: in 1972, when Opryland opened, Nashville had around
five thousand hotel rooms; in 1977, when the hotel opened, there

were nine thousand rooms. Across the street from Opryland, John Hobbs headed a group of investors who built a Fiddler's Inn with 114 rooms and put in a putt-putt golf course, wax museum, car museum, and a country music night club, The Nashville Palace. All were doing thriving business.

Because of problems with their insurance company—the type of insurance the company had concentrated on was quickly becoming less appealing to consumers, and the company had been slow to shift into new types of policies—the chairman of the insurance company, Rusty Wagner, told other executives with the company that the company desperately needed to find a way to boost their stock. The idea of a cable television network, to be called The Nashville Network, came out of this.

Bud Wendell had arranged a partnership with the Westinghouse Electric Corporation, based in Pittsburgh, to do the marketing for TNN in exchange for a percentage of the ownership in the network. In 1982, National Life was the victim of a hostile takeover by the Houston-based insurance firm, American General. American General was not interested in the country music business and set about getting rid of the Grand Ole Opry, Opryland Theme Park, the Opryland Hotel, and the proposed cable network. Local businessman Bronson Ingram had agreed to buy the properties, but, at the last minute, the company was sold to Edward Gaylord, an Oklahoma City–based newspaper and TV station owner. If Ingram had purchased it, the companies would have remained locally owned.

After the purchase, Gaylord in Nashville, now headed by Bud Wendell, was committed to keeping the properties operating in Nashville. The Nashville Network, which was moving forward with plans for going on the air, had hired a staff and crew and was developing programming.

The centerpiece for TNN's programming was to be a nightly show, *Nashville Now*, hosted by popular disc jockey and local TV personality Ralph Emery. The Grand Ole Opry would be broadcast on Saturday nights, and a show called *Tumbleweed Theater*, which would show old western movies, was set to run as well. Hosting the *Tumbleweed Theater* would be Riders In The Sky.

In January 1983, the Riders began taping their segments for the *Tumbleweed Theater*, which consisted of introducing the western movies and then doing skits and songs to fill in time between breaks in the movie and when the movie ran out.

Chapter 18

On March 5 and 6, 1983, the day before their debut on The Nashville Network, the Riders were in Alexandria, Virginia, to record a live album for Rounder at The Birchmere.

They began their set with "Cowboy Jubilee," their theme song at the time and the title of their second album. Next came "The Yodel Blues," written by Johnny Mercer and Robert Emmet Dolan, which Ranger Doug had learned from an Elton Britt album.

This was followed by "When the Bloom Is on the Sage," which Ranger Doug had first heard when Red River Dave sang it. That song came from The Happy Chappies, also known as Fred Howard and Nat Vincent, who were on a radio broadcast on KFRC in San Francisco, California, in 1930.

Vincent was an original member of the Happy Chappies when they were formed in 1926; Howard joined a few years later, replacing Vincent's original partner. The group was popular on KRFC radio and Columbia recordings. Vincent was born in Kansas City, Missouri, in 1889 and loved playing Sousa marches on a paper-covered comb; he taught himself to play piano and moved to New York City in 1909 to write songs. "I'm Forever Blowing Bubbles" is the best known of the early Vincent songs.

Fred Howard Wright was born in 1896 in San Diego; he later dropped his last name and went by his first and middle names, Fred Howard. He was a member of the *Ma Perkins* radio cast from 1935 to 1940.

"After You've Gone," an old pop song written by Turner Layton and Henry Creamer, is performed as a fiddle tune by Woody Paul. This is followed by Woody's "Cowboy Song" from their first album, then a session of "varmint dancing" by Too Slim while Woody plays fiddle tunes.

A Bob Nolan song, "Hold That Critter Down," is followed by Billy Hill's "The Last Roundup," one of the most popular cowboy songs of all time. It was originally published during the Great

Depression, where it first achieved fame in the *Ziegfeld Follies* of 1934.

Songwriter Billy Hill was born in Boston and studied violin; as a teenager he visited the West and worked briefly as a cowboy and miner. In 1931 he wrote "The Last Round-Up" when he was penniless. When his wife gave birth to their daughter in an elevator because a hospital refused to admit them without payment in advance, Hill almost sold "The Last Round-Up" for twenty-five dollars but was advanced two hundred dollars by Gene Buck, head of a performing rights organization (ASCAP) just in time. In 1933 Shapiro, Bernstein, and Co., a top New York firm, published the song. This is the first western song Gene Autry recorded while he was still on WLS in Chicago.

"I Grab My Saddle Horn and Blow" is a Bob Nolan song, and so is "When Payday Rolls Around," which the Riders had recorded on their first album. Too Slim's version of "Cielito Lindo" was followed by Woody Paul doing "Blue Bonnet Lady," then "When Payday Rolls Around" before concluding with "So Long, Saddle Pals."

On March 7, 1983, The Nashville Network (TNN) went on the air. This was a national cable channel, based in Nashville, that broadcast country music shows nationwide. It offered national television exposure for the artists connected to the Opry as well as country music artists in general. Riders In The Sky were major beneficiaries of this network, which featured them on a regular show, *Tumbleweed Theater,* from the very beginning.

Knowing that the network would debut, the Riders put together a two-hour pilot show, taped at the Tennessee Performing Arts Center (TPAC), featuring their stage skits and some songs along with guests Buddy Spicher and Kathy Chiavola. The pilot was of poor quality, and TNN's director of programming, Elmer Alley, passed on the show. Meanwhile, Steve Arwood, Ned Ramage, and Randy Hale had formed Celebration Productions and were working on an outdoor show. That show wasn't panning out well, so, while Arwood was discussing the problems of the outdoor show with Alley, they hit on the idea of showing old western movies, with the Riders as hosts.

The copyrights to these old movies, many featuring singing cowboys, had lapsed, so they were in the public domain and thus would not cost the network anything to broadcast. Alley suggested that a show be ninety minutes long, and Arwood wrote the pilot, with input from the Riders.

"At first it would be Ranger Doug, Slim, Woody, and I all in a room. Those first three or four scripts had a lot of input from all of the Riders, but, as the show progressed, Woody would always have to leave and Doug would fall asleep," remembered Arwood. "Doug would then wake up and perhaps add something. But mostly it was me and Slim writing the shows."

The budget for each show was $7,500—miniscule by TV standards. They had to tape twenty-six shows in three weeks, so the Riders could wear only three different costumes—to save money and keep a continuity as the shows were edited. They would tape twenty-six songs in one outfit, then twenty-six songs in another. They would do generic "wrap-arounds"—for instance, "Stay tuned, we'll be right back to this exciting movie" or "We've had a great time today—gotta go. See ya next time on *Tumbleweed Theater!*" They'd also tape wrap-arounds to specific movies, but there had to be a lot of flexibility for the tape editors when they put the shows together.

The shows usually began on a bunkhouse set, with the Riders doing a song on the porch. The next shot would be a different set—in the bunkhouse—as Ranger Doug welcomed the viewers to the show. Then there would be one of the phony commercials the Riders were noted for—"Udder Butter" and the like. During breaks in the movie, the Riders would do songs and skits.

The film editor was Russ McGowan, who got the movies from a mysterious source named "Packy Smith." The Riders and Arwood would watch the movie in a conference room and work up the script from there.

At first, the idea was to present singing-cowboy movies, but the movies they received had been heavily edited for television and, when cuts were made, it was usually the songs that were cut. And so there were a number of singing-cowboy pictures, starring the likes of some of such lesser lights as Bob Baker or Smith Ballew, where there was no singing.

The directors for the show were Jim "Moose" Edwards, who was a big Gabby Hayes fan, and Randy Hale; Arwood was the producer and floor director.

The *Tumbleweed Theater* show inspired the Riders to create characters such as Sergeant Dudley, Sidemeat and Slocum and Charlie out of that show. "We were trying to get stuff past the censors and it was hard," remembers Slim.

The show did not receive big ratings—none of the TNN shows did—but when the station ran "per inquiry" ads, where viewers responded by ordering something, there was always a large response. And, even though the official ratings services didn't have the Riders as a blip on the radar screen, they received a great deal of fan mail, proof that a lot of people were watching. More important, *Tumbleweed Theater* was a major boost to the Riders' career, giving them national exposure on television each week.

The Riders appeared on Ralph Emery's early-morning television show on January 18 and February 18. This connection with Emery—and all those appearances on his early-morning TV show—would pay off as Emery would have the Riders on often as his guests on his popular *Nashville Now* show on TNN.

The premier of TNN was a big event, and the Riders performed at a party at the Opryland Hotel. The centerpiece of the broadcast was the debut of *Nashville Now* hosted by Emery, but TNN rolled out the carpet for all of its stars during the debut broadcast.

On April 12, the Riders appeared on TNN's *Nashville after Hours* show, and on the fourteenth they joined Ralph Emery on *Nashville Now.*

On April 22, the Riders performed at the University of Texas and found a dedicated fan, Jamie Amos, who started a fan club for them. For the next ten years, Jamie would send out quarterly newsletters, keeping Riders fans informed of what they were doing.

The Riders also appeared—albeit briefly and not as Riders In The Sky—in a major movie in 1983. *Sweet Dreams*, the story of Patsy Cline, starring Jessica Lange, was filmed in Nashville and the Riders were cast as the Jordanaires, the background singers who sang on so many great recordings. (The group in the movie was never called the Jordanaires, but that's clearly who they were intended to portray.)

"They needed harmony singers, so somebody thought of us," said Ranger Doug. "In the scene where Patsy Cline debuted on the Opry, they had us—with a studio singer named Gary Pigg—on camera."

There was a bigger part written for them—including a studio session scene—but a tour of Holland came up and the Riders had to leave. "We got to meet Jessica Lange," said Slim. "But mostly we stayed backstage and practiced."

From May 21 through May 28 the Riders were in Europe, appearing in Holland at Merselo, Dordrecht, Gouda, Hilversam, Ede, and Slagharen. The tour was organized by Ruud Hermanns, who had met the Riders one night at the Opry. Riding around in a van in Holland, the Riders thoroughly enjoyed themselves, checking our some museums when they weren't performing or traveling. Hermanns had a band and sometimes performed with them.

"I thought Europe was opening up for us," said Ranger Doug. But it was not the case—the audience was "appreciative and polite," said Slim. In other words, they didn't get it. "Most of the audience reaction in the early years was stupefaction," countered Ranger Doug. "And the European audience reaction was twice as stupefied because they didn't have the tradition. If you play out in Colorado, even though this is the modern age, people have a sense of the western tradition—at least a little glimmer back there that this comes from something. But in the East and in Europe it comes from Mars. Anybody with a cowboy hat over there reminded them of the TV show *Dallas,* so it was 'Hey, J.R. Ewing.' That was their idea of it."

On December 30 they celebrated their one-thousandth appearance with a guest spot on *Nashville Now* with Ralph Emery. They finished 1983 by performing on New Year's Eve at the Grand Ole Opry.

The Riders had made 197 personal appearances during 1983; seven had been on national television, aside from being seen each week on their own show. This would mark the beginning of regular national exposure for the Riders and create a demand for personal appearances, so their income jumped as their booking fee increased.

Chapter 19

On May 14, 1984, the Riders boarded a flight for London and began a British tour with an appearance on *Breakfast Time* on BBC-TV on May 15. The next day they began their tour of England, beginning in Southsea, then going to Burnemouth, Hertford, Boston, Chatham, and Brean Sands. On May 24 they continued their tour in Scotland, performing at Saltcoats, Aberdeen, Elgin, Dundee, and Edinburgh before playing in Londonderry, Northern Ireland, on May 30, then finishing their tour in Bridlington, England, on May 31.

"It was booked and promoted by this crazy Scottish promoter, Drew Taylor," said Ranger Doug. "We toured with Roy Drusky, who still had a name in England at the time. Roy is a Seventh-Day Adventist, and he was very adamant about not playing any dives. Also, from sundown Friday night to sundown Saturday night we couldn't play because of Roy's religion. If we went on Saturday night, it was after sundown. He wouldn't do a sound check or talk about music or the show. That frustrated the heck out of Drew, because Friday night was a good night for him."

"We rode around in a little van," remembers Slim. "It was a tin death trap."

"The audiences really varied," said Ranger Doug. "Where we did radio shows or where the audience was hip enough, they liked us very much. And in Scotland they really liked us. I found that strange and wonderful—how we connected with them. In England a lot of the places we played were very traditional country places, and if you do comedy over there you've got to have a blacked out tooth, baggy pants, and a red wig. I mean, you've got to be real obvious that this is COMEDY! They understand the old vaudeville type of comedy, but, if you try to intersperse it, they just don't get it."

The Riders did a lot of sightseeing and "wandering around." In London—where they stayed several nights—they saw the Albert Hall. And in Edinburg they walked the Royal Mile. "The seaside towns were always good," said Ranger Doug, "because they always reminded me of those Graham Greene novels."

Back in the States the Riders were working on their show—trying to find a lineup where each could hear the other.

"It's a tough thing because, if you see the way the Pioneers lined up, Bob Nolan was in the middle," said Ranger Doug. "And he had one arm around Tim Spencer while Lloyd Perryman was on the side where his guitar was out of the way. Visually, Bob belonged in the middle. But for a guitar player to be in the middle, that's a whole different thing because the instrument is just awkward, although not as awkward as the stand-up bass. So we went through a thing where we would get the guitar out of the way—I stood on the left side—so the other guys could hear it well."

"Balancing a trio to adjust for hearing is a tough thing," continued Green. "But we finally decided that visually I belong in the middle. Because I'm the Ranger! Also, for a while Woody was emceeing the shows, but that didn't last long. I'm not a great gifted public speaker, and I was falling all over my words, which I still do, so Woody said, 'Hell, I can do better than that.' In some ways he didn't do that bad a job. But it just didn't feel right."

"For awhile, Woody stood in the middle," said Slim. "But we quickly realized that Ranger Doug needed to be in the middle." And with that realization, the stage lineup of the Riders was fixed.

By 1984 the Riders had discovered that a number of kids were coming to their shows, brought by their parents. The Baby Boomers—the Riders' original audience—were booming with babies and brought them along, often dressed in cowboy and cowgirl outfits.

"We had to drop the drugs and sex humor when kids were sitting in the front row—it just wasn't appropriate," said Slim. The Riders also had children of their own growing up who loved the show and the music. The Riders knew firsthand that their own kids loved Raffi and Sesame Street, so "it seemed like a great market to go after," said Slim. "We'd say to ourselves, 'We've got to have a kids' record,' and that idea just took hold. The Riders have always been about finding little niches and markets, and this seemed like another one. We didn't want to be a kids' act exclusively, but we thought it could all work together and give us another slant on the Riders thing."

On August 16, 1984, the day after appearing on *Nashville Now* on TNN, the Riders went into Studio 19 in Nashville and recorded "The Biscuit Blues" and the old standard, "Get Along, Little Dogies." This would be the beginning of their first children's album.

"The Biscuit Blues" was written by Bob Nolan and sung by Pat Brady when he was a member of the Sons of the Pioneers. It's a humorous song that fits well with Slim's Sidemeat character, whose biscuits are "the hardest substance known to man." The song was heard in the 1938 movie *West of Cheyenne*, starring

Charles Starrett. "Get Along, Little Dogies" was first published as "Whoopee Ti-Yi-Yo, Git Along Little Dogies" by John Lomax in his landmark book of western folksongs, *Cowboy Songs and Other Frontier Ballads*, in 1910. A couple of lines from this song had also appeared in *The Log of a Cowboy* by Andy Adams in 1902, which was a book about an 1882 cattle drive from Texas to the Canadian border. Lomax had heard the song sung by a gypsy woman in Fort Worth. The journals of Owen Wister, author of the novel *The Virginian*, also recorded some verses to this song in 1893.

> As I was out walking this morning for pleasure
> I spied a cow puncher a riding along
> His hat was throwed back his spurs was a-jingling
> And as he rode towards me he was singing this song
> Whoopee-ti-yi-yo, get along you little dogies
> It's your misfortune and none of my own
> Whoopee-ti-yi-yo, get along you little dogies
> You know that Wyoming will be your new home

The Riders returned on the twenty-first to record "The Old Chisholm Trail" and a song written by Lou Robino, Joe Estella, and Dick Manning, "There's a Great Big Candy Roundup."

"The Old Chisholm Trail" is a true folk song, changing with each singer. The couplets are easily made up, and often coarse lyrics were sung by cowboys; the refrain remained the same, but outside a handful of verses the song has a number of different variants. Perhaps the original tune belonged to an old Stephen Foster song, "Old Uncle Ned," or perhaps the old railroad song "Drill, Ye Tarriers, Drill." Too Slim used the couplet, "Now some cow pokes can make any song rhyme, But as for me I could never get the hang of it!" (A take-off of the parody: "Roses are red, violets are blue, some poems rhyme, this one doesn't"). "There's a Great Big Candy Roundup" was popularized by Gene Autry. The next day they recorded two more old chestnuts, "I'm Going to Leave Old Texas Now" and "Betsy from Pike."

An old song, "The Trail to Mexico," was the origin for "I'm Going to Leave Old Texas Now." It is sung like an old religious song when the song leader would "line out" the song—singing the line, which would then be repeated by the congregation—

and was collected by John Lomax. It was sung by Tex Ritter in his 1937 movie *Trouble in Texas*. The Riders often get kids to come on stage for this song as Too Slim sings a line, which the crowd of children then repeat. Slim then begins singing verses about patronizing the mercantile—which the children dutifully repeat to their parents. It's a cute way to involve children in the show—and advertise the merchandise table.

The origins of "Betsy from Pike," known most often as "Sweet Betsy from Pike" are not known, but the song was sung before the Civil War.

> Oh do you remember sweet Betsy from Pike
> She crossed the wide prairie with her lover Ike
> With two yoke of oxen, a big yellow dog
> A tall shanghai rooster and one spotted hog

On October 24, the Riders went into Audio Media Studios and recorded "Slow Poke." This song was written by Chilton Price, the music librarian at WAVE radio where Pee Wee King and the Golden West Cowboys were working. According to King, Chilton gave him an envelope filled with songs, and he played some on the piano at home. King states in his autobiography that "Chilton wrote complete songs, and they were beautiful, but since she doesn't sing, she didn't know how they would sound."

King and Redd Stewart, a member of King's band and the co-writer, with King, of "The Tennessee Waltz," "took her songs and played them, singing and humming, changing words and notes here and there until we'd get a version easier to sing." That's why King and Stewart share co-writing credit on "Slow Poke," which was a number-one country song for King's group in 1951 and the only million-seller the Country Music Hall of Fame member ever had as a recording artist.

On December 17, the Riders went into Studio 19 and recorded three songs written by Ranger Doug: "'One, Two, Three,' Said the Miner," "The Cowboy's A-B-Cs," and "Down the Lullaby Trail." They recorded Woody's song, "Blue Bonnet Lady," as well as a medley of fiddle tunes that Woody had arranged before concluding the session with "Even Texas Isn't Big Enough Now," a song written by Kerry Chater and Patti Dahlstrom.

"'One, Two, Three,' Said the Miner" is a cute song about a miner who lit a fuse to blow open a vein of gold but didn't step back far enough when the dynamite blew.

"Four, three, two" said the miner
Not quite far enough from the well
"One and" . . . And blew himself clean to Oregon

"The Cowboy's A-B-Cs" is a children's alphabet song ("A is for the antelope, B for buffalo," etc.) that the group members edited after Ranger Doug brought a version in twice as long.

"There was a full line (instead of a half line) devoted to explaining every letter," said Ranger Doug. "It was not a bad song, but would have been seven or eight minutes long! One of the great things about working in a band is the editing process that takes place on my songs. Woody and Slim have had a good deal of influence on many of these songs—sometimes the suggestion of a word or tempo change, sometimes revisions the size of this one. We almost never write as partners, but many songs with individual writer's credits are, ultimately, a group effort."

"Down the Lullaby Trail" was also written by Ranger Doug. "When we began collecting material for our kids' album *Saddle Pals*, the initial thought was to record the old Roy Rogers classic, 'My Little Buckaroo,'" he states in his songbook. "Although a lot of people love it, I always felt that it induced a little sugar overload, and I never liked the way the stresses fell; it was unlike the natural rhythm of speech, and for better or worse making the lyrics of songs fall into the rhythm of speech has always been important to me." And so he wrote "Down the Lullaby Trail."

Lay your sleepy head on my shoulder
Close those tired eyes.
Take off that hat and those little brown boots;
It's time for the cowboy to say "Good night."

"If ever a song was written from real life, this is it," notes Green. "The hat and the little brown boots are still laying around the house somewhere. Like many parents, some of my most tender memories are of rocking the kids to sleep, singing and telling stories. One of my favorite lullabies was Tim Spencer's 'Out on the New Frontier.'"

On January 9, 1985, the group went into Studio 19 and recorded "Yippie Yi Yo and Away We Go," written by Woody Paul and Too Slim, which finished up their children's album. The song was written as a theme song and leads off the finished product.

Yippie-yi-yo and away we go
With a gallop and a cowboy yell
Swinging in the saddle, herding the cattle
With a song and a story to tell

The album, *Saddle Pals,* was released in 1985 and voted "Children's Album of the Year" by the National Association of Independent Record Distributors.

Chapter 20

The Riders were on the periphery of country music—part of the Grand Ole Opry with a presence on The Nashville Network—but they were not country stars. In country music, the way to achieve fame and fortune is to have hit records on the radio. By 1985, two of the Riders were actively seeking a way to have a hit on country radio.

Woody Paul was the one most determined to have that. "He wanted a country album—he's always leaned that way," remembered Slim, who added, "I fell for it too, but Ranger Doug was always skeptical."

"It's never been what I wanted," said Ranger Doug. "If it happens by accident—a hit on country radio—well, that's great. I'm not going to run from it. But to go chasing the hit record—God, who needs that?

"Our records were selling about the same," continued Green. "So our label, Rounder, and the producer, Robby Adcock, said, 'Let's do something different to get on the charts if we can, blah blah blah.' So we sold out. But nobody bought it."

On April 8 they went into Studio 19 and recorded two songs

by Woody Paul, "Soon As the Roundup's Through" and "Cowboy of the Highway" as well as Johnny Bond's "Cimarron" and a song written by Lee Domann, Pete Sebert, and Ralph Whiteway, "Trail of Tears."

Woody Paul's "Cowboy of the Highway" sounds like an Eagles song; there's a heavy drum and an electric lead guitar that pierces through the speaker. The theme of the song is the truck driver as cowboy; recording a truck-driving song certainly marked a major departure from the grandeur of the West songs of Bob Nolan.

Movin' on thru the break of dawn
A thousand miles from yesterday
Rollin' on, goin' home
One last stop in Santa Fe
Cowboy of the highway
Feel that eighteen-wheeler makin' time
There's a rainbow on the Rio Grande
She waits for you across the Texas line

"Soon As the Roundup's Through," which was originally recorded for their *Cowboy Jubilee* album, has a nice, loping Eagles-esque feel about it as well. "Cimarron" was written by Johnny Bond and published in 1942. Bond wrote the song after realizing there was no song by that title although there was a hit movie named *Cimarron* in 1931, based on the book with the same title by Edna Ferber. Back in Oklahoma a singing group known first as the Cowboy Trio and then the Bell Boys, comprised of Bond, Jimmy Wakely, and Scotty Harrell, had crossed the Cimarron River a number of times during their travels. This group had often commented on the fact that "Cimarron" would be a good title for a song, and in 1938 Bond wrote a song in his room at the YMCA in Oklahoma City. The trio began performing it during appearances in and around Oklahoma.

The group moved to Hollywood in 1940 and changed their name to the Jimmy Wakely Trio and joined Gene Autry's radio program, *Melody Ranch*. In 1941 they performed "Cimarron" in the movie *Twilight on the Trail*, which starred Bill Boyd. In the 1942 Gene Autry movie *Heart of the Rio Grande* they performed the song

again, and Jimmy Wakely recorded the song for Decca. Later, Les
Paul and Mary Ford and the Billy Vaughn Orchestra both had hit
recordings of this song.

The original singing cowboys—Gene Autry, Roy Rogers, Tex
Ritter, and others—made their mark in the movies. That was the
ticket to their success. In the spring, the Riders appeared in a TV
singing-cowboy movie starring Kenny Rogers. On May 23, they
were on a ranch outside Sheridan, Wyoming, filming *Wild Horses*.
"We played as if we were a band at a dance," said Ranger Doug.
"It was just like an old western where Roy Rogers walks into a
saloon and there's the Sons of the Pioneers playing on the band-
stand. Only it was Kenny Rogers walking in the room and Riders
In The Sky on the bandstand. It was wonderful. Kenny Rogers
and Richard Farnsworth were in the scene. That's the first time
we met Farnsworth, and he became quite a fan through the years."

The group did "Blue Bonnet Lady" and "Here Comes the Santa
Fe." "Kenny Rogers definitely got it," said Slim. "He's a musician
too, and he's a very intelligent entertainer," added Green. "He
quickly saw what we are all about."

"Ranger Doug had bought four copies of Kenny Rogers's book
How to Make It in the Music Business while we were playing at the
Wind in the Willows," remembered Slim. "He said we all needed
to read it, so I read it—and so did Tommy. So when we met Kenny,
we told him we'd read his book!"

On June 10, they were back in Studio 19 to record two songs,
an old Fred Rose number, "I'm Satisfied with You" and Ranger
Doug's "All Those Years."

Fred Rose is a seminal figure in both country and western
music. Rose, a pop songwriter born in Chicago, moved to Nashville in the mid-1930s and had a program on WSM, *Freddie Rose's
Song Shop*. In 1938 Rose moved to Hollywood, where he wrote
songs for Gene Autry; among the songs he wrote were "Be Honest with Me," "Tweedle-O-Twill," and "At Mail Call Today." When
Autry went into the armed services in 1942, Rose moved back to
Nashville and formed Acuff-Rose Publishing Company with Roy
Acuff. This was the first major music business company outside
the Grand Ole Opry and played a key role in Nashville's development as a music center. Rose signed Hank Williams as a
songwriter and produced his recordings; he wrote numerous

songs (sometimes under the pseudonym Floyd Jenkins) and published others, including "The Tennessee Waltz."

Rose wrote a number of western swing numbers, and "I'm Satisfied with You" is one of them. In 1978, a version of this song by Leon Rausch, a former member of Bob Wills and the Texas Playboys, reached the country charts.

"All Those Years" was a departure for Douglas Green as a songwriter. "I often work better on assignment, knowing we need material, rather than just sitting around the bunkhouse waiting for the muse to drop by," states Ranger Doug. "I wrote a couple of the few non-Western songs of my career for this project, but this is the only one that everyone—the producer and my partners—liked."

> If I'd thought of you first just a couple of times
> Instead of chasing those dreams in the air
> Maybe tonight I'd be holding you close
> Instead of reaching and reaching
> For something that just isn't there

"People are often curious as to whether a song is autobiographical," said Green. "In this particular case the answer is no, nothing specific. I was simply trying to achieve some of the same feeling of poignant regret Willie Nelson so beautifully caught in 'You Were Always on My Mind,' which had been popular not long before."

Actually, if the "you" in the song "All Those Years" is read as "western music" or the original vision Green had for the group, the song is definitely autobiographical.

The setting seemed right for the Riders to get country radio air play, and Lord knows country music needed to get back to its roots at this point. The previous October Julio Iglesias had won a CMA Award (for "Best Duet" with Willie Nelson). During 1985 country would get back to its traditional honky-tonk roots with the success of Randy Travis, but it was not quite ready to get back to its western roots.

If any western artist could have become a country star, it would have been Riders In The Sky. The album, *New Trails*, is a good, solid work for the commercial country market. The major drawback, it seemed, was their label; Rounder Records is an independent that does not have the same resources major labels use in order to get air play on country radio. The major labels dominate that medium, and Rounder could not find a way to break down those barriers.

Looking at the evolution of an act, it is important to look at turning points. But the Riders, although they tried to evolve at different points in their career during the 1980s, never really did. And that is a key to their success. Once they decided to quit flirting with country stardom, they set about becoming what they started as: the preeminent western music act in America. Success comes to those who narrow their focus and pursue a single goal relentlessly, not allowing themselves to be distracted by other opportunities outside this goal. The Riders wanted to be known as the top western act in the country. Although this album would be viewed as a distraction later, a side road in their quest, it served a valuable purpose: it taught them to focus on who they really are and to do what they do better than anyone else.

On June 17–21 the Riders were at the TNN studios taping their parts for *Tumbleweed Theater*. The next week, on June 24 and 25, they taped more appearances for *Tumbleweed Theater*. On August 25, after an appearance at the Kentucky State Fair, the Riders flew to Peterborough, England, for a country music festival there. Then they hopped on a plane and headed back to the States, where they appeared at the Minnesota State Fair in St. Paul.

"We were worn out—jet lagged," remembered Slim about the appearance in England. "Bobby Bare was there. It was in a big tent in a big field. I remember that after the show I went back to the hotel and watched the movie *Nashville* on English TV. It was a new perspective seeing that movie over there."

"I remember Billy Walker over there," said Ranger Doug, "because I borrowed his guitar when we played. I didn't want to fly over and carry a guitar for just one date. It was a country music festival—people had figured out who we were and were interested in seeing us again. And once again, they didn't particularly get it."

Chapter 21

The Riders began 1986 with an appearance on the Opry on January 3. On January 21 they were on *Nashville Now*, then headed out to the Cowboy Poetry Gathering in Elko. "The first year of the Cowboy Poetry Gathering—1984—we were in Alaska," said Slim. "We'd known Hal Cannon, one of the founders of the gathering, for a while—and he invited us. It was the beginning of the Cowboy Renaissance. There was some initial skepticism about us—some thought our tongue was too far into our cheeks. Some of the old poets were put off by us initially. I remember Wallace McCrae saying, 'What the hell is this?' but then he saw us and we got his vote."

It was a memorable time for Ranger Doug and Too Slim—but not for Woody. "Woody doesn't like free gigs," said Slim. "The only time Woody came out of his room was to play our gig."

"We got a per diem but didn't get regular appearance money," remembers Ranger Doug. "I thought it was really fun, and I remember having a blast. I remember Woody holed up in his room and wouldn't come out until the exact moment we had to be on stage. Then after the performance he would disappear again. But I really enjoyed it—especially when it was real fresh. We hung out and jammed—that's what I remember. Those nights sitting up with Babe Humphrey and the Bar J Wranglers and Cy Scarborough. Some of those chuck wagon people came too, and we sang those old songs all night long. It was so much fun.

"Woody's so strange about that," said Doug. "It's against the rules to have fun and enjoy yourself. He loves to play only when he's playing. He doesn't jam, he doesn't sit around and play with other people. He likes to figure out the seventeen notes he's working on and play those twenty thousand times. That gets pretty tiresome after awhile. Some guys will play one tune after another—but not him!"

On August 27, the Riders began a six-day run at the Minnesota State Fair in St. Paul. On August 30, they appeared again with Garrison Keillor on the *Prairie Home Companion*. On November 4, the Riders taped "Shotgun Red's Christmas Special" for TNN.

"We'd worked with Steve Hall—the guy who had Shotgun Red—at the Minnesota State Fair and shared the stage," said Slim.

"He would come out with his band, then do a Shotgun Red thing. On the last day of the fair, we got a big garbage can and painted 'Deep-Fried Cheese' on the side and stole Shotgun and put him in the garbage can. Came time for the Shotgun Red portion, and Steve couldn't find him. We pulled him out of the barrel. Steve was really mad."

"At the fair we'd announced to the crowd that we'd stolen Shotgun Red and deep-fried him in cheese," said Ranger Doug. "Because at the Minnesota State Fair everybody eats their deep-fried cheese sticks—they fry everything in cheese. So we decided we'd fry Shotgun Red in cheese. That's where I came up with a great line. Steve always closed his show: 'I was backstage at the Grand Ole Opry and a nondescript fellow came up to me and said, "Pleased to meet you, Steve. I'm the most important person in country music." And I was ashamed to say that I didn't recognize him. He didn't look like anyone I'd known. I said, "I'm sorry, Sir, I'm pleased to meet you too but I don't know who you are." He said, "I'm the fan." Then they'd play 'God Bless America' or something in the background—the end of his shows were real big. So on our show, I knew he was out there listening, and I said, 'I was backstage at the Grand Ole Opry and a nondescript fellow came up to me and said, "Ranger, Doug, I'm just proud to meet you. I'm the most important man in country music." I said, "I'm pleased to meet you too but I don't know who you are. He said, "I'm Steve Hall's fan."'"

During the time they were at the Minnesota State Fair—over the Labor Day holiday—another event was occurring in Colorado that would have a major impact on western music: Michael Martin Murphey held his first WestFest at Copper Mountain. Murphey envisioned a showcase for the American West in the heart of the American West. He wanted to emphasize western culture—arts and music and cowboy poetry. The first WestFest had an Indian village, a Mountain Man Rendezvous, booths of collectibles, western art, and country and western stars. The festival had taken a year of planning, and although only three thousand showed up that first year, a lot of people sat up and took notice. Murphey wanted the Riders to perform at that first WestFest, which would become the model for Western festivals in the years ahead, but they had already committed to the Minnesota booking.

During 1986, the Riders acquired a new manager, David Skepner. Skepner was born and grew up in the Los Angeles area; he worked for MCA Records, then began managing Loretta Lynn, an artist for that label. Skepner saw that Loretta could be more than just a country star, that she had major appeal in American music. Lynn became a country superstar, sold millions of records, wrote a book that became a best-seller, then saw that story of her life, *Coal Miner's Daughter*, become a major motion picture.

"The guy who got us Skepner was my ex-brother-in-law, Ned Ramage," said Woody. "Ned had a friend who lived next door to Dave, and they'd all go whooping in the evening after dinner over to where David lived. Loretta Lynn was quitting or in one of her metamorphoses and David didn't have an act, and so Ned went and talked to him and arranged a meeting between me and him. I was gung ho—I was ready to sing Eagles-type stuff or whatever the hell it took to make us some money, be successful. I think Rounder kind of dropped the ball."

David Skepner had strong connections in the music industry and immediately set out to make some changes in the career of the Riders. Skepner was also managing country singer Judy Rodman and had an appointment with Tony Conway at a booking agency, Buddy Lee Attractions, to discuss their booking Rodman. Skepner convinced Conway to book Rodman, and as they were chatting after the agreement, Skepner mentioned he had just signed Riders In The Sky, who were being booked by APA out of Los Angeles.

Paul Lohr, a relatively new agent to the company, happened to be walking past Conway's door as Skepner said that. Lohr, a long-time fan of the Riders, stopped in his tracks, stuck his head in the door, and said, "Riders In The Sky? I could book the shit out of that band!" As Skepner looked toward the door, Tony Conway introduced him to Paul Lohr. After the introduction, Skepner looked at Conway and said, "Looks like you've just signed another act."

Paul Lohr would play a major role in the career of Riders In The Sky in the years ahead. Born in Baltimore, he received a degree in journalism from the University of Missouri, then landed a job as an advertising account executive at WLAN radio in Lancaster, Pennsylvania. Lohr also began booking and managing an act, the Johnny Neel Band; Neel, a blind keyboardist, had a rock 'n' blues band. Lohr and Neel both came to Nashville to further their careers.

In Nashville, looking for a job, Lohr prepared a press kit on himself instead of a resume. He met Tony Conway at Buddy Lee, who told him there were no job openings at the agency; however, about a month later, Conway called him on a Thursday and offered him a job beginning Monday. Lohr, who was living in Wilmington, Delaware, at the time, was going through a divorce and needed to pack up his house; two weeks later he started work for Buddy Lee.

Paul Lohr had come across the first Riders In The Sky album in 1980 when he worked for Record Bar; he became a lifelong fan. After getting them a contract with Buddy Lee—which Ranger Doug thought was "a step down. I mean, we were booked by APA out in Hollywood, and I thought Buddy Lee was just a Nashville agency at the time"—David Skepner went to MCA Records, where he knew the executives from years of working with Loretta Lynn, and got the Riders signed to that major label.

The album *New Trails* had not broken the Riders into the country market—primarily, it was thought, because it was on a small, independent label. But a major powerhouse like MCA was sure to launch Riders In The Sky into country music superstardom. At least that was the prevailing wisdom around the Riders camp.

In December the Riders were on a USO tour, organized by Skepner, that took them to Greenland, where they played two air force bases. "Skepner got us that—he was big in the USO," said Slim. "We flew up on a C-130 and brought letters to Santa that had been written by kids from a school we sponsored. An air force guy took 'em and promised to deliver them to the North Pole. It was really cold and dark there. Never got light. We drank a lot of North Sea Crude, and all of us wound up playing electric instruments back at a bar—we did a bunch of country tunes."

"They have a way of toasting you with Aquavit," remembered Green. "And the toasts start at ten in the morning and they don't quit toasting you. I remember they had a little gym there, and I went and worked out drunk. I'd never worked out drunk before!"

Ranger Doug's other vivid memory of the Greenland dates was that it was "really cold and dark. Really cold. And really dark."

David Skepner was a divisive figure—people either loved him

or hated him. He endeared himself to a number of people—and totally turned off others. Some just didn't want to have anything to do with him. By the spring of 1986, the Riders had been on *Tumbleweed Theater* for three years. Elmer Alley had left his position as director of programming for TNN and was replaced by Paul Corbin. When Steve Arwood went into Corbin's office to renegotiate the next season for *Tumbleweed Theater,* Corbin asked, "Aren't the Riders being managed by David Skepner now?"

Arwood replied that they were. "Well, we don't really like David Skepner around here," replied Corbin. And thus the Riders were dropped from TNN's roster. However, the previous three seasons of shows would be repackaged and continue to be shown on TNN for the next two years.

Chapter 22

The contract with the major label, MCA, led to discussions of what their first album should be. Since they were such a strong act live and since they toured a great deal, the decision was made to record a "live" album in the studio. By recording in the studio, they were assured of a good sound; also, they were able to do mostly songs they'd never recorded before, along with a few old favorites.

The Riders began their set with a Cindy Walker song that Bob Wills and the Texas Playboys had done, "Miss Molly," then played Green's "Lonely Yukon Stars" followed by a song Slim wrote, "Ride with Me, Gringo." The classic Bob Wills song, "Faded Love," was next; followed by "Cherokee," written by Ray Noble; then the Stuart Hamblen classic, "Texas Plains," which they would use later to open their shows. This was followed by three more classic cowboy numbers: "Back in the Saddle Again," "(Ghost) Riders in the Sky," and "Don't Fence Me In," all from their first albums. Then Slim did his humorous "Salting of the Slug" before the Riders continued their presentation of classics, doing Bob Nolan's "One More Ride" and the Billy Hill classic, "The Call of the Canyon."

"Sidekick Heaven," a parody of "Hillbilly Heaven" written by Eddie Dean and Hal Blair with additional lyrics from Slim, came next. The original has the singer dreaming of "hillbilly heaven," where he meets all the stars who have passed away. The singer then asks who's coming in the future and a list of names is read until the reader announces the singer's name, who then wakes up. "That song started out as 'Stand Up Heaven,' about all these stand-up comedians," said LaBour. "It evolved into 'Sidekick Heaven' with the Sidemeat character."

This was followed by the cowboy poem, "Reincarnation," written by Wallace MaCrae. Ranger Doug's "That's How the Yodel Was Born" was followed by "The Wayward Wind," written by Herb Newman and Stanley Lebowsky and originally a hit for Gogi Grant; then "My Oklahoma," a song written by Terrye Newkirk; and "Stone's Rag," an instrumental by Oscar Stone.

Two more classics, Johnny Bond's "Cimarron" and the Smiley Burnette–Gene Autry number, "Riding Down the Canyon" were followed by Green's "Ride with the Wind," before the Riders finished with four western classics: "Cattle Call," "Carry Me Back to the Lone Prairie," "When Payday Rolls Around," and "Happy Trails (to You)."

Not all of the songs recorded made the album; those that didn't were "Cattle Call," "Cherokee," "Cimarron," "Don't Fence Me In," "Faded Love," "Ride with Me, Gringo," "Ride with the Wind," "Sidekick Heaven," "Stone's Rag," "One More Ride," and "The Wayward Wind."

Of these songs, the Riders had never recorded "Cattle Call," "Cherokee," "Ride with Me, Gringo," "Sidekick Heaven," "The Wayward Wind," or "One More Ride" but would record them again later. The Riders had previously recorded "Cimarron," "Don't Fence Me In," and "Ride with The Wind," which were on earlier albums. The Riders had never recorded "Faded Love" or "Stone's Rag" before and would not do so again.

"Back in the Saddle Again," "(Ghost) Riders in the Sky," "That's How the Yodel Was Born," and "When Payday Rolls Around" had all been on previous albums. The songs that made the album that had not previously been recorded by the Riders were "Carry Me Back to the Lone Prairie," "Concerto for Violin and Longhorns," "Happy Trails," "Lonely Yukon Stars," "Miss Molly," "My Oklahoma," "Ridin' Down the Canyon," "Texas Plains," and "The Salting of the Slug." "Reincarnation" is a poem that Slim learned in Elko during the gathering out there.

"Carry Me Back to the Lone Prairie" was written by Carson J. Robison, inspired by the old folk song "O Bury Me Not on the Lone Prairie." The song was introduced in the movie *Stars Over Broadway* in 1935. Robison was born in Kansas in 1890, where his father was a cowboy fiddler and dance-caller; Carson learned to play the guitar and harmonica. He worked for the oil industry in 1920, then began performing at WDAF in Kansas City, Missouri, before he moved to New York in 1924. Robison helped write "Barnacle Bill the Sailor" and made a number of recordings with Vernon Dalhart, whose recording of "The Prisoner's Song" b/w "Wreck of the Old '97" in 1925 was the first million-seller in country music. Later, Robison wrote "Life Gits Tee-Jus, Don't It?" which was a hit for Tex Ritter in the 1940s.

The Riders' version of "Miss Molly," a classic song originally recorded by Bob Wills and the Texas Playboys and written by Cindy Walker, featured the guitar solo of super musician Mark O'Connor.

"Texas Plains," which became the Riders' theme song and led off the album sequence, was written by Stuart Hamblen and first recorded in August 1934 by Hamblen and his Covered Wagon Jubilee. Hamblen was the biggest western radio star in Los Angeles and a major influence on the Sons of the Pioneers and other Hollywood singing cowboys. A native of Texas, Hamblen didn't achieve the national recognition of performers like Gene Autry or Roy Rogers, but several songs he wrote—"It Is No Secret (What God Can Do)," "This Ole House," and "I Won't Go Huntin' With You, Jake (But I'll Go Chasin' Women)"—all became major hits in the late forties and early fifties.

"Ridin' Down the Canyon" was written by Smiley Burnette in the backseat of Gene Autry's car as the two were traveling to Hollywood in 1934 for an appearance in their first movie, *In Old Santa Fe*, which starred Ken Maynard. According to Burnette, he wrote the song quickly—as the car covered about five miles—and Autry gave him five dollars for half credit and half the royalties. According to Burnette, the song earned him about a dollar a mile.

"Happy Trails" was written by Dale Evans as a theme song for her husband. Roy Rogers had often used the phrase "Happy Trails" when signing autographs or as a parting phrase. In 1950, Dale began humming the phrase "Happy Trails" and then com-

posed the song, which was soon adopted as the theme song for
The Roy Rogers Show. It is the most perfect "good-bye and so long"
song ever written.

"The Salting of the Slug" was sung a capella by Slim, introduced as an authentic folk song from Joelton—a suburb of Nashville where he lives. The story of the song actually goes back to a
luncheon party in Santa Cruz that the Riders had with John
Sandidge, a concert promoter. During the party, Sandidge's dog
brought up a mole while everyone was eating, laughing, and drinking. One of Sandidge's friends picked up the mole and threw it out
in the creek on his property. Ranger Doug then composed a tune,
"The Flipping of the Mole," about that incident and then, according to Doug, "Too Slim took that and transmogrified it into his own
experience."

> I watched each creature swell and pop
> Did thrill me to the core
> And every slug did learn that night
> That when it rains it pours

"Lonely Yukon Stars" begins with a breathtakingly beautiful
yodel. "I had been working on a song, a notion or concept really,
called 'The Echo Yodel' for some time, but it never came together
for me," said Green. "I had the idea for this yodel in my head, but
it was inchoate, unformed." Green acknowledges that "the unusual chord structure, though not the melody, tempo, or feel, is
exactly the same as Bob Nolan's gentle and haunting 'A Summer
Night's Rain.'" The song was inspired by the Riders' visits to
Alaska to perform as well as "the association with Sergeant Preston
and Yukon King" said Green.

> Lonely Yukon stars gleaming high in the sky
> Scattered careless and loving by an artist on high
> To their silent song the sighing wind adds its part
> A song that can only be heard by the heart

Although Ranger Doug has a natural affinity for yodeling, he
has also studied and practiced yodeling assiduously. From his
first days in Nashville he's listened and learned from recordings

by "Elton Britt, Roy Rogers, Montana Slim and Rusty Richards, Gary McMahan and David Bradley. Also some of the great Bavarian and Swiss yodeling—Franzl Lang—thanks in part to Dr. Leland Hansen, who has kept me well supplied with an astonishing variety of European yodeling on tape." Although his yodels seem effortless, they come after long sessions of relentless practice and study.

After an appearance at Harrah's in Nevada and an appearance on TNN's *Nashville Now,* the Riders went to England, where they played the Silk Cut Festival in Wembley on April 18 and 20 and appeared at The Mean Fiddler, a club in North London, on April 19. The Silk Cut Festival was promoted by Mervyn Conn and featured David Allen Coe, Patty Loveless, and Rex Allen Jr. in addition to the Riders.

Green remembers that "Mervyn had big plans for us, but we didn't click with that audience. In that huge auditorium, I don't know if it was our accents or our whole approach—but they just didn't get it." As further proof of that, the Riders played a club in north London, The Mean Fiddler, during that trip, and an audience member came up to them and asked, point-blank, "Are you pissing on us?" (meaning "Are you making fun of us?"). It was obvious the Riders and the English audiences didn't click.

Although the Riders had appeared at Fan Fair—the annual gathering of the tribes for country music fans held in Nashville each June—they were on the "Independent Label" show and did not attract the huge crowds that come to see superstars. When they joined MCA, that label put them on their shows—in prime time with a host of superstars—to appear before around twenty thousand fans. It was a mixed blessing.

"I've been pretty happy with our Fan Fair shows," said Ranger Doug. "Given the fact the fans have come to see a lot of different artists. But, as a general rule, I think there's a point after about fifteen hundred or two thousand people, our effectiveness diminishes. You need to be right on top of us to enjoy us. A few people are going to get it," continued Ranger Doug. "But most people seeing us perform think they're changing sets and need somebody out there."

Chapter 23

In the summer of 1987, Battle Ground Academy High School in Franklin, Tennessee, held its twentieth-year reunion for the 1967 graduating class. Woody Paul was a member of this class, and so was Billy Maxwell—but they hadn't seen each other since around the time they'd graduated. Woody and Billy had gone through elementary and high school together (they'd been to different junior highs) and lived close to each other. At the reunion the two sat down and began talking—and didn't stop until everyone else had left. During the conversation, the two agreed to keep in touch. This led to Billy going on the road with the Riders.

Billy is a golf pro at a state park in Tennessee, and during the winter months he often has time to go on the road with the Riders. Since that first time, he has gone on a number of road trips with them, handling their mercantile and taking a shift driving and becoming a semiofficial part of their organization. He's also kept a journal of these travels, documenting life on the road with the Riders.

Here's the story from Billy Maxwell of his first encounter with the Riders. "I had heard of Riders In The Sky but I had no idea that Woody was part of the group. I wasn't real familiar with them—but I had heard of their name. At that time Woody was playing a lot of golf—and he thought what I was doing was pretty neat—so I invited him to come up and visit and play some golf. It just so happened that the week after the class reunion he had that week off so lo and behold he and his family showed up in the park to spend five or six days. He and I played golf every day and had a really great time. As he was getting ready to go, he was telling me about being on the road and that always fascinated me. I've always liked to travel and so I said, 'Las Vegas is my favorite town in the world. Sometime if you're going to be in Vegas, let me know because I want to go with you.' So he said, 'O.K.' and went home, and we didn't have any more contact for a couple, three months. Then one day, out of the blue, Woody called about 3 A.M. That's his business hours—5 o'clock in the afternoon until 4 A.M. Usually he's working in the early part of the night, so when he does his phone calls and his paperwork—paying bills and stuff—its 4 or 5 A.M. So he calls one night and said, 'Look, we're going to be in Las Vegas in November.' I said, 'Great, I sure would like to go.' He said, 'Well, this is the deal. This is at the end of a three-week road trip, and we're coming from Seattle, so why don't you get a ticket, fly to Seattle, meet us there—we're doing a couple of shows at Harvest Festival in Seattle—and then we're coming back to Vegas and doing a couple of shows there. Then we're doing Grand Junction, Colorado; Pueblo, Colorado; and then we're coming home.' So that was my first trip."

On November 27, 1987, Billy flew to Seattle. "I got a cab from the airport," he said. "They were playing at the convention center at the old World's Fair site. That was at the time when they used to have the old bread truck with the mural on the side of it that said 'Riders In The Sky.' That very night at the hotel I stayed in a room with Woody. There was only a king-sized bed—so we both had to sleep in the same bed. He wanted to go to a movie that night. I said I was too tired, so he goes to the movie *Planes, Trains, and Automobiles*. In that movie, they all got stuck in one room and had to sleep in the same bed—same as us. And he thought it was really funny. All these big guys were all sleeping on one bed."

That night, after playing, they left Seattle. "We left Seattle about 10 P.M. with Woody driving," said Billy. "And after about a hundred miles, we ran out of diesel. He had to get out and thumb back with a can to get some diesel. This took about an hour. Then Ranger Doug started driving around 3 A.M. Ranger Doug had a girl with him, and she didn't want to go home. Ranger Doug was trying to put her on a bus, on a plane—tried everything in the world. See, the deal was that he had another girl waiting for him in Las Vegas who'd already checked into the hotel. Finally, we were down to Sacramento and getting ready to cut over to Las Vegas. So we went to a bus station and Ranger Doug said, 'This is it' and gave her a bus ticket. He was on a deadline—had to get rid of her before we got to Vegas.

"In that bread truck they had, there weren't any curtains on the bunks. I guess it didn't bother the guys, and, if the girls wanted to go bad enough, they just overlooked the situation. A lot of 'em did. It was nothing to walk back in the bunk area and see something pretty rich, pretty rich.

"We got to Las Vegas around 2 A.M., and Woody and Ranger

Doug both had girls already there, so they went on in. Slim and I were a little early—so our complimentary rooms for the show didn't start until the next night. Woody and Ranger paid for their rooms, but Slim and I decided to sleep in the bus and check in the next morning to save money on a hotel room. We couldn't check in until 11 A.M., so I went in and played Keno and picked three numbers, playing for a dollar. The first time I played I hit and won $175. I was just killing time.

"They played at a Fair Buyers Convention where all the fair buyers come in and buy their entertainment. It was the MGM Grand, and somebody invited us to dinner at the really nice restaurant where people dressed for dinner—like tuxedoes. And we didn't have any of those kinds of clothes with us. But we got special permission to eat there. And at the end of the meal, the waitress brought around the tray with little French pastries where you could choose what you wanted. And Woody said, 'Just leave the tray,' so she left them—about twenty-five small things. Woody proceeded to eat five or six and then passed the tray around. It didn't matter—he wasn't paying for it. Those desserts were probably seven or eight dollars each.

"About midnight Woody called me up in the room and said they were all down at the casino—so I went down and we gambled until about 4 A.M. We were supposed to leave at 10 A.M., but Ranger Doug's and Woody's girlfriends' planes didn't leave until 1 P.M. We had to wait for Ranger Doug to get back from the airport.

"We left Vegas and Ranger Doug drove till about two in the morning and then I started driving out through the desert. Drove from Southern Utah to Green River, and they did a show that night in a little bar in Grand Junction, Colorado, that seated probably forty people. They were working for a thousand dollars a night. Then we went through Vail to the Eisenhower Tunnel to Denver and stopped in Castle Rock to see a friend of Woody's—they'd gone to M.I.T. together—and he was equally as weird as Woody.

"We went through Colorado Springs to Pueblo, where Ranger Doug had another girl—the third one in three days—coming in to see him, and she had a friend who needed to travel with her. So Doug had arranged for the friend to see Woody. Woody wasn't real receptive to the situation, but he accepted the challenge. One of 'em's name was Dale, so we got to calling them Chip 'n' Dale.

When the girls got there, we all had separate rooms, but Woody was going to work out, so he sent her to my room for me to entertain her while he was gone. He stayed gone for hours and hours—but finally came back. Woody really didn't treat her too well—and after she left, Ranger Doug confronted him about that.

"We left Pueblo at 5 P.M., dropped the girls off at Wichita, came back through Kansas City and St. Louis and on back home. We got back on December 5."

The Riders were in a national commercial for Levi's 501 jeans in 1987. They did the singing but did not appear in the advertisement, which was televised. "Somebody called us and gave us very specific guidelines of what they wanted in the song for the ad," said Ranger Doug. "I wrote one, and Woody and Slim wrote one together. They liked mine, and we recorded it. The run of that commercial didn't last long. It was a very peculiar juxtaposition because the tune I wrote was very western—as western as it could be—and they put it up against a bunch of young guys who were in an urban area like Chicago or Detroit or New York stacking tires and stuff. It isn't the image I'd have put with it."

On December 8 they appeared on the *Crook and Chase* TV show; the following day they were on *Nashville Now* again. On Christmas evening, the Riders went down to the Opry and played there; they played on the Opry again the next night. They had made 187 appearances during 1987.

Chapter 24

In January, Billy Maxwell went on the road with the Riders, driving the bus and selling merchandise. "We were going to Elko; it was a neat deal," he said. "We flew into Salt Lake City and had to rent a bass for Slim and then get it over to Elko, which was about 250 to 300 miles away. Woody had called around for two days before we left home to find the cheapest van we could rent, and we ended up with a mini mini mini van—really small. It was Ranger Doug, Slim, Woody, me, and this big bass fiddle—and I had about four inches of seat because the bass fiddle was in the back with the neck sticking into the front seat.

"When we first started doing Elko it was a very intimate thing with the poets and a little music thrown in," continued Billy. "Everybody knew everybody, and the town was very small. There were three casinos in town. But over the years it's grown to be such a big thing, and it's not as much fun as it used to be. The Riders used to really love to go, but now they don't go unless they get paid. But this was the third or fourth one, and people would listen to poetry all day and then come listen to the Riders at night in the casino. Lots of old people from the early days were still there. In Salt Lake City we stopped at Bill and Nada's, one of their favorite places to eat, and Slim took me by the place in Salt Lake City where he wrote 'Ride with Me, Gringo.' That van smelled like sardines. We were at the Cowboy Poetry Gathering for about a week, then we flew to Dallas where Woody's wife, Liza, met us at the airport."

From the beginning, the Riders had used the old western radio shows of Gene Autry, Roy Rogers, and others as a basis for their stage shows. They would mix serious songs with humor, feature a variety of entertainment, and include short skits in their performances. After *Tumbleweed Theater*, the Riders had developed several characters for their act—Slim was "Sidemeat," Woody was "Drywall Paul," and Ranger Doug was "Sergeant Dudley." So it seemed logical for the Riders to present a full-fledged radio show—an ear movie, actually—for their second MCA Record. Titled *Riders Radio Theater*, the album—which came when the cassette was most popular—was perfect for putting in the car tape system for a long drive.

On March 7, 1988, the Riders entered Emerald Studios on Music Row in Nashville and began recording their *Riders Radio Theater* album. The term *Riders Radio Theater* had come from former member Tommy Goldsmith, who simply thought the phrase fit what they were doing back during their Wind in the Willow days.

"The idea came from a show called *Radio Mystery Theater*, hosted by E.G. Marshall," recalled Goldsmith. "It was on public radio. I was a musician on the road, and every now and then I'd come across that program. It was a real treat to find it on a long drive at night. It made the hour pass pretty quickly."

Back when they were playing the Wind in the Willows club every Tuesday evening, Tommy wrote a "radio" play, "The Cowboy Who Hated Christmas." That was the first skit the Riders did, although they always "had some shtick," said Tommy. "We were all doing little bits of humor," but that was the first radio script they'd done—although there was no radio station to carry it.

This MCA recording also brought in someone for the sessions who would become an essential part of Riders In The Sky in the years ahead: Joey Miskulin joined the Riders for this recording.

Joey's reputation had preceded him. "We'd known about Joey because Woody had a tape of a guy singing 'I Wish I Was Eighteen Again,'" said Slim. "We thought he was singing and playing the accordion—and the guy was a great, great accordion player, and we thought, 'That's what we need to fill out our sound—an accordion player, to do twins with the fiddle and capture that Andy Parker and the Plainsmen sound and Sons of the Pioneers sound. A guy named Jay Brodersen kept telling us, 'You need to meet this guy, Joey Miskulin, and finally we heard this guy singing 'I Wish I Was Eighteen Again,' and we said, 'He sounds like an old man.' Woody said, 'Yeah, he sounds weird but he really plays great.' It turns out that we found out much later that it was Frankie Yankovic doing the vocals—we had thought it was Joey— but he has a fine, mellow baritone voice. In fact, I think he has one of the finest voices of the four of us, if not *the* finest—just a really great voice—can do anything with it.

"Anyway," continues Slim. "I was doing a benefit with Dickey Lee down at the Station Inn. This was long after I'd left Dickey, but he called his old band back together to do this benefit and Joey was there playing at this benefit with Cowboy Jack Clement. That's where he and I met, and we just stayed in touch. When we did the *Riders Radio Theater* album we called him up to come in, and it turns out he has this great ability to do stings and a great dramatic sense and knew every theme song in the world. He knew how to add cartoon music behind a chase scene and could do dramatic stings—he was the whole package."

On the first day of sessions, the Riders recorded five songs: the "Riders Radio Theater Theme," written by Too Slim; "So Long, Saddle Pals," written by Woody; "Sundown Blues," written by Ranger Doug; "Chant of the Wanderer," written by Bob Nolan; and "Cattle Call," written by Tex Owens and made famous by Eddy Arnold.

On "Cattle Call," Too Slim begins talking while Ranger Doug is strumming in the middle of the song and concocts an elaborate shaggy dog story that culminates with a train wreck of circus animals. "The idea came from the Smothers Brothers," said Slim. "I wanted to do something like they did—start off with something and then let it twist and turn into some illogical story with a disastrous ending. I had the idea in my head and walked around a little town in Kansas somewhere working it out."

The next day the Riders were back in the studio and recorded comedy bits and skits; on March 13 they recorded some more comedy bits and skits. In between those sessions they played the Grand Ole Opry on Friday and Saturday night.

The album is filled with quintessential Riders humor; Too Slim gave "Trail Traffic Reports" where he parodied the traffic reports heard on morning and afternoon drive-time radio for a different kind of drive time—a cattle drive. They advertised bogus products—like "Udder Butter on a Rope" and "Saddle Whiz"—and included a long drama where Ranger Doug's yodel saved the day—in true, unlikely hero fashion, reminiscent of the old Gene Autry and Roy Rogers movies—to get them out of a jam.

The album is as classic as any radio show ever done by Gene Autry or Roy Rogers. It captures the Riders in their breadth and depth and was a harbinger of their next big career move.

Joey's Story

I was born on January 6, 1949, in Chicago, Illinois. I am the only child of Joseph John Miskulin, who worked in the printing business, and the former Mary Ann Baskovic. They were married in Chicago in 1948.

My parents were divorced when I was a youngster—under five—so I lived with my mother and her parents. There was always a lot of music in our home. The first records I can remember were seventy-eights of Frankie Yankovic and His Yanks on Columbia Records and also some country groups, like Lulu Belle and Scotty. There were also the pop records of the day, people like Frank Sinatra, Doris Day, things like that.

My grandparents and my mother certainly had an interest in music. My grandparents were of Slovenian descent and had various folk records and of course many records by Frankie Yankovic, who had his first million-selling record in 1948 with "Just Because," followed by another gold record in 1949, "The Blue Skirt Waltz." Although my dad and his brother Louie played in some of the Croatian string bands in the Chicago area, I would say I was mostly influenced at that point by accordion music from Slovenian people and also by the pop music on the radio.

My dad had brought back a twelve-bass accordion from Italy, where he had been stationed in World War II. One weekend while I was staying with him I picked up the instrument and started picking out the rudiments of some very simple songs. I enjoyed the instrument and the music I was trying to make. It was bedtime when my father asked me—I was about four and a half years old—would I like to take music lessons? I thought that would be really, really great because I thought it would be a bridge to connect me with my dad—it was his accordion. I thought it would also connect me with my grandparents and my mom and with the accordion music of Slovenia.

That's what led me to take formal music lessons—I started when I was five, and the joke at our house was that I could read music before I could read English. The lessons continued in earnest until I was maybe eleven years old and then I put the accordion down because I decided I wanted to play trumpet in the school band. So I did that for about a year until I started reaching the higher octaves in the trumpet, which is when I discovered I had a problem. I had perforated eardrums, and the pressure that was building up was not painful but made me a little bit dizzy. So I put the trumpet down. It was just about that time that my mother was asked by the folks where she worked at Argo Corn Starch—some of them knew I played accordion—if I would play at a shop picnic. So she asked me, and I said, "I guess so." And she said it would be nice because there would be food there and things like that. So I brought my accordion and played the songs I knew, and the people liked it. Picnics were different back in those days—it was at a little pavilion and people danced to what I was playing even though I had a very limited repertoire. But at the end of the day I had eaten potato chips, pretzels, and barbecue chicken and drank pop and I got paid on top of that—I got twelve dollars. I thought, "This is really, really cool." It was fun to make people happy and get paid. That was in 1960, and that was a lot of money to me then.

So I started listening to accordion records at home and took an interest in some of the bands that played around the Chicago area—one of which was Joe Kovich. My mom or my grandmother used to take me to hear that band—it was a Slovenian polka band, and it consisted of an accordion, a banjo, a drummer, and a bass player. Joe was nice enough to let me sit in with my little accordion and play some. And I must admit I was a very quick learner. I would watch what Joe did and go home that same evening and practice and practice. I just had an aptitude for quick learning, and they were just amazed that I was a young kid and could do it.

While I was sitting in with Joe Kovich one night, there was another fellow by the name of Ronnie Lee, and he came and spoke to me as I sat at the table after having played a set. He asked if I would be willing to play in his polka band in Chicago. Ronnie was originally from Montello, Wisconsin, but he had settled on the north side around Addison, Illinois, and wanted to get a polka band started. I thought it was a good idea. I was about twelve years old. Ronnie was a nice guy and asked my mom, and she

didn't see any harm in it. That was my first real professional playing experience. There were times when I made five or ten dollars
a night. Sometimes we played for the door and made good money,
and other times we played for the door in a dance hall or bar and
made almost no money. It all depended on the size of the crowd.

It was while I was playing with Ronnie Lee that I got my first
chance to do some live radio broadcasts. WTAQ was a community radio station in La Grange, Illinois, and they used to go on
location to some of the restaurants in the area and do on-location
shows on Sunday afternoon. One of the places I remember playing—it could have been my very first professional radio show—
was Texas Tommy's Steakhouse in Naperville, Illinois. Of course
it was very thrilling for me to do that. I had played on the radio as
a young kid, maybe five or six years old. At that time the accordion schools had so many students—this was right before rock
'n' roll happened. The accordion schools were able to buy time on
the radio and perhaps on a Sunday at eleven o'clock in the morning or something like that they would have all of their students
do a song. It was great because it gave the parents a chance to
hear their kids on the radio, and the kids thought it was really a
big deal. It was a great sales tool.

The very first song I played on the radio was "Melody of
Love." I was a young boy—this was 1954 or early 1955. When I
was with Ronnie Lee, we would play a half-hour or hour radio
broadcast that was really, really fun. I felt great because all my
friends and relatives in Chicago listened to it, so I felt like I was
on top of the world.

While I was playing with Ronnie Lee, Roman Possedi heard
me. Roman had the best-known Slovenian polka band in the Chicago area. Roman had been on TV and had made appearances on
the *Frankie Yankovic Show.* You've got to understand that Frank
Yankovic had television shows in various parts of the country.
He'd fly all over the country and do these shows, although he
never had an actual network show. But he had a show in Buffalo,
New York; one in Cleveland, Ohio; and another in Chicago. Roman became friends with Yankovic, and Frank would have him
do a performance now and then, maybe once every three or four
months, on his television show in Chicago. I'd seen Roman on
TV—you must remember that, in those days, anybody who was

on TV was a big star in anybody's mind. It was just a lot different than it is now. Anyway, Roman saw me playing with Ronnie Lee and came and asked if I'd be willing to play with his band. You can see that everything was happening really, really quickly. I'd gone from playing a shop picnic to playing with Ronnie Lee and then Roman asked if I'd play with his band. I agreed, and my mother and grandparents were really happy because Roman had such a great reputation for being a wonderful person as well as this was *the* premier Slovenian polka band in Chicago. We all agreed it was a super idea.

I think it was at that time that I decided I really wanted to become a good player, although at that time I was only interested in polka music—polkas and waltzes and ethnic music. Roman would pick me up after school on a Friday, and we'd go to his house and have dinner and then go and play on Friday evening at a dance. Or even, back in those days, you might do appearances at the movie theaters before the movies or between movies. Anyway we'd do something on a Friday night and then I'd stay over at Roman's house and practice all day Saturday. Roman would have to work on Saturday—we'd stay up until about one o'clock in the morning after the job on Friday, and Roman would wake up at five o'clock and go to work on the railroad while I'd stay at his house with his kids and his wife and his stepson, Stephen, who was also interested in music. It was great because I used to practice. I would sit by the record player—Roman had a very extensive library of records—and I would practice. Then he would come home and we'd have dinner at his house, and we would go and play Saturday night. If we had a job on Sunday, I'd stay over Saturday night. I'd then practice again on Sunday and play the job. So I was working as many as three days a week back when I was twelve.

It was while I was with Roman that I made my very first recording. I recorded on the Balkan Record label, which was owned by Lou Hlad. It was the biggest independent label of ethnic music in the Chicago area at that time. They recorded a lot of Croatian bands, Slovenian bands—not as much Slovenian music but a lot of Croatian music and a lot of Czechoslovakian music. Chicago has a large Bohemian and Czech population. So anyway that was my first record, and I made that just as I was turning from twelve to thirteen. It was a marvelous experience for me—I thought I was on top of the world once again.

I started going to see Frank Yankovic when he came to town. We might be playing somewhere on Friday, so we'd drive to where Frank was—Frank of course traveled the United States extensively coast to coast, border to border. Frank had heard me play with Roman, but not much happened as a result of that. However, the banjo player, Adolph Pozatek, who had played in Joe Kovich's band—the first band I ever sat in with—joined the Yankovic band. And I remember going to see Frank at the Carousel Ballroom in Chicago, and Adolph said, "There's Joey—remember Joey?" Frank said, "Let's have him sit in," and so Yankovic got off the band-stand, introduced me, and I picked up his accordion and started playing. Shortly after that, Frank asked if I wanted to go on the road with him. I asked my mother if it would be okay for me to play with him, and of course this was the ultimate. Not only was Yankovic the most famous polka band leader, this is a guy who was so popular that he beat Duke Ellington in a battle-of-the-bands contest. He was on Columbia and had two million-sellers but was continuing to sell hundreds of thousands of records. I think at the time I joined Frankie he had sold eight million records. Plus he was on television, played in Hollywood, played in New York, played everywhere! I begged and begged my mother and grand-parents to let me do this. It meant I would be going on the road, but they felt that if Adolph Pozatek, the banjo player, vouched for the moral character of the guys in the band and, because they were thirty to thirty-five years older than me, they would watch out for me, then it would be okay to travel with the Yankovic band.

While I was on the road, I disciplined myself to study music theory and counterpoint and things like that. I did most of my studies in the back of the bus. I got college textbooks, and it was a tedious job to say the least initially, because I was trying to teach myself and when they talked about theory I'd just stare at the page. There was no one to say, "It's simple." Once I started get-ting in the groove it started making sense, and I could apply ev-erything. In Frank's band, we'd play the Nevada circuit—Vegas, Reno, and Tahoe—and I paid absolute attention to what was go-ing on with the other musicians. Also, because I was a kid I couldn't gamble, so there were only a few places to go. I either had to go outside and get something to eat or go back to the hotel room or hang out in the rehearsal area of the casino, which I did. I did eat, but most of the time I was at the piano practicing or reading the college textbook. So that's how I learned the rudiments of music theory and harmony.

That road gig with Yankovic led to an association that continued for thirty-six years. During that time I recorded many, many albums on Columbia, RCA, MCA, and Polygram with Frank Yankovic and produced his very first Grammy award–winning polka album called *70 Years of Hits with Frankie Yankovic, featuring Joey Miskulin.*

Once I joined the Yankovic band my whole musical career really changed—it went into high gear, although I was not quite in high school yet. It meant doing television shows, recording on Columbia Records and later RCA, MCA, and Polygram. It also led to me producing four Grammy-nominated records for Yankovic, one of which won the Grammy in 1986. That *70 Years* was the very first Grammy awarded to a polka record. And it was during those years with Yankovic that my musical tastes really began to become diverse. I started really listening to the radio, listening to all kinds of music—rock 'n' roll, country—a lot of country—to lots of jazz. I decided that I needed to become a well-rounded musician if I wanted to continue in this business and make it a career. During those years we traveled to Nevada and worked with some of the greatest names in show business. We appeared on the same bandstands as people like Red Norvo, Homer and Jethro, Trio Los Panchos, Spike Jones, Bill Haley and the Comets—the list goes on and on. I was so fortunate to get in on the tail end of that era where you could go to a lounge in Nevada and hear the most wonderful music. There was Louis Jordan, Scat Davis, Esquivel, the Brothers Castro. It was so wonderful. Not only was I able to work with those people, but I had a chance to see some really great acts that we didn't work with. Like Harry James and his big band with Buddy Rich on drums—in the lounge! I believe that was at the Flamingo Hotel. To see Louis Prima and Keeley Smith with Sam Butera and the Witnesses. What an education I got just from keeping my ears and eyes open in the early sixties.

I left the Yankovic band in 1968 and joined the Hawaiian Jazz Revue and played in Hawaii, Japan, Hong Kong, China, Vietnam, Thailand, Okinawa, and back to Hawaii. I got an offer from Don Ho to stay with him and live in Hawaii, but at that point I decided it was too far away and I wanted to get back to the mainland.

I got back to the U.S. mainland in March of 1969. I was going to stay on the West Coast, but Frank called and said, "We've got three more albums to do on our RCA contract," so I decided to come back with him. I stayed with him until I got married in 1970 to my first wife, Joanne. I tried for a very short period of time to lead a normal life. I worked in a factory office keeping records on steel—log it in and log it out. First week I wore a white shirt and tie, the second week I didn't have the tie, and the third week I didn't even shave. It was ridiculous. So it was the old wife's ultimatum—music or me—so what can I say?

The primary reason for wanting to perform was strictly the music. Once I decided that I wanted to play music, it swept me up. To play with these groups and understand how wonderful it is for four people to make something that is so great. Or five or six people or whatever was in the band. The rest of the things came later. When I saw people react to me when I was on TV with Roman or later with Frank, that was great, and it made me feel good. To hear crowds applaud a twelve- or thirteen-year-old kid. Fortunately I never let it go to my head. I never stopped learning, and I think it's because of the music. I didn't say, "Well, these folks like me; I'm a big shot or whatever." I just wanted to improve musically. The crowd didn't seem to make that much of a difference to me. It was all great—don't get me wrong—it was all great that they enjoyed it, but that wasn't my stimulus. It was the music itself—to make it all work, to have that band sound as great as it could be. Travel, meeting girls, the money all came later, but the reason for wanting to play was to hear and feel and express myself through music.

In 1978 my wife, Patti, and I opened "Joey Miskulin's Lounge" in Cleveland. It had two bandstands and a big dance floor; we featured polka music on Wednesday, Friday, and Saturday nights with jazz on Tuesday, and I played a variety of things on Thursdays. A whole lot of people came to that club—politicians, musicians, dancers, and every kind of music lover. I also produced a show on WCLQ-TV, *Polka Time USA*. We had that club for six and a half years, and it was really one of the premier nightclubs in the Cleveland area.

Then I moved to Nashville in 1986. I'd been on the road with Frank Yankovic for many, many years, then started doing a lot of studio work in the seventies and through the eighties. I recorded with lots of groups, lots of big-name people, and was expanding my horizons in terms of becoming a recording studio musician and a producer. Jack Clement invited me down to Nashville, and he went more than the extra mile for me. First, he invited me to stay with him while my wife, Patti, stayed in Cleveland and worked two jobs. She was incredible. We didn't want to move before I knew if I could make a living doing studio work.

Jack would let me sit in his office, and everybody came through there and I got to meet them. And not just meet them—Jack would make sure they knew what I did. And then I decided to buy a house right behind Jack's, and Jack moved in with me and paid rent—said he needed a place to live when he had his own house. But he did it to help me and, man, that was a huge help. He didn't have to do that, but he's such an incredible human being. Next to Frank Yankovic, I owe everything to Jack Clement and Steve Popovich. Those guys did more for me than anyone. And, of course, Patti, my wife, for working two jobs and keeping the house in Cleveland while I was getting started in Nashville.

So I moved to Nashville and started recording with Johnny Cash and the Everly Brothers and Emmylou Harris and even did a recording with Paul McCartney on one of Johnny Cash's albums. Also arranged and recorded three cuts on U2's *Rattle and Hum* record and appeared in their movie. I was doing a lot of session work in Nashville.

At that point, believe it or not, I had not heard of Riders In The Sky, and of course they hadn't heard of me. The guy who brought it all together is Jay Brodersen. Jay had played banjo and guitar with the Yankovic band for a little while, and he was a big fan of Riders In The Sky. Jay liked the way I played—we'd worked together and done some things—so he sent me a tape of the Riders and sent the Riders a tape of me. We did not meet until I was doing a benefit at a little place called the Station Inn in Nashville.

Jack Clement and I were playing along with Vic Willis and his trio. At the same time Too Slim was making an appearance with the Dickey Lee band. He had played with Dickey before starting with Riders In The Sky. So Jack had introduced me and told the audience a little bit about me. Dickey introduced the guys who were working with him that night. After the show Slim was sitting, having a drink, and I walked over to him and said, "I know who you are—our friend Jay Brodersen told me about you," and he said, "Yeah, and you're Joey and Jay told us about you." That was our first meeting. I don't recall if it was right after that or right before that, but I actually played with Doug and Slim on a Gary McMahan record, but it was an overdub, so I never saw them. That's how it is sometimes in the record business—you will work with someone on a record—maybe five or ten records—and never see them. So that was the first meeting for Slim and me.

Time passed and I got a call from, I think, Woody, who introduced himself on the phone and said they were doing a record called *Riders Radio Theater* for MCA. He asked if I'd be interested in doing some recording with them, and I thought, "Sure." That was my business. So I came to the studio with my accordion, and that was my first meeting with Woody and Ranger Doug, and we recorded *Riders Radio Theater*. The next thing I remember is that a little time had passed and I got a call from, I think, Slim—or maybe it was Woody again—and it was, "Would you like to make an appearance on *Riders Radio Theater* itself," which was being broadcast and taped by WPLN in Nashville as well as other parts of the country. And I thought, "Sure, great." I didn't have a cowboy hat, but Ranger Doug or Woody said, "Don't worry, we'll get you one." It was such great fun to play with them. We did a radio show, then shook hands and I left. It wasn't long after that they called and said, "How'd you like to be on the radio show for every taping?" I thought it would be great, and that was really my start with the Riders.

Chapter 25

The idea for a radio show had been brewing for quite a while. According to Ranger Doug, "When we'd gotten done those three years on The Nashville Network doing *Tumbleweed Theater,* we thought the whole idea would translate well with radio because, from the start, I had gotten so much of the sensibility of Riders In The Sky from those old radio shows—the Sons of the Pioneers Teleways transcriptions, the Foy Willing and the Riders of the Purple Sage transcriptions, and Gene Autry's *Melody Ranch* shows. I'd listened to a lot of that stuff while I was working at the Hall of Fame. As a kid I did too, but it didn't stick with me as much then. So we'd always come out and performed like it was a radio show— we'd been doing that for years. Some of the guys who'd worked on the *Tumbleweed Theater* shows—the producers, Steve Arwood and Randy Hale—thought what we did would work as a radio show too. At one point we'd gone in and cut a radio demo, just to see what would happen. Took it to WPLN, and it sat there in complete invisibility. And then I ran into Henry Fennell, a staff announcer at WPLN, the Nashville public radio station, at the old record store on Elliston Place, and we got to talking about this, that, and the other. And he said, 'Have you ever thought about doing a radio show of what you guys do, because we're trying to create more Nashville-based stuff for our station.' And I said, 'You've got a tape there somewhere. We've done that—it's there somewhere.' And it developed from there. We did our first year there."

Actually, the idea for a radio show initially came from Bruce Nemerov, who had seen them at Wind in the Willows and loved their show. He suggested they record a "demo" radio show. The Riders have always been careful with their money—they've never been a big-money act—so keeping expenses down, watching carefully where their money goes, has long been part of their life. This is especially true with Slim, so it was appropriate that the first question Slim asked was, "Is this going to cost us anything?" Nemerov replied that he would foot the bill, so the Riders went into Tom T. Hall's studio in Franklin, "The Toy Box," and recorded the demo. Nemerov first took the demo to executives at American Public Radio, which distributes the *Prairie Home Companion*, and included a budget for the show. They turned it down, saying, "It costs too much money" and "There's no classical music on it." Nemerov and the boys were dumbfounded. "It's in our charter," stated the executive. "We have to promote classical music." True, the *Prairie Home Companion* occasionally has classical performers on—but it's not really a classical music show.

When the show was turned down, Nemerov then took it over to WPLN, where it sat on the shelf until Ranger Doug's chance encounter with Henry Fennell. Two WPLN supporters, Brenda Loftis (later she married and became Brenda Batey) and Judy Liff, who had produced a pilot show for the station, *The Hungry Ear*, agreed to obtain the financing for the show and the *Riders Radio Theater*.

"Steve Arwood came over to Ranger Doug's house on Natchez Trace, and we sat around the table throwing out ideas," said Slim.

"All the guys took part in writing the first show, called 'Dialing for Dogies,' but as the show progressed, Slim became the major Rider writing. It was like writing the TV show," said Arwood. "Woody would show up, then have to go somewhere, and Ranger Doug would be there but usually fall asleep. Most of the time he'd add some key sparks at the end when he woke up and Woody would add some good ideas when he came back. But this became Slim's baby—he really took ownership. He really loved writing those shows."

The first *Riders Radio Theater* was taped at the Johnson Theater in the Tennessee Performing Arts building in Nashville on April 25, 1988. They did two shows during an evening.

On May 19 they were in St. Louis for a Public Radio Convention, promoting their new show on NPR. "We did a concert at 9:30 A.M.," said Slim. "Some loved it, and a number of stations picked it up. That's where the folks with WVXU in Cincinnati first heard it. We did fifty-two shows that first year. Around the seventh or eighth show Joey came on—and that was a big step."

"Actually, the professionalism didn't really kick in until the fifth or sixth shows," said Arwood, who became the announcer on the show and took the handle "Texas Bix Bender." Part of the problem was Slim's frugality; he didn't want to hire a sound-effects person. "We'll do it all ourselves," he said. But after the fourth taping it was obvious the show wasn't quite working, so the group had a meeting. Arwood knew a sound-effects person was desperately needed but thought that Slim would still be against it. But the meeting of the group opened with Slim asking, "Don't you think we need a sound-effects guy?" And so Bruce Nemerov, operating under the handle "Zeno Clinker," took on the job of doing sound effects.

Also, the group called Joey Miskulin, who acquired the handle "Joey the Cowpolka King," to add some punch. "Getting Joey kicked it up about ten notches," said Arwood. "He was the secret weapon to really make that show happen."

Arwood, as Texas Bix, had no cowboy clothes, so Ranger Doug provided him with a western sports coat and a ten-gallon cowboy hat. "The hat was too big for me," said Texas Bix. "Doug's head is bigger than mine. But I wore it during the shows."

David Skepner, who had contacted Brenda Batey and Judy Liff about the show, wanted to be the director. "But he didn't know what he was doing," said Arwood. "Still, the audience loved them, so it all worked."

The Riders just wanted to do a radio show, so they agreed to doing one a week—fifty-two that first year. It almost killed them.

The Riders would do two shows an evening. Arwood would write the shows while the Riders were on the road, then when they got back into town, would go over the shows with the guys. After the first read-through, Slim would inevitably say, "Okay, now let's go through it again and put some jokes in." That's when serious rewriting began. The shows were always too long "because I wanted to have too much and not too little," said Arwood. Ranger Doug remembers that at the rehearsals it was always "cut, cut, cut."

On the day of the taping, the Riders would gather at the Tennessee Performing Arts Center and run through the whole show—editing, rewriting, making adjustments, and tweaking the timing, because each show had to be exactly twenty-eight minutes long. They would usually finish rehearsing just before the audience came in. Then they'd do the two shows, back-to-back, with a new audience for each show.

On August 1, 1988, the Riders were at the first Western Music Association Festival, held in Las Vegas. The night before they had been in Welches, Oregon, at the Rippling River Resort and the next night would be in Corvallis, Oregon, at the Benton County Fair. But that day in Las Vegas was the first convention for a key organization to promote western music. Part of the reason the organization had come into existence was because of the success of Riders In The Sky.

"Bill Wiley played a big part in our life for a number of years," said Ranger Doug. "He said, 'Let's get these people who play western music together if we can.' He'd been intimate with the Sons of the Pioneers for a number of years. It was really his dream to get this together. Those who loved cowboy music—and there were so few of us at that time—1988—got these people together for some jamming. I don't think it was meant to be more than a reunion. To get the people who love the stuff to talk about it. I'm sure it developed rather quickly into 'How can we get this to promote western music?' Make it something that America will pay to see again. It started to develop into something else when it moved to Tucson and Tom Chambers stepped in and took control.

"It's just my gut feeling, but I think when Bill started it, he wanted it to be just a reunion," said Green. "But because so many of the members are performers, they wanted an organization that would further western music in general. Those people wanted an organization that would materially advance their careers. And that's what a trade organization ought to do."

That first convention of the Western Music Association laid the groundwork for a thriving trade organization that represents western music. It holds an annual convention, has a quarterly publication, and sponsors an awards show and hall of fame.

In September, the Riders were back in Nashville, performing on the Opry and doing *Riders Radio Theater* shows on September 20, October 11, October 25, November 1, and November 8. They appeared on *Nashville Now* on November 15, then did *Riders Radio Theater* shows on November 22 and 29.

In November, Billy Maxwell went on the road with the Riders again. "We all met at Woody's house and left at ten o'clock at night and drove to Phoenix," he said. "Woody had a girl who came in from California. We stayed at a Hyatt Regency, and they played at a Harvest Festival. After the last show on Sunday they flew to San Antonio for a Moe Bandy Golf Tournament. I took them to the airport and thought Woody's girl was flying out with them. Woody never has his stuff packed until you're at the gate ready to go, so you've got to wait for him. The girl was sitting there on the bus, and Woody said to me, 'Her plane ain't leaving until sometime in the morning. Do whatever you want to with her.' Then he shut the door and walked into the airport. So I had to get her a hotel room before I could drive to Oklahoma City.

"I got in Oklahoma City around 6 P.M. and checked into a Motel 6, then picked them up at the airport the next morning," continued Billy. "There was a big windstorm—it was blowing down signs. We headed to Woodward, Oklahoma, and did a show there, then drove to Boulder, Colorado, on November 16. We checked into our rooms, and Woody had another girl who met him there. She was about nineteen. We checked into a little hotel, and the showers were about waist high. You had to get on your knees to get a shower. I don't know what the deal was, but Slim said it was because it was a mining town and they were used to having these short miners stay there. They were 'miners' showers,' he said. Liz Masterson came to the show, and the waitresses were on roller skates.

"The next morning we were supposed to leave at 11 A.M. but when that time came, it was snowing hard. Everybody was on the bus except Woody. Somebody said, 'We'd better go get him,' so Slim and I went and knocked on the door to his room, and he wasn't up yet. He finally opens the door—the wind's blowing and snow is coming in—and he's standing there buck-naked. Ain't got nothing on. Slim said, 'Woody—it's time to go. We're supposed to leave at 11 o'clock and it's twenty after now.' Woody said, 'Nobody told me—I didn't know.' Slim said, 'Get your clothes on and let's go.' Woody said, 'Well, I ain't had anything to eat. Slim, would you go across the street to that health food store and get me some of them whole wheat croy-sonts.' That's the way he said it—croy-sonts. Slim, said, 'Yeah, just get your clothes on.'

"So we went across the street, walked into this place, and it's a college town so there's college kids in there working. Educated kids. And Slim walks up to the counter and says, 'Give me a couple of them whole wheat croy-sonts.' Just like Woody had said it. And I just lost it right there. Slim didn't bat an eye, but I'm sure the girl on the other side of the counter is thinking, 'Where did this idiot come from?'

"We finally got Woody on the bus about a half-hour later and drove to Houston. We checked in the Wexford Hotel, and Woody had another girl meet him there. There's a guy in Houston who always comes to their show—Ranger Doug doesn't like him 'cause he sits in the front row and gets a couple of drinks in him, and he's seen so many shows that he always yells out the punch lines three or four seconds before anybody on stage says them. Kills an act. He's a big loud-mouthed guy—you can hear his voice over anybody else's in the crowd.

"A guy came to the show who made custom boots—name's David—and he smiles all the time but doesn't say a whole lot. He had some samples of the different types of leather or animal skins he used on different boots, and he had them in this notebook. He would turn the pages so the guys could pick out a type of skin for a pair of boots. The next day Woody woke up and said, 'I had this dream last night that something had happened to everybody and this guy was showing me this notebook. And on the pages he'd say, 'This is Ranger Doug's skin' or 'This is Too Slim's skin.' That's typical of what goes on in Woody's mind.

"We had to go to Bay City, Texas, for a show, so Woody rides down with his girl and gets there late, of course. A woman drove up with some seafood gumbo, and we had it backstage. Outside of town, they'd put up this big huge billboard advertising that Riders In The Sky was going to be at this harvest festival. It was a huge, full-sized billboard on the side of the road with their pictures on it, so we had to stop and take their pictures with that billboard in the background. They'd never seen themselves ten times life-sized before."

On December 2, they were back at the Opry, then did *Riders Radio Theater* shows on December 6 and 13, then an appearance on the Opry on December 17.

It was a big year for Riders In The Sky. Their 191 appearances included a number of national television appearances, the launch of the National Public Radio show *Riders Radio Theater*, and the release of the MCA album, also called *Riders Radio Theater*.

Chapter 26

On January 10, 1989, the Riders taped two shows for *Riders Radio Theater* and the next day appeared on *Nashville Now*. The day after that they were in Jack's Tracks studio with Kathy Mattea recording "Here's Hopin'." The next two days—Friday and Saturday—they played on the Opry.

On Monday morning they were at TNN working on a "Country Comedy Special." They spent three days that week working on that show, then, early on Thursday morning, were on Ralph Emery's local TV show. Friday night they performed at their Hospital Hospitality House benefit, and on Saturday night they were on the Opry.

In January, an article in *USA Today*, "Hip Country Pops a Clever-Humor Cork," written by David Zimmerman, states, "Their humor, including the ongoing serial 'Meltdown on the Mesa,' is Western wacko. . . . What makes the act work is the mix of note-perfect harmonies—Woody Paul really does know his way around a fiddle—and off-center humor."

The Riders then took off for Elko, Nevada, where they spent two days at the Cowboy Poetry Gathering before flying to Ann Arbor, where they appeared at a folk festival. "That was a great return," said Slim. "Hometown Boy makes good. We played at the Hill Auditorium, where I'd seen Simon and Garfunkel, Lovin' Spoonful, the Byrds, the Beach Boys, and Segovia. It was such a thrill, and it broke open the Ann Arbor market."

On February 27, 1989, an article on the Riders appeared in *People* magazine. Titled "Riders In The Sky Lasso Listeners by Poking Fun at Cowpokes While Singing Sweetly of the Prairie" and written by Steve Dougherty and Jane Sanderson, the article states, "Roll over, Randolph Scott, and tell Gabby Hayes the news: Riders In The Sky, the music-comedy stars of Public Radio's *Riders Radio Theater*, are suddenly seeing their career rise like—well, allows Too Slim, 'Not like a rocket. Maybe a hot-air balloon.' They mockingly describe themselves as the Springsteens of the Sagebrush and the Marx Brothers of Western Music. . . the Riders prefer spoof on the hoof. Beneath the parody, there's a genuine love of the lore. 'Without that,' says Slim, 'you've got three overeducated guys with their tongues so far in their cheeks it's not funny.'"

One of the people who read that article was Alan Sacks, an independent TV producer in Los Angeles who had developed the TV shows *Welcome Back, Kotter* and *Chico and the Man.* He also produced the documentaries "Du-Beat-e-o" about punks; "Thrashin'" about skateboarders; "The Color of Friendship," a story about racial conflicts in South Africa; and the TV movie "Women of West Point."

"I saw the picture of three singing cowboys and children around them," said Sacks. "My mind kind of stays open, and I thought this could be developed into something for TV. So I immediately contacted David Skepner."

Skepner happened to be in L.A. at the time, so they had breakfast. Sacks tossed out some ideas, and Skepner said the TV producer needed to meet the Riders to see if they clicked. On April 12 the Riders were playing in San Francisco, and Sacks went up to meet them. "We hit it off immediately and began collaborating," said Sacks.

Originally, Sacks had the idea of a TV sitcom based on the old Beverly Hillbillies show—only it would be "Riders go to Hollywood," a "fish out of water" idea. He took the idea around to some TV executives but none were excited about it.

On March 14 the Riders were at 16th Avenue Recorders taping some comedy bits and skits as well as six songs. Ranger Doug wrote "Riding the Old Front Range," Too Slim wrote "Ride with Me, Gringo," and the group arranged "The Queen Elizabeth Trio."

"Ride with Me, Gringo" was inspired by a poster on the wall of a restaurant in Salt Lake City. The song begins:

Last night I saw Pancho Villa,
He came to me in a dream
He said he would wait in the mountains
He would wait for me by a stream

The song is filled with allusions to the Mexican Pancho Villa, who led a raid into the southwest United States in the early twentieth century. The song concludes:

Today I ride on a dream
To a rendezvous in the mountains
They're waiting for me by a stream

Ranger Doug's "Riding the Old Front Range," has an easy, loping feel to it.

Lazy clouds and lazy cattle
Lonely hours in the saddle
Life's a joy, life's a battle
Ridin' the old front range
Where endless plains and endless skies
Meet silver mountains as they rise
To greet the lazy clouds on high
Ridin' the old front range

The "Queen Elizabeth Trio" is a song sung in falsetto. "Joey had a *Hooked on Polka* album that had 'The Happy Wanderer' on it," said Slim. "And I loved that song and was walking around singing it. Then at a sound check we all started singing it in real high voices—and that's where that come from."

The other three songs were "There's a Blue Sky Way Out Yonder," written by Fred Hall, Bert Van Cleve, and Arthur Fields; "No Rodeo Dough," written by John Jacob Loeb, Cy Coben, and Lewis Harris; and the old classic, "Along the Navajo Trail," written by Larry Markes, Dick Charles, and Eddie Delange.

"Along the Navajo Trail" was originally titled "Prairie Parade," but Lou Levy, head of the music publishing firm Leeds Music, disliked the title—the "p's" often popped when sung into the microphone. Also, another song titled "Prairie Parade" was in the movie *Laugh Your Blues Away* in 1942. The first song was written by Larry Markes and Dick Charles, who worked as page boys at the NBC Studios in New York. When Levy asked for a new title and rewritten lyrics, bandleader Eddie DeLange came up with the title "Along the Navajo Trail." Levy asked the songwriters if they would share songwriting credit and royalties with DeLange; the pot was sweetened when Levy promised that Bing Crosby and the Andrews Sisters would record the song with the revised lyrics. The songwriters agreed, although the first recording was by Dinah Shore.

Larry Markes, born in 1921, served as a fighter-bomber pilot during World War II; stationed in England in 1945, he was unaware that "Along the Navajo Trail" was featured in a Roy Rogers movie that carried that same title. According to Jim Bob Tinsley, in his book *For a Cowboy Has to Sing*, Markes took a British girlfriend to the movie in London. When the song came on, Markes said, "I wrote that song!" The girl, thinking that Markes was trying to impress her, said, "Oh, that's all right, Yank. I like you anyway."

The Riders continued their concept of putting radio on record with this album, which would be titled *Riders Go Commercial*, a fervent hope and prayer as the Riders once again tried to capture a massive audience with their niche music and humor.

On March 15 the Riders went back into the studio to record some more comedy bits and skits. The comedy skits begin with a faux boardroom conversation where record company executives discuss their future big ticket items, then discuss the Riders—and how they can face the challenge of getting them into the big sales column. The conclusion is to put commercials on their album. In this conversation the Riders show a keen awareness of who they are and how they are perceived by the major-label music industry. They don't kid themselves—they're not in the same league as the musical superstars, yet they have a certain undeniable appeal. They also parody as well as sympathize with the problem label execs have of trying to market them. What do you do with an act so far out in left field that all the traditional methods of marketing don't apply?

In the "commercials" the Riders push products such as the "Accordion Repair Course," "Udder Fantastic" and "Cow Paint and Body Shop." It was another gambit to get on country radio—but, once again, it didn't work. Big sales didn't come their way either, although the Riders continued to sell good, steady numbers. But not good enough for a major label, which wants and needs gold and platinum sales figures to stay in business.

In May, an article in *Country Music Magazine*, which Ranger Doug used to write for and which had sponsored the infamous softball team that Ranger Doug, Too Slim, and this author had all played for, published an article by Patrick Carr titled, "Riders In The Sky: Have a Dream Job." The article states, "At the Tennessee

Performing Arts Center . . . [a] horse's skull is wired together somewhat conspicuously and beside it stands a placard bearing the
legend *De Mortius Nil Nisi Bonum:* 'Let nothing be said of the dead
but what is good.' The cacti are cheap, cheesy-looking two-di-
mensional plywood cutouts . . . [in] front of the stage is a Pee Wee
Herman doll, wearing a sombrero, mounted on a stuffed armadillo. . . . Woody Paul on the fiddle is obviously a few buffalo
chips light of a load." The article concludes, "The serene, golden-
throated Ranger Doug is the kind of man they don't make anymore: handsome but not pretty, tough but not mean, kind but not
soft, bright but not smart, a man's man and a lady's dream: a
straight shooter, plain talker, lifelong friend and protector of
women, children and animals. 'The Idol of American Youth' in
the flesh."

The article notes that the Riders "are exhausted, as they often
are these days" because "the pressures of writing and recording a
weekly radio show while also keeping their act on the road are
extreme." In answer to the query about Woody Paul having a Ph.D.
from M.I.T, Ranger Doug states, "Not many people know this,
but many of the great fiddle-players—Sam Bush, Johnny Gimble—
have doctorates from M.I.T. It's a program they have up there."
He then adds, "I'd say that Riders In The Sky is the most need-
lessly overeducated band in North America."

In the article Ranger Doug notes, "The band is still just a delight to me. . . . You see, what we do is really a great joy. People go
through a lot in life and for them to come for two hours and alter-
nately laugh, crack up, and then be really moved by a song like
'Blue Montana Skies' or 'Streets of Laredo,' which touches them
somewhere and takes them away from their mortgage and their
marriage and their teenage druggies and whatever else bothers
their life . . . that's a very satisfying job."

Ranger Doug concludes, "As people we're kind of at one with
our music. We're not having to put on an act to promote something that's not really us. We really do love this music. We love
the tradition. We love to write in it. We love to dress up and be
cowboys; it's like we're six years old again. And I think the audience senses that: both the commitment we have, and the joy we
feel doing what we do. That's why we've survived."

On June 13 the Riders appeared on *Hee Haw,* then went to

Branson, Missouri, where they appeared at Silver Dollar City June 19–22. Their two-thousandth performance came a few days later, on June 25, in Bellevue, Colorado, at the Double Diamond Stables, which is Gary McMahan's ranch.

Back in Nashville, the group recorded *Riders Radio Theater* shows on June 27, July 6, and July 26. On June 28 and 29 they taped appearances on *Hee Haw*. On September 3, the Riders were at Copper Mountain, Colorado, for WestFest.

"We couldn't be at the first WestFests because we had a scheduling conflict. We always played the Minnesota State Fair on Labor Day, which was when WestFest was scheduled," said Slim. "But for this WestFest we didn't go to Minnesota." He added, "The audience totally got it—the energy was picking up. I remember a whole lot of people and hearing Robert Earl Keen by himself."

Feeding off the audience, the Riders got quite wacky on stage, even launching into "Surfin' U.S.A." Things got really crazy, and Ranger Doug announced from the stage, "I've lost control of this show!"

"I remember walking around and seeing the crafts and thinking this was a great idea," said Ranger Doug. "Some of those WestFests were glorious—the ones in Colorado especially."

Chapter 27

 On the Road with Riders by Billy Maxwell

We left Nashville on October 10, 1989, driving on I-65 North, headed to Montana. Everybody was into working out then, so we stopped in Minneapolis, where everybody worked out at the YMCA. I stayed in the bus, and while I was in the parking lot somebody backed into the bus, but it didn't do any damage. We went through Fargo, North Dakota, to Plentywood, Montana, where Woody and I played golf. We only played three holes because the wind was blowing so hard you couldn't even stand up to make your shot. Plentywood is about sixteen miles from the Canadian border, and the Riders did a radio station interview that afternoon, then played the high school auditorium for a show that night.

Then we headed to Billings, where we stayed at the Rim Rock Inn. Ranger Doug had filled up the diesel tank with gasoline, so we had to siphon the gas out of the bus, but we didn't have much luck. So we went back to the Rim Rock, where Woody said he was going to an AA meeting. We all went to a Mexican restaurant and had some bad food, so we got some frozen yogurt, went back to the hotel, and watched TV. Finally, we had to take the bus to a service station, and the guy had to take the tank off to get the gasoline out of the tank. That bus had two tanks so you could switch to the other tank. We were late for the show and had to borrow a truck to get to the show. We drove through Butte in the middle of the night, and there was nothing open in downtown Butte.

It was Slim's turn to start driving, so he said, "I'll just find something further down the road," so I pulled into this closed service station to let Slim drive. It was a split highway with a median in the middle, and Slim got out there and had to turn the wrong way so he made a U-turn to get back going the right way. As soon as he made that U-turn— it was three o'clock in the morning with nobody on the streets—here comes this cop and pulls him over. Slim said he was talking to him and thought he was doing some good. Said he was with Riders In The Sky, and the guy said he'd heard of Riders In The Sky, so Slim thought he wasn't going to get a ticket. But the guy just kept on writing and handed Slim a ticket and then gave him one of them deals. Said, "You don't have to stay and appear here. You can just give me forty dollars, and I'll pay your fine." I'm sure it was one of those deals that the guy made forty bucks and that was the end of that.

We drove on in to Big Fork, Montana, and got there about eight-thirty Sunday morning and checked into the Timbers Motel. About ten-thirty Woody said, "Let's go for something to eat." We were at the edge of Glacier National Park, and we rode around in the bus—it was cold, snow on the ground. After awhile Woody said, "Let's drive up in the park." And as we got closer he said, "Let's drive up the 'Going to the Sun' Highway." This road is very narrow with a lot of switchbacks, and we're in the bus. We drove the bus almost to the top before we turned around and came back—the road was so narrow we couldn't go any farther. We had to turn that bus around on one of those narrow, crooked roads. It was ridiculous to ever try and do anything like that, but we did.

We had a great meal and show that night and left about seven-thirty the next morning and drove past the southern boundary of Glacier National Park. We arrived in Great Falls about one-ten that afternoon and went to the Charlie Russell Museum, but it was not open so they decided to go work out. We went to the auditorium and Buckeye Blake, who did the Riders In The Sky poster, came to the show that night. We went to an Italian restaurant for dinner and had some bad food.

We loaded up that night and headed to Concordia, Kansas. This was the night the earthquake hit California. We were driving, and Slim was trying to get the World Series on one of those little hand-held Sony portable TVs, and he couldn't get it to come in. So he said, "Something's wrong with this TV. Every time I want to watch something, it won't come in. It never works at the right time." Finally, he did get the World Series and found out the earthquake had knocked them off the air. So then we changed our plans and stopped in York, Nebraska, where we got a room so we could watch TV and find out what was going on. It was some bad stuff. We spent the night there and then the next day went on to Concordia, Kansas.

Did a show there and then left Concordia about eleven that night and drove on to Cheyenne, Wyoming, then Laramie, where we stayed at the Annie Moore Guest House in Laramie. It's a great little place, and lots of interesting people have stayed there. Anybody that's speaking or entertaining at the university—that's where they put them up. Woody stayed in the basement.

Woody decided to go to the golf course and hit a bucket of balls. After the show we went to a little bar with the promoters. The next day we went to the public radio station to help them with a fund-raiser—people call in and talk to Riders In The Sky, you know, and pledge some money. While we were on the radio show something came up about pizza, and all the guys commented on how much they love pizza.

We left Laramie and went north to Casper and stopped at a little place called Shirley Basin—the road goes in there, but it doesn't go any farther. The whole town consists of trailers with a little Quonset hut grocery store, and I guarantee you that you could take three hundred dollars in there and buy everything they had. They didn't have much stock on the shelf, so of course they didn't have no diesel fuel. But we found somebody who had five gallons of diesel there and we paid them like ten bucks for five gallons of diesel. Put it in the bus and barely made it on into Casper.

We went to the event center in Casper, and when we got to the show there were about eight pizzas—one of every kind you can imagine—

from the local Pizza Hut. It was enough pizzas to feed twenty people. The bunch in Casper had called ahead and told them that the Riders love pizza.

The next morning Woody and I played golf in Casper, but the wind was blowing hard and somehow we missed a hole—we played eight holes but finished on the number nine. Don't know where that other one was—we lost it somewhere.

Woody wanted to go to a department store in downtown Casper for some perfume for Teresa—this is in the early days with her—so we did. So Woody goes into this really nice department store and into the ladies' perfume section with all these girls in their make-up—looked like they just walked out of a magazine. He's in there with a hooded sweatshirt on with his hood pulled up around his head—'cause it's cold—and he asked, "Got any of that Passion perfume?" The girl said, "Yes, I've got some here," and she got out a bottle. Then Woody says, "Oh, I didn't want to buy any—I just wanted to smell it. My wife said she liked it, and I just wanted to know what it smelled like." So she sprayed a little on his hand and he said, "Yeah, that's all right." But he didn't buy any there.

We headed down the road and stopped in at a barbecue place in Kansas City, Arthur Bryant's, where the Riders always eat anytime they're through there. Great place. We'll actually schedule leaving time so we can get there before they close. After that, we drove on back to Nashville.

On September 1 the Riders were at the Emery Theater in Cincinnati for a fund-raiser for the public radio station, WVXU. While there, they were asked about the coming season of *Riders Radio Theater* shows.

"The folks at WVXU said they were looking forward to the upcoming season of *Riders Radio Theater,* and we told them there wasn't going to be a next year—it was over," said Fred. "So they rallied to the cause. We had lunch at the Quality Inn in Norwood, Ohio, with them and talked it over. They wanted to pick up the show. On that September 1 show, a bat was in the audience, flying through the house. So we started doing the Batman Theme, then the theme to the *Bat Masterson* TV show and made a lot of bat jokes. After that we had a bat rigged on a fishing line and played with that when we were at the Emery."

The radio show in Nashville had been successful—although

a grind on the Riders—but manager David Skepner had some run-ins with the folks at WPLN, and they didn't want to work with him anymore. So they canceled the show. Fortunately, WVXU picked it up, but the Riders had learned an important lesson: they would not do fifty-two shows a year anymore. That first year they did half that many.

 ON THE ROAD WITH RIDERS BY BILLY MAXWELL

December 7, 1989: We left Nashville and stopped east of Memphis for lunch—had barbecue. They did a show in Little Rock that was pretty uneventful and then drove to Austin, Texas. We arrived about 8:00 A.M. and checked into the Rodeway Inn, and they worked out. There's a great restaurant they always go to in Austin—El Azteca—that has great Mexican food. They played a big outdoor rodeo arena for the Texas Highway Patrolmen, and it was so cold that Woody said he couldn't even feel his fingers on the strings. The sound and lights people didn't show up—so it was really bad—not really a good show. Ronnie McDowell was on the show too.

Before we went back to the motel we all went to the Broken Spoke, and there was TNN on in the bar. The Riders were the grand marshals for the Nashville Christmas Parade that year, and this was right before the parade. They were advertising the parade on the TV and showed a picture of Riders In The Sky on the screen while they're sitting at a table with their street clothes on. The people in the bar were watching this on TV, and they started looking at the screen and then looking at these guys at the table and all of a sudden it dawns on them that the Riders are sitting right there at the next table. So everybody comes over and wants autographs. That was pretty neat.

Chapter 28

On January 22, 1990, the Riders taped their first *Riders Radio Theater* shows in Cincinnati. By this time, the Riders had a strong team working with them. Steve Arwood—Texas Bix Bender— wrote the first draft of the scripts on his typewriter at home, then met them in Cincinnati, where they edited the show and pulled it together. During the show, he did the announcing. Joey, "the Cowpolka King," performed onstage with the Riders, while Roberta Samet—"the Fair Roberta"—did "whatever needed to be done." She worked on their make-up, costumes, and generally pitched in whenever needed. David Skepner was always at the shows, and his assistant, Lisa Harris, worked daily with the Riders. After Paul Lohr had booked a date, Lisa went over the contract with the promoter, booked the hotel and flight arrangements (if necessary), and checked on the special provisions in the contracts about catering food backstage, the sound check, and whatever else the Riders needed to put on their show. Since the Riders never had a road manager—although Billy Maxwell functioned in that role when he was with them—Lisa had to advance the dates.

Part of advancing the dates was working on publicity. "Most of the time, that was easy," said Lisa. "Because a lot of their dates were repeats—they'd been there before, and the crowds loved them. It was a lot harder in the big markets because they're so saturated with entertainment. Then I'd have to 'sell' the Riders to the entertainment writer. But we had a great press kit, and we included fun things like bumper stickers, Too Slim's marketing catalog, and a badge. So most of the writers called back."

After an interview was set, "the Riders always sold themselves," said Lisa. "They were always great doing interviews, and the writers loved talking with them."

There was a guest on each of the Riders shows, and Lisa or Skepner booked those. Although the pay for an appearance was only scale—$113—a number of major acts called and wanted to be on the show. Garth Brooks, Kathy Mattea, and Marty Stuart were just a few of the guests who appeared.

During the radio shows, Lisa would type up the scripts after the editing, type up commercial breaks, and do any necessary promotion on site, from calling the media to making sure VIPs had seats. There were always two shows done back to back, with the guest performing a set in between the shows.

"They are the epitome of entertainers," said Lisa. "They're so professional and easy to work with, and whenever an audience sees them, they love them. And they were like my uncles—it seems like I grew up with them!"

She also acknowledged that the Riders are incredibly smart. "You've got a rocket scientist, an environmentalist, and a literary scholar!" she said. "What other group fits that bill?"

After these first tapings, they headed out to Elko for the annual Cowboy Poetry Gathering.

 ON THE ROAD WITH RIDERS BY BILLY MAXWELL

January 29, 1990: We played at a high school in Idabel, Oklahoma, but there was nothing really memorable. Then we went to Pittsburg, Texas, and after the show we went to this guy's home because the Arts Council or something was having a reception, a meet and greet. It was a log home, a beautiful place. After we left, Woody was driving, and he got in a big fight with Teresa over the phone while he was driving home. So every exit he would stop and call her and she would hang up on him, then he'd get back in the bus and drive like a mad man to the next exit, stop and call her again. This was after Joey had started. And Joey was supposed to drive the next shift after Woody, and they got into a big argument in the middle of the bus. Joey said, "How do you expect me to drive next when I can't get any sleep because you're driving all over the road at ninety miles an hour, stopping at every exit?"

The Riders were back in Cincinnati on February 12 and 14 to tape two more *Riders Radio Theater* shows. On February 22 they appeared on TNN's *American Magazine* show, on March 6 they were on *Nashville Now,* and on March 14 they were on TNN's *Tennessee Outdoorsman* show.

"On *Tennessee Outdoorsman* they took us fishing up on Tim's Ford Lake," said Slim. "None of us are really fisherman so we didn't think there'd be much to it—but it turned into a blast. Woody was roping fish. There was some comments about Bill Dance—who hosted a famous fishing show. Woody thought it was the Bill Dance show—and thought the guy with us was Bill Dance. He never did realize it wasn't. Years later, people would come up and say they saw us on that fishing show."

On April 10 and 11 the Riders were at 16th Avenue Recordings. On the first day they recorded five songs: "Ride, Cowboy, Ride," written by Rex Allen Jr., Curtis Allen, and Denny DeMarco; "The Call of the Canyon," written by Billy Hill; "Sidekick Heaven," written by Eddie Dean, Hal Blair, and Fred LaBour; "Homecoming Yodel," written by Ranger Doug; and "The Arms of My Love," written by Woody Paul.

"The Call of the Canyon," published in 1940, was written by Billy Hill, the same songwriter who wrote "The Last Roundup." Hill suffered from depression and wrote "The Call of the Canyon" while in one of his low moods. It was his last published song. The song was recorded by popular dance bands led by Kay Kyser and Guy Lombardo, and Gene Autry sang the song in his 1940 movie, *Melody Ranch*. On Christmas Eve 1940, Billy Hill died. In 1942, Autry starred in a movie, *The Call of the Canyon*, that featured this song.

"Sidekick Heaven" had been recorded before but hadn't been released; this version would be released. Based on the song that was a hit for Tex Ritter in 1961, where Ritter meets the country stars of the past in "hillbilly heaven," Too Slim included the great cowboy sidekicks from the B Western era in his song.

"Ride, Cowboy, Ride" was written by Rex Allen Jr. and his brother, Curtis Allen—both sons of singing cowboy Rex Allen, along with Denny DeMarco. Rex Allen Jr. had originally recorded the song, which was a chart record for him in 1982. Allen Junior was one of the few country artists trying to revive the western tradition; before his release of "Ride, Cowboy, Ride," he was on the charts with "Last of the Silver Screen Cowboys" (which featured guest appearances by Roy Rogers and Rex Allen Sr.) and "Cowboy in a Three-Piece Business Suit." He also wrote "Can You Hear Those Pioneers?" a song honoring the Sons of the Pioneers, which featured harmony vocals by that group and Rex Allen Sr., that reached the country charts in 1976.

"The Arms of My Love," written by Woody Paul, has an achingly beautiful melody that captures the feeling of a lonesome cowboy by a campfire on the prairie. On this album, the song is an instrumental; later Woody Paul added lyrics and rerecorded it.

The next day they recorded six more songs: Ranger Doug's "Someone's Got to Do It"; "Texas Echo," written by David Ball; the Elton Britt song, "Maybe I'll Cry Over You"; Woody Paul's "What Would I Do Without You?"; "Living in a Mobile Home," written by Ronnie Scaife and Rory Michael Burke; and Ranger Doug's "The Line Rider."

"Maybe I'll Cry Over You," a ballad written by legendary yo-deler Elton Britt, allows Ranger Doug to sing a plaintive yodel to a slow song. "Living in a Mobile Home" was done by the character Drywall Paul, played by Woody Paul. "That character was born on the radio show," said Slim. "Woody would do a Stonewall Jackson impression on the bus—and it was hilarious—he was dead on with Stonewall. Then on the radio show he became Sheriff Drywall—a would-be country singer. That song was pitched to us—and we said, 'Drywall could do that.' We also did a photo shoot with me in drag."

"What Would I Do?" by Woody Paul is a western swing number.

When I need love and understanding
No one satisfies me like you do
You're not just my girl
You're my life, you're my world
What would I do without you?

A. Swinburne Slocum, played by Too Slim, and Charlie, played by Ranger Doug, were two characters the Riders developed doing *Tumbleweed Theater* and appeared in continuing roles on *Riders Radio Theater*. Ranger Doug enjoyed writing songs for Too Slim's characters—both Sidemeat and Slocum—and captures the latter's character in "Someone's Got to Do It."

"Slocum got his name from some cheesy 1950s western TV melodrama, wherein a staunch but cowed landowner finally stood up to the local bully, telling him, 'Slocum, git off my land,'" states Ranger Doug. "His flannel-mouthed delivery became a family joke repeated endlessly. The A. Swinburne I liked just because it is alliterative: it is actually the name of the Edwardian poet Algernon Charles Swinburne, a connection that no Riders fan has yet picked up. Charlie is a direct reference to the great character actor and legendary movie bad guy Charles King."

I've got a pencil-thin moustache
and a reptilian demeanor
If I could squeeze a nickel profit,
I'd take your grandma to the cleaners
I love forgery, extortion, and changing cattle brands

But mostly I'm in love with making big and evil plans
Because the plot demands an evil man
To prove the good are good
Someone's got to put them through it
Even Shakespeare in his glory
Put good villains in his stories
It's a dirty job, but someone's got to do it

"Too Slim claims this is the most Broadway of all the songs I've ever written," said the Ranger.

"I've always felt that "The Line Rider" was the first song of mine that spoke in my voice, that was not a conscious or semi-conscious extension of the Nolan-Spencer-Parker-Whitley-Jones oeuvre," wrote Ranger Doug in his songbook. "The only derivative thing about it is the yodel: we had enjoyed so much acclaim for 'Lonely Yukon Stars' that I was looking for another place to add a sad, aching, staggered three-part yodel."

There's a broken-down saddle on a peg on the wall—
Who knows how long it's hung there?
Like the hole in the soul of the lone buckaroo
It's just too far gone for repair
Still his longing's as wide as the deep midnight sky
And as silent as breaking of day
So he saddles his pony and rides down the line
It's the best he can do for today

"I was going through an awfully difficult time when I wrote it: a crumbling marriage, estrangement from a child I adored, the crushing financial burden of two daughters in college at the same time," states Ranger Doug. "It was a time of enormous self-doubt. 'The Line Rider' certainly reflects the weariness of spirit I felt then, as well as the inner strength we all have to muster from time to time, the determination it took to plow through a tough time just by putting one foot in front of the other and moving on. The line-riding cowpoke was my vision of that inner strength, and I sketched his portrait in this song." The song would win a Western Heritage Award from the Cowboy Hall of Fame for "Best Western Song" that year.

In August, an article in *Cincinnati Magazine*, "Urban Cowboys: It's Happy Trails to You at the Emery Theater" by Linda Pender, was published. The article states

> The tiny lobby at the Emery is cheek-by-jowl with boots and string ties. Inside the auditorium, the audience proves less homogeneous: graying counterculture types, punky teens, retirees, parents with kids. Lots of parents with kids, even though it's a school night. . . . *Riders Radio Theater* . . . earlier this year was offered a home at the Emery Theatre by its broadcasting champion, WVXU. The program is taped in Cincinnati two nights a month, two shows a night. . . . The Riders have sung a happy birthday, commented upon Jesuit basketball prowess, and welcomed the rest of the company on stage: The Fair Roberta, stage manager; Big Zeno Klinker, sound effects; and Bix Bender, announcer. . . . During the intermission there's a Too Slim look-alike contest. A 3–year-old in chaps and a moustache wins by a mile.

On September 21 they were in Washington for an appearance on CBS's *Nightwatch*. Here, "a great moment in cultural history" (according to Too Slim) occurred when Ranger Doug got to meet Anthony Burgess, author of the futurist novel *A Clockwork Orange* and the topic of his English master's thesis at Vanderbilt.

"I was taken aback," said Doug. "It was like meeting Roy Rogers. It was like, 'Whoa, what can I say to this guy?' I told him I'd written a thesis on him. He was very nice—I think he was in ill health. He wasn't garrulous at all, but his wife was very garrulous. She's Italian—a real fireball. It was in the Green Room and it was like when we met Dr. Heimlich of the Heimlich maneuver. We were just backstage—one of those West Coast shows. And there he was. But Anthony Burgess, I knew quite a bit about. If I'd known he was going to be on the show I'd have gone back and reread my thesis and gotten sharp. But the thesis I'd written about him was in 1971, and he'd written a lot of books since then. I'd kept up on his writing—had read all his books. He's so erudite—with James Joyce especially. And I didn't dare open that can of worms and display how ignorant I am. You know the old saying, 'It's better to keep your mouth shut and be thought a fool than open your mouth and prove it.' I had no idea he was going to be on. It was kind of big for me."

On October 2, the Riders were in Roy Rogers's hometown, Victorville, California, where they appeared at The Cocky Bull.

"Roy and Dusty Rogers came to that show—and we were just glowing," said Slim. "It was the best—we were so excited with our hero in the front row. And he was loving it. I did the 'Sidekick Heaven' song, and we knew he had worked with those guys— knew 'em all. We were just beaming. We met for breakfast next morning with Roy and Dale at an IHOP. Typical Roy—just a down-to-earth guy."

"You know, I don't get nervous anymore," said Doug. "But on that show I was shaking. To do this stuff before the master, the guy who started it all, the guy who put together the Sons of the Pioneers. The King of the Cowboys. And he loved it and was so gracious. It was just overwhelming."

On October 10 they were at the Music Mill Studio, recording vocal overdubs on "Happy Trails (To You)" behind the previously recorded vocals of Roy and Dale.

 ON THE ROAD WITH RIDERS BY BILLY MAXWELL

October 27, 1990: Woody was into running at this time, and we were playing at the Cactus Cafe on the campus of the University of Texas in Austin. Before the show that afternoon, Woody went out for a run and was gone a long time. We did the sound check that afternoon and he wasn't there, which was not unusual, but it was getting close to the show and he still wasn't there, and everybody was getting a little concerned. All of a sudden he comes in and his face is all dirty and his clothes are pretty grimy and you could tell he was really shaken. He said, "You'll never imagine what happened to me." He was out running and the river runs right through Austin and there are lots of railroads. He got on the other side of the river and it was a long way back to the bridge, so he decided to run across this railroad trestle to get back to the other side. So he gets in the middle of the railroad trestle and here comes a train and he has to climb down into the timbers of the railroad trestle while the train goes by. He says his head was only like eighteen inches from the wheels when this train was going by. He had grease all over him. You just never know what's going to happen to Woody. It's always something.

Then we went to Houston and there's this great place we always eat at in Houston—Los Dos Amigoes. It's just a concrete-block building and you could drive by and say, "Man, I'm not going into that place," but the food is just unbelievable. So we'd eat there two or three times a day when we were in Houston.

On November 19 and 20, the Riders were at TNN taping the TV special "Christmas the Cowboy Way." The rift between Skepner and Paul Corbin had been patched up by then, and Skepner had negotiated a contract where the Riders would do six television specials for TNN. The proviso was that a major country star would appear on each show.

"Suzy Bogguss and Minnie Pearl were on that first show," said Slim. "Minnie did a cameo at the end. We wrote the story about a bus full of kids waylaid by snow and so they had to come to the ranch house and we had to entertain them. Boguss was the school marm."

Bogguss was really into her part—so much so that she bought a dress just like Miss Kitty wore on *Gunsmoke* to appear on the show. The only problem during the taping was Suzy getting a series of phone calls from her husband, whose car had broken down. As soon as the taping finished, she had to go pick him up.

On November 26 they went back to Austin to tape another appearance on *Austin City Limits*. Then it was back to Cincinnati on November 28 and 29 for some more radio shows. On December 4 they appeared on both *Crook and Chase* and *Nashville Now* on TNN.

Chapter 29

Michael Martin Murphey did a guest appearance on *Riders Radio Theater* and shortly after that—in mid-1990—hired Joey Miskulin to go on the road with his band. Joey had been on the road with the Riders since the middle of 1989, but "I always got a weird feeling with David Skepner," said Joey. "I never felt that David Skepner wanted me involved with the Riders, although I could not have been treated better by Doug, Slim, Woody, or anyone else involved with them. I just felt that Skepner looked at me like I was someone interfering or a fifth wheel. That was a feeling I'd never had before in my life. It just played on my mind, and I seriously thought that I was never going to be a firm part of this organization. Skepner never told me that directly, but I felt it very strongly. We had talked about me producing a record, but it never happened. I can't really blame Skepner for that—he'd only heard polka records I'd produced. Anyway, I went with Murphey, and we produced some records together, but my heart was always with the Riders."

Even though Joey did not perform on the road with the Riders, he always came back for their radio shows. "I'd hire someone to take my place with Murphey," said Joey. "I think I only missed two radio shows."

 On the Road with Riders by Billy Maxwell

December 6, 1990: We drove to Grand Forks, North Dakota, where we opened for Robin Lee—she did "Black Velvet." We got out of there pretty early and drove to Idaho Falls, where we stopped because Woody had "The Rash." He had these little red dots all over him. It was for real. I remember we were somewhere in some major town—a big city but I can't remember where it was—we stopped at the Y downtown so Slim and Ranger Doug could work out. Slim told Woody that if he'd clean his bed out and wash his sheets that maybe he wouldn't have those kinds of rashes. So Woody got all mad at Slim and was out on the side of a street in this downtown area—this is where you got people walking by with business suits on and briefcases in hand—and he was shaking out his sheets and bed clothes to see if he could get rid of the bugs or whatever it was. He wound up having to go to the hospital. It wasn't nothing dangerous. They said it was almost like a diaper rash that a kid gets. I don't know if they gave him some medicine or what. Of course he came back and told us all it was highly contagious and we was all going to get it, but nobody ever did.

We stopped in Elko for some diesel fuel. We were going to California, but when we got to Reno we found out we had a wheel that was broken on the bus. From the lug nut on out it was just split. It was probably a good thing we stopped. When we slowed down you could hear it crunching. It could have caused us to have some real problems if we'd been running seventy or eighty miles an hour on the interstate.

That old bus had some strange-sized wheels on it, and we never could find another one to fit, so we had to put the spare on and go on. So we was out of a spare. We got to Hampton, California, about 5 P.M., got rooms, and had a quick shower. It was an old bed-and-breakfast—really neat. Everything there was antique. The next day we went on to Vasalia and did a show there, then went to a guy's house—he played fiddle for the Reinsmen—and he had these orange trees in the back of his house. We went out and picked oranges and brought them in and his wife squeezed them and made us a glass of orange juice fresh right off the tree. That was pretty neat.

After the show we headed toward Klamath Falls, Oregon. We were headed north on the interstate, and I was driving and noticed the lights kept getting dimmer and dimmer and dimmer. I pulled off the interstate and went to the front of the bus, and they were glowing like little pumpkins, so I knew there was something wrong. At the next exit we pulled into a service station, and sure enough they'd had some work done on the bus and the mechanics didn't tighten the bolt that goes through the generator, so it had worked its way out and the generator slid down.

We pulled in there, but there was no place to get it fixed. Finally, we called a mechanic and he said he'd have to get one and come out there the next morning. Meanwhile, we had to sit there all night in that service station. Then about two or three in the morning Woody thought he could fix it.

Woody said, "If I could just find another bolt I could get it running," because the fan belt wasn't lost—it had fallen down and was hanging in the motor. All we needed was that bolt that went in the generator.

We were at a little service station off this remote interstate in northern California. And the guy that owned the service station had a bunch of old cars around there. Woody said, "There's got to be a bolt in those cars around here." So Woody went over to the guy in the service station and asked, "What if I can find a bolt on one of those cars?" And the guy said, "Those are the boss's cars—you can't take a bolt off one of those. Oh, no, no." So we walked out the door, and Woody said, "Come on over here and help me take a bolt off one of these cars." So we took a bolt of one of 'em and tried to put it on the bus.

Then Woody goes back into the service station, and the guy says,

"What are you going to do?" And Woody says, "Well, we got a bolt that we think might do." And the guy says, "You didn't take one off one of those cars, did you?" And Woody says, "Oh, no, no. We wouldn't do that. You told us we couldn't do that."

It ended up that bolt didn't work, and we had to wait until morning when the mechanic came and got it fixed. This was north of Sacramento, so we headed up to Klamath Falls that morning, but then we split another wheel on the bus. We've got the spare on, so we can't replace it. So we pulled in a place and go to a junkyard. It's a wide wheel, but it's not very big around—a special wheel that goes on the bus so it doesn't lift the bus up too high off the ground.

We go through that junkyard and find two wheels, but they charge us something like two hundred dollars apiece for them. But we were stranded—what can you do? It was one of those deals. So after several hours we get them on the bus and go to Klamath Falls, but now we're going to be really close on time.

Slim was driving as fast as he could, and then it started snowing. We didn't get to Klamath Falls until five o'clock, and the show was at seven so we were cutting it pretty close. We did the show, and everybody was so tired that we decided to stay there that night.

We drove on to Boise, Idaho, the next day and checked into the University Inn and did a show. That's where Woody's wife, Teresa, is from and where her parents live. We went to dinner with them that night. Teresa was in Nashville, and she was pretty homesick through that whole situation. Woody called Teresa that night and told her we were all in Boise and were going out with her parents, and it didn't make her very happy to know she was sitting in Nashville homesick with nobody while we were going to dinner with her parents. After he hung up, Woody said, "I made a big mistake with that call. I wish I'd never told her that. I really caught it."

Woody had met Teresa on the road—in Sun Valley, Idaho. It was a pretty short relationship—they got married out there. It's hard on the women married to those guys. When they're home they're home, then when they're gone they're gone. And they may be home for just a few days then they'll be gone for a few weeks. Lots of women want to marry a "star," and then they do and find out they've married some guy that ain't around. Further, there's all these other women out there on the road just dying for a one-night stand with 'em so for the rest of their life they can tell all their girlfriends what they did with a big star.

Then we went on to Casper and had to leave the bus running all night because it was so cold we didn't think we could get it running again if we cut it off. Did a show and then went to Fort Collins, Colorado, where everybody decided to go to Winter Park skiing. This was when we stayed at Baxter Black's—we had about three days off.

Baxter was living just north of Denver, and we went out to eat with Baxter in his limousine. He'd bought this limousine—forgot who he said it belonged to but it was some famous person. It was about twenty years old, and he was having the interior of it redone. But he wanted to take all of us out to dinner, and he said it was the only thing he had big enough to carry us all. The inside was all stripped out of it, so he had lawn chairs and hay bales inside to sit on.

The whole downstairs of Baxter's place—like the basement—was built like a bunkhouse. It had about eight beds in a row in there, had a bathroom with like three sinks. Two commodes, a couple of showers. It was like three double beds and three single beds. It was just one big room—like a bunkhouse. Slim and Bert—she'd flown in—stayed in the guest bedroom. But me and Woody and Ranger Doug stayed downstairs.

Baxter's wife, Cindy Lou, cooked dinner for us. Next day we got up and it was eight below zero and we had not left the bus running. This was a diesel, and it would not start. So Woody takes a shovel full of coals from the fireplace at Baxter's house out through the front door of the house. I just knew he was going to drop 'em and burn the rug or the floor or something. He puts the shovel of coals under the engine of the bus, and he works on that for awhile but that's not heating it up enough. So then he starts putting cardboard and wood and stuff down there under the engine. Now he's got flames coming up the side of the engine. So I think, "This is it. He's gonna burn up the bus, and we're gonna die right here. And we're gonna have no transportation." Finally he does get the bus started and we head on down to Colorado Springs where its fifteen below zero. So Woody said, "We can't cut the bus off—we've got to leave it running." We're in Colorado Springs for three days and two nights and we leave the bus running the whole time. There's a big snow on the ground, and about every three hours one of us gets up and goes out to check on the bus to make sure it's still running. Every afternoon at four o'clock we take the bus to the gas station and fill it up with diesel.

We did the show there and left and we're on a little cut-through road that goes from Colorado Springs to the interstate—Woody, Ranger

Doug, and me. Slim and Bert stayed out there because they were going somewhere for Christmas. We were about an hour outside of Colorado Springs, and all of a sudden the bus just quits. Just dead. Ranger Doug was driving. It was cold—still fifteen below zero. Severely cold. I remember getting up from my bunk and looking out the window of the bus, and I could not see a light—street light, house light, any light in any direction, 360 degrees. I mean, here we were in the middle of nowhere. And it's fifteen below zero. You can't put on enough clothes to survive. I thought, "We're gonna die right here. Freeze to death."

It's two o'clock in the morning. Nobody on the road. Woody gets out, says, "I know what it is, the fuel line has frozen up." We had two tanks on the bus, and he says "It's right where you switch 'em over. I've had this problem before." So he's outside, cold, snow on the ground, and he's got a rolled-up newspaper on fire and he's running it up and down the fuel line on the bus. It's diesel, but it's still fuel. And I think either he's going to catch the bus on fire or we're gonna freeze to death. But the King comes through—a few minutes of doing this, and the bus starts and we're on our way again. Headed on down the road. And that was that. From there it was just straight on home to Nashville.

Chapter 30

The year 1991 began with a bang. On January 6 they were in Washington, where they appeared on NPR's *Weekend Edition*, interviewed by LeAnn Hansen. "That was a very scripted show," said Ranger Doug. "She had her questions and stuck to them. It wasn't a free-ranging interview, which we're known to do. She wasn't into the silly part of it at all. Which is okay—that's public radio.

"You know me, Mr. Historian," continued Green. "I've always been concerned about keeping the tradition alive. But I've always resisted pigeon-holing us as a revivalist act, because we aren't. But she stressed the 'keeping the western tradition alive' aspects of us."

On January 10 they were on the "Grand Ole Opry Sixty-fifth Anniversary Special," televised nationally. The Riders did not have a featured spot. "They said we could show up and sing in the chorus," said Green. "Well, heck, you get network scale—and what else are you going to do on a Wednesday night?"

"We typically stood in back with the legends," said Slim. "Gatemouth Brown and Johnny Gimble were on that show—and we spent the whole day in the dressing room jamming. At the end we came out with the crowd and sang 'Will the Circle Be Unbroken.' As we were walking back with Grandpa Jones, he said, 'Well, I don't believe they could-a done it without us!'"

On January 20 and 21 they were in Cincinnati for *Riders Radio Theater* tapings. From January 30 through February 2 they were at the Elko Poetry Gathering, where they also performed at the Red Lion Casino.

 ON THE ROAD WITH *RIDERS* BY BILLY MAXWELL

January 30, 1991: The Riders came in to Salt Lake City from California and then drove to Elko. Joey was playing with Michael Martin Murphey, but they were there. So was Alan Sacks, David Skepner, Paul Lohr, and of course Murphey and Joey. That's when Slim married Bert. The wedding was at 12:30 P.M. in a little wedding chapel just down the road from the Stockman Hotel. After the wedding we all went out on the street and made pictures. Prostitution is legal in Nevada, and a prostitute was wandering up and down while we were taking pictures. There was a drunk out there too. It was quite an affair. After the wedding, we all went down to the Stockman and had dinner. Later on that day, we ran into Slim and he told us he was going to be a daddy again. Woody had already predicted that.

"Let's just say that we wanted to get married to start our family," said Roberta. "We'd known each other for ten years, had lived together for four years, and we were happy that way. But we wanted a traditional family."

"Actually, we were too chicken to get married unless it was spur-of-the-moment," said Slim, who'd actually proposed to Roberta on New Year's Eve. "But my biggest regret in all that is that my two older kids, Lily and Frank, weren't there for the wedding. I really wish I'd planned it so that they could have been there."

Elko was picked, according to Roberta, "because so many of our friends would be there. There were about 150 people at the wedding. So many of our friends in western music went to Elko that it just seemed like the best place to get married."

On February 5 and 6 the Riders were in the Music Mill Studios recording vocal overdubs on songs recorded by Roy Rogers, "When Payday Rolls Around" and "Little Joe the Wrangler" the first day, then "Tumbling Tumbleweeds" and "Alive and Kicking," a song written by Roy Rogers, on the next day.

On May 13 and 14 the Riders were at Nightingale Studios in Nashville recording. On the first day they recorded "Press Along to the Big Corral," "Great Grand Dad," "Ballad of Palindrome," "Come and Get It," "Cody of the Pony Express," "How Does He Yodel?" and "Face: The Music."

"Come and Get It" was written by Tim Spencer with his brother, Glenn. Tim, born Vernon Spencer in 1908, was one of the founding members of the Sons of the Pioneers. Born in Missouri, Spencer's family moved to New Mexico when he was a child, then moved to Oklahoma, where he became involved in school musicals and purchased a banjo ukulele. After finishing school, Spencer moved to Los Angeles to try and break into the movies. He landed a job at a Safeway warehouse, where he was working when he saw an advertisement in the newspaper in August 1932 for a singer who could yodel. The ad was placed by Leonard Slye, who needed to replace Bob Nolan, who had just quit the singing trio. Spencer auditioned, was accepted, and soon the group was part of Benny Nawahi and the International Cowboys. The group then adopted the name "O-Bar-O Cowboys" and went on a tour of the southwest from June to September 1933. Although the trip was musically a disaster, Spencer met his future wife, Velma Blanton, in Lubbock, Texas, during this tour.

The group disbanded when they returned to Los Angeles, but Slye still wanted a trio. So he contacted Spencer, who agreed to try again, and the two then convinced Bob Nolan to give it another shot. The group rehearsed for several weeks, then joined Texas Jack and His Outlaws. Calling themselves the Pioneer Trio, the group was heard on radio station KFWB, where one day the announcer introduced them as the "Sons of the Pioneers," explaining later they looked too young to be "Pioneers."

In 1936 Spencer left the group and was replaced by Lloyd Perryman. He returned in 1938, after Slye had left to become singing star Roy Rogers, and remained with the group until 1949, when he retired. He rejoined as a singer in 1955 when they re-signed with RCA Victor but never toured with them as a performer after his retirement.

Spencer was the driving force behind the Sons of the Pioneers during most of his time with the group. An outgoing person, he conducted the day-to-day activities and business affairs of the group and helped produce their recording sessions through 1957. Later in his life Spencer formed a religious publishing company, Manna Music, and published the gospel standard, "How Great Thou Art."

Spencer was a prolific songwriter who wrote "The Timber Trail," "The Everlasting Hills of Oklahoma," "Silent Trails," "Sagebrush Symphony," "It's a Cowboy's Life for Me," "By a Campfire on the Trail," "Down the Trail," "A Cowboy's Sweetheart," "Moonlight on the Trail," and other Western greats, mostly for singing-cowboy movies.

Of the song, "How Does He Yodel," Ranger Doug states, "I had worked a number of these cowboy and European variations into our stage version of the yodeling showoff standard 'Chime Bells,' and when the time was right, it was natural enough to adapt these experiments to a children's song."

How does he yodel?
When does he yodel?
Why does he yodel?
It sure beats me!

One of Too Slim's unique "talents" is playing his face; by creating an open hollow in his face and slapping the side of his face, Too Slim manages to produce melodies. This routine is a regular part of the Riders' stage show, and Slim even wrote a song for it.

I am the cowboy that's known as old Too Slim
And when they see me ridin' by, they say "Hey, that's him,"
He can sing and varmint dance and play the bunkhouse bass
Yeah, but what he does the very best is play his face

Of the "Palindrome" song, Slim said, "I collect those—and so does Woody. He is always coming up with some. He'll wake me up in the middle of the night and tell me of one he's created. We were going through the airport at Nashville, and I started singing the Palladin Theme and using Palindromes. It became a character in the radio show. That show was a spawning ground for comedy."

Some examples of Palindromes (which are exactly the same phrases or sentences read forward or backward):

Too hot to hoot
Gug Gug Gug-Yo! Bottoms Up! U.S. Motto Boy! Gug Gug Gug
Evil is a name of a foeman, as I live
No evils live on
Draw, O coward

On their second day in the studio they recorded "Harmony Ranch," "I Always Do," "One Little Coyote," "Prairie Lullaby," "The Cowboy's A-B-Cs," "Pecos Bill," and a "Fiddle Medley" arranged by Woody Paul.

Explaining the genesis of the song "I Always Do," Ranger Doug wrote in his songbook, "I was dropping my daughter Annie Laurie off at her mother's one spring and gently and rather matter-of-factly explained that I'd be gone for a while on a two- or three-week road trip. She turned to me, her enormous blue-green eyes welling up, and said, 'Daddy, I just don't think I can stand it if you're gone as much as you were last summer.' I tried my best to reassure her that my love surrounded her wherever I was. I wrote her this poem in an effort to show by example that her father's love was endless as the sea, sure as the sunrise."

My love flows endlessly,
As endless as the blue-green sea
Hold to your heart my promise true:
I'll be coming back to you;
I always do

On "One Little Coyote," Ranger Doug decided to "write a cowboy counting song like 'The Twelve Days of Christmas.'"

As I rode my pony across the Western plains
We stopped and heard a sweet and sad refrain

It filled the sundown sky with a mournful tune

It was . . . ten cowboys singing loud, nine buffalo stampede, eight mustangs, seven geese, six beaver slap, five prairie dogs, four little dogies, three big elk, two wise owls, and one little coyote howling at the moon.

"Prairie Lullaby," by Woody Paul, is a beautiful bedtime song.

The silver moon is sailing
The starry heavens deep
And all of nature's children
Are nestled down to sleep
So say your little prayers now
Close your eyes now
Go to sleep now
And tomorrow we'll ride the trail together again

"The Cowboy's A-B-Cs" had been previously recorded on *Saddle Pals*, their first children's album for Rounder.

These songs would comprise their first album for Columbia, another major label. When it looked like the Riders might be dropped from MCA, Skepner scrambled over to CBS and made a deal for the Riders to appear on that label. It was their second shot at the Big Time on a major label, but the results were the same: a great album *(Harmony Ranch)* by a great act but no country music superstardom for the boys.

On May 21 they were in Omni Studio with Michael Martin Murphey, recording "Riding Home on Christmas Eve" and "Christmas Yodel." "I used the Sidemeat voice on that song," said Fred. "So when they did a video they wanted to use Sidemeat, but we had a scheduling conflict. So they used another guy as Sidemeat. I still hear about that today!"

On June 7 they were in Omni Studio with Michael Martin Murphey recording "Good Night Ladies/Auld Lang Syne," "Riding Home on Christmas Eve," and "The Cowboy's Christmas Ball." On June 9, they were at WestFest in Indianapolis; on June 15 they were at WestFest in Red River, New Mexico; and on July 5, they were at WestFest in Osage Beach, Missouri.

"Those WestFests were Murphey's," said Slim. "He had them

in a lot of places, but they didn't really work in the East. We didn't get a crowd at places like Indianapolis and Osage Beach. At Osage Beach there was Williams & Ree; at Indianapolis was the Judds."

They taped *Riders Radio Theater* shows on June 10 and 11 and July 1 and 2. On July 3 they were in Ann Arbor at the Power Center. The Riders spent July 4, 1991, on The Mall in Washington. "It was at the foot of the Washington Monument," said Slim. "Our families came along for that one."

Chapter 31

After the idea of doing a "Riders Go to Hollywood" sitcom, based on the old *Beverly Hillbillies* show, didn't get much response from TV execs, Alan Sacks developed the idea of a children's show starring the Riders. On May 27, 1990, the Riders did a showcase for TV executives at McCabe's in Santa Monica, and Judy Price with CBS was immediately interested. "There was also a guy in Business Affairs at CBS that was a big fan of theirs," said Sacks.

CBS insisted that a writer for the show be hired, "and that was a big mistake," said Sacks. "We should have had the Riders writing." Instead, writer George McGrath was hired to write the show. Texas Bix thought he was going to get the job of announcing on the show; his voice was perfect on *Riders Radio Theater.* But the writer got that job as well.

Too Slim agrees with Sacks about the writing. "Everything we've had a hand in writing has been a success," he said. "We didn't have a hand in that, and it wasn't."

"He was a nice enough man, but he didn't have any feel for us and what we do," added Ranger Doug. "Also, I don't think he had any confidence we could carry it off. So he added all these extraneous characters. Some were good, but the show got all clotted. If you look at children's shows that are popular, they've got four, maybe five, characters. You don't have ten. That writer just didn't have a feel for what we do. He was a funny guy but he wasn't us."

From July 17 until September 14, the Riders spent most of their time in Studio City, California, where they taped their CBS Saturday morning children's show, *Saturday Morning with Riders In The Sky*. It took twenty-three days of taping to come up with thirteen shows.

"At the end of May we went out and had to take acting classes," said Fred. "Then we cut the tracks for the tunes—and they'd play the tracks while we sang live. It wasn't good audio. We'd get our scripts on a Monday morning, block it out and rehearse for three days—then tape on Friday. It was on the old Republic lot—in Studio City. Off Ventura past Sportsman's Lodge. They put us up at the Oakwood Apartments. Baby Alice was born on August 24. We watched the full moon rise over Hollywood—and the next morning she was born. Bert was in labor, and we were filming outside. Unbearably hot. And everybody knew if she went into labor, it was over. So they were trying to hurry us up, and hurry her up."

That fall *Saturday Morning with Riders In The Sky* was on CBS. But it didn't draw the ratings. "The network kept changing the time period each week," said Alan Sacks. "And the audience couldn't find it."

"CBS lost faith in the show very early, in the third or fourth week," said Slim. "We were pre-empted on the West Coast by college football. It was on at six in the morning East Coast time. Then it came on at nine-thirty, then eleven-thirty. The rumor was that one of the key CBS exec's little daughter didn't like it. [Slim imitates a whiney kid's voice:] 'Daddy, I want that show off the air. NOW!' When they lost faith, it was just a matter of time and it was gone."

Still, the show gave them another boost—especially with the children's audience. That CBS exec's daughter might not have liked it, but parents of kids across the rest of America did—and brought their kids to Riders shows.

On Thanksgiving, November 28, the Riders appeared on *CBS This Morning*, then in the Macy's Thanksgiving Day Parade. "That was part of our CBS Show deal," said Slim. "We got the Macy's Day parade out of all that. We like to froze to death. We were on a little stage at the corner of a street. And we thought we were doing a run-through and I kept saying 'My fingers are freezing!' And we thought they were going to do the on-camera stuff in a little bit—turns out the run-through, when we were loose and cutting up, is what they got on camera!"

After the parade, the Riders and their families had dinner at the Plaza Hotel; baby Alice slept under the table while the grown-ups ate. "I remember being heartbroken at that time because I was breaking up with Laura Harris," said Doug. Doug had begun his relationship with Laura in 1988; his second marriage had ended that year.

The Saturday morning show was later awarded a Daytime Emmy for costume design. Roberta Samet had worked on their show designing their clothes but wasn't a union designer—so she only received a certificate. The trophy went to Jacqueline St. Ann, who was a union designer.

"They even altered their jeans for that show," said Roberta. "You know—like if the Wranglers didn't fit absolutely perfect, the costume department would get them altered. It was an amazing experience."

 ON THE ROAD WITH RIDERS BY BILLY MAXWELL

December 2, 1991: We were in Nashville with Michael Martin Murphey doing the "Cowboy Christmas Show" with Ralph Emery on *Nashville Now.* After the show we left around midnight, headed east up through Knoxville to Arlington, Virginia. We were going to work at the Birchmere. Next morning we went to the CBS studio in Washington to tape a spot on *Nightwatch* to be shown that night.

Then Woody and I went down to the Smithsonian and up to the music department where they had the Stradivarius. And it just so happened that a music class was in there and they had all the Stradivarius instruments out of their cases and all these music students were getting to play them. So Woody was very interested in this, and we were just out in the hall—we weren't part of the group—but he saw what was going on, so he just opened the door and walked in. And I guess nobody paid much attention to him until all of a sudden he picked up one of these violins and everybody let out a gasp—'cause Woody looked like a street person. He picked it up and put it under his chin and started playing, and everybody said, "Wow." He played for quite a while in there, and it was a pretty neat deal. It was real unusual to see that. Afterward, I said, "Man that was really great," and Woody said, "That thing was so out of tune couldn't nobody play it. I was afraid to tighten the strings up too much."

After that we were headed for New York City and we like to have never found a place to park the bus—it cost us sixty bucks to park the bus for two hours. The deal was we had to leave the keys there and we didn't want to leave the keys there with nobody there just to park there. So I had to stay in the bus—but I didn't want anybody to know I was in there. After Woody came back we did some sightseeing and then went to the Bottom Line and did a show there.

The New York audience still didn't get it.

It is difficult, if not impossible, to capture such a fluid act as Riders In The Sky in a fixed form. Their live shows alternate between the silly and the serious, there is expert musicianship in the midst of extreme humor, and the shows present a well-oiled machine. *Riders In The Sky: The Book* was published in 1992 and attempts to capture the Riders in their *Riders Radio Theater* personas, with Sidemeat's cooking recipes, some faux ads, cartoons, a radio script of "Meltdown at the Mesa," a guitar lesson from Ranger Doug, a mini songbook, and a brief but straightforward history of Riders In The Sky.

The Riders saw themselves as a product to be marketed, and this was another part of their marketing plan. It was humorous and a nice souvenir but could never serve as *the* book on the Riders because it glossed over their genius as musicians and instead emphasized their characters and cleverness. The latter are certainly an important part of the Riders, but it is far from a complete picture of who they truly are.

In January 1992, "20 Questions with Ranger Doug" by Michael Bane was in *Country Music Magazine.* Some of the questions and responses:

> QUESTION: What is your least frequently asked question?
> RANGER DOUG: "Is that the guitar player's new Jaguar parked out front?"
> QUESTION: Did CBS give you any guidelines for the TV show?
> RANGER DOUG: No, not really. The one thing they did ask, in the wake of the Pee Wee Herman debacle, was that we keep our pistols in our holsters!

QUESTION: What is the Cowboy Way?

RANGER DOUG: Well, in this year of situational ethics and difficult moral places, when you're caught between the rock and the hard place of bad ideas, just ask yourself, "What would Gene, Roy, Tex, or Ranger Doug do?" That's the cowboy way.

QUESTION: What was the first cowboy movie you ever saw?

RANGER DOUG: It was Gene Autry in *Riders in the Sky*. The second one, which really stands out in my mind because it was the first one I ever saw in color, was *The Lone Ranger and the Lost City of Gold*, which I rented recently to show my kids, and I couldn't believe what a piece of junk it was! Boy, it was important when I was a kid!

QUESTION: Tell me the difference between cowboy movie music and cowboy music.

RANGER DOUG: I think most of the music, before the movies was . . . well, if you know the songs, you'll know what I mean—"Little Joe, the Wrangler," "Strawberry Roan," "When the Work's All Done This Fall." They were all about the ranch. All about work. Some of them were kind of tragic or about some deed of heroism. I think that what Bob Nolan and Tim Spencer—the two great writers of our genre—essentially did was give the West a vision that America believed in. Suddenly, it wasn't just a work song, only about horses. It was a song about being free—like the Cowboy National Anthem says, "Lonely but free I'll be found, drifting along with the tumbling tumbleweeds." That song encapsulates everything. It's the Cowboy Way. It's a code of honor. It's a love and appreciation of nature and of the West. If that sounds serious, by golly, it is!

QUESTION: Is the Cowboy Way creeping east?

RANGER DOUG: I would hope so. But we don't play the East much. Sometimes in the East, we're anomalies or weirdos or guys who forgot it wasn't Halloween anymore. You cross the Mississippi, and suddenly, people begin to get it. In the East, a lot of people think we're making fun of the music; in the West, they understand. We're having fun with it, sharing a lot of laughs about something we all love. When we played a lot of colleges, people would come up and ask what the real cowboys thought of us, didn't they hate us making fun of them? But all the real cowboys, and people like the Sons of the Pioneers, they said, "This is great! You're bringing it back with a sense of fun and anybody can understand it."

Alan Sacks describes Ranger Doug as the "sweetest, nicest, most gentle guy in the world." He says Too Slim is "one of the funniest guys in America," and Woody Paul is "the smartest guy I ever met in my life." During the taping of their TV show, Sacks said that Woody came off the set one day and admitted that while he was fiddling he was "figuring out some quantum theory."

Sacks became fast friends with the Riders and loved going shopping with Ranger Doug as he picked out his shirts; the Riders introduced Alan to Manuel, the popular Hollywood tailor who made many of the Riders' costumes. The Riders told Sacks about the Elko Poetry Gathering and invited him to come along; he did and was entranced. Sacks produced an album of cowboy poetry for Rhino Records and made a documentary of the tenth annual Cowboy Poetry Gathering at Elko, which was shown on PBS.

 ON THE ROAD WITH RIDERS BY BILLY MAXWELL

February 2, 1992: We was playing blackjack at the Red Lion in Elko; it was late, after midnight. Quentin Pope was standing there watching us. Slim had had a couple of drinks, and Slim isn't really a great blackjack player. Neither am I. But we always have fun doing it, and we always try to play late so we don't mess anybody else up. So Slim, he's playing and he says, "Hit me," and then Slim says, "Oh, I busted." And Quentin leans down and whispers in Slim's ear, "Slim, did you realize you'd already hit twenty-one?" Slim says, "Yeah, I figured that out but it was too late. Don't say anything 'cause maybe the dealer didn't notice." The dealer said, "I noticed." Slim already had twenty-one in his hand when he took the hit, so that busted him. He had a couple of aces, so that makes it hard to count.

Another unofficial member of the Riders team began traveling with them in the early 1990s. Mike Mahaney had moved from KCRW in Santa Monica to KCSN in Northridge, California, in

1983, where he did a show called "Trail Mix" that featured a good dose of Riders music. When the Riders were on the West Coast, Mahaney often traveled with them, helping out with the mercantile and generally pitching in like Billy Maxwell did when he traveled with the Riders.

On his first road trip with the Riders, Mahaney learned a valuable lesson. "It was about three in the morning," he remembers, "and Woody and I were the only ones awake. We stopped at a truck stop, and I got up and went to the rest room—barefooted. When I came out, the bus was driving off. I panicked—ran after the bus screaming and waving my arms, but the bus kept going. I didn't have any shoes on, didn't have my wallet with me—I was stranded. About five minutes later the bus comes back, going real slow. Woody was smiling, but he told me real quietly, 'Whenever you get off, let somebody know.' That taught me a big lesson."

Mahaney remembers traveling from Las Vegas to Torrance, California, with Slim driving and the bus doing only thirty miles an hour because it was overheating so much. "We went through Death Valley," said Slim. "And there was a big thermometer that said '125 degrees.' But we just had to get to the gig—couldn't get it repaired until after we'd played."

"Woody would go to bed and leave me notes of things to do the next day," said Mahaney. "Some of those things were not possible to do. I could get the oil changed or buy some oil or some snuff for Woody. But sometimes there was no dealer to be found to repair the bus or get parts for the bus. That bus is another member of the band."

Mahaney witnessed a major disagreement among the Riders on one of his trips with them in California. "They had set up for an afternoon show in Felton, California," said Mahaney. "Then we took a break and had lunch. Woody and his son Jake walked to the store for some snuff. Everybody knew the show was supposed to start at 3 P.M., but Woody wasn't around when the show started. Didn't show up until about half an hour after the show started. The Riders joked about it, but after the show when the guys were back on the bus Ranger Doug said very quietly but firmly to Woody, 'We're supposed to be a professional band. If you don't show up, what does that make us?'

"Woody said he thought the show was supposed to start at

four, and, although it was real clear that everybody was informed of the three o'clock starting time, Woody insisted, 'Nobody told me.'

"It's pretty amazing these guys can work as hard as they do," said Mahaney. "That was the biggest argument I ever saw them have. Doing what they do looks delightful from the seats out front, but it's a very physical thing. It's a very hard job to get from point 'A' to point 'B' and then to point 'C.' To drive all those miles, find the venues, be on time year after year after year. People just don't know how much hard work it takes just to get there."

Chapter 32

 ON THE ROAD WITH RIDERS BY BILLY MAXWELL

March 21, 1992: They were getting the Western Heritage Award for "The Line Rider," so we went to the Cowboy Hall of Fame in Oklahoma City. We were on the plane going in with Sam Elliott and Katharine Ross, and we got there and had breakfast. Skepner was supposed to go, but at the last minute he canceled. It was a black-tie affair. So at the last minute Woody called and said, "You need to go," so I ended up having to buy a tuxedo for the deal. We checked into the Worthington Hotel, and they all had rooms provided by the Cowboy Hall of Fame. So I check into the room on the third floor, and it's a suite—really laid out. Hugh O'Brien and Jack Palance were there.

They all went over to the Cowboy Hall of Fame for a rehearsal, then they took us to Remington Park for lunch. We rode in the limousine with Jack Palance. That night Richard Farnsworth, Ben Johnson, and Steven Ford from *The Young and the Restless* were there. We went back and put on the formal affair for the cocktail party and awards ceremony. Next morning we went back out to the airport. Then we flew on to Austin, and the plane was overloaded. We were flying from Oklahoma City to Austin, and they were offering just unbelievable deals for people to get off. And we would all have liked to have gotten off and taken one of the deals, but we had to be in Austin—couldn't miss the show. They were offering like two round trips and three hundred dollars in cash.

On April 20 and 21 the Riders went into Nightingale Studios in Nashville and recorded their Christmas album.

On the first day, they recorded seven songs: "Riding Home on Christmas Eve," "Sidemeat's Christmas Goose," "Rudolph the Red-Nosed Reindeer," "Christmas at the Harmony Ranch," "Navidad Y Año Nuevo," "Jingle Bells," and "White Christmas."

"Christmas at the Harmony Ranch," written by Woody and Karen Ritter, has a sprightly melody and fits the Riders perfectly.

> There's a cabin on the prairie
> With its window glowing brightly
> My homecoming pony starts to prance
> For the door is open slightly
> Where the snow sprinkles lightly
> It's Christmas at the Harmony Ranch
> Oh the wreaths are made of sagebrush
> The goose is on the table
> The boys have asked their ladies for a dance
> And their singing loud and merry
> Can be heard across the prairie
> It's Christmas at the Harmony Ranch

"Sidemeat's Christmas Goose" was written for a Riders' Christmas Special on TNN, "Merry Christmas from Harmony Ranch." The song, written by Ranger Doug, proved to be so catchy, they recorded it for their album. The song uses the Sidemeat character, whose lack of cooking skills is legendary.

> Look at them running 'round the pen
> He's chasing it, it's chasing him
> "I'm gonna rope and tie that on'ry Christmas goose!"
> Feathers flying there and here
> He's got its neck, it's got his ear
> "Now hold still you old dad-blasted Christmas goose"

"Rudolph the Red-Nosed Reindeer," first released in 1949 by Gene Autry, was that singing cowboy's biggest hit of all time. That song followed "Here Comes Santa Claus," which was a hit for Autry the previous year. Autry, who co-wrote the latter song with

Oakley Haldeman, got the idea when he was grand marshal for the Christmas parade in Hollywood. Riding down "Santa Claus Lane," Autry heard the kids shouting, "Here comes Santa Claus!" and that idea sparked the song. The second day in the studio the Riders recorded "Here Comes Santa Claus" as well as "Christmas Medley/The Greatest Gifts," "Silver Bells," "Just Put a Ribbon in Your Hair," and "Christmastime's A-Coming."

On May 8, the Riders were in Oklahoma City at the National Cowboy Hall of Fame, where they were honored for their election to the Western Music Hall of Fame. They also won a Wrangler award for their "First Cowboy Song," which was voted "Outstanding Western Song." "We hosted that awards show," said Fred. "Woody wouldn't go—it didn't pay."

On September 15, the Riders sang the national anthem in Cincinnati at Riverfront Stadium before a baseball game between the Reds and the Dodgers. "It was an incredibly hot day," remembers Fred. "WVXU was out there. We'd spent so much time in Cincinnati that folks thought we'd moved there. I called it our 'Menstrual Tour'—once a month we were in Cincinnati. That show was nerve-wracking, and I was exhausted. But it was great."

The next two days were spent recording *Riders Radio Theater*. By this time, Ranger Doug had a new love in his life, Dianne Rau. As manager David Skepner observed, "Ranger Doug is a true romantic—he always has to be in love."

 ON THE ROAD WITH RIDERS BY BILLY MAXWELL

November 27, 1992: Friday: We all went over to Woody's house to attend Ranger Doug and Dianne's engagement party at 3 P.M. After the party we went to the Opry, where they played. Then we had to pack up, and it was 3 A.M. before we were on the road. We had a universal joint going bad, so Woody and I took the bus to a Ford dealership to get it fixed. We went into a McDonald's in Missoula, Montana, and Ranger Doug walked in and said, in his deep voice, "My dear lady, what would the chef recommend today?" We've been saying that line ever since.

December 3, 1992: Around 7 A.M. I woke up just as the bus went off an embankment and skidded into a cow pasture. Woody had run off the road. We had to wait about two hours for a wrecker to come from Billings, Montana, to pull us out. We were coming from Casper, heading to

Sheridan, and he had come off the exit on the interstate really fast and it was snowy and icy. When he got to the bottom to stop and turn right, he couldn't stop and he couldn't turn. He couldn't do nothing, so he went right off that embankment right into a cow pasture. 'Course everybody was skidding off the roads there. After we stopped me and Slim went into a little restaurant and sat down. Waitress came over and poured us a cup of coffee and said, "You the guys in that big RV in the field over there?" We said, "Yep." She said, "We were all standing here by the window. Saw you come off that exit and everybody said, 'They ain't gonna stop,' and sure enough you didn't stop."

That same morning Slim and I were in the back of the bus getting something out. We had the back door open, had the plywood cactus out, and they were leaning up against the side of the bus. I was in there digging around trying to find whatever it was Slim was looking for when all of a sudden Woody just drives off in the bus. Drives off in the parking lot and leaves us standing there running across the parking lot carrying the plywood cactus. Nothing was hurt, so we continued on to Sheridan, Wyoming.

The period between 1988 and 1992 is critical in looking at the development of western music in the last decade of the twentieth century. In 1986, Michael Martin Murphey created WestFest in Colorado, but it didn't really hit its groove until 1988; from that point on, it was a major attraction in the West, drawing thousands annually. This celebration of the West inspired a number of people to pick up guitars and fiddles and rekindle their love for western music, which had mostly been forgotten.

The Cowboy Poetry Gathering in Elko, Nevada, which began in 1984, was finally attracting some major attention by 1988, and so was cowboy poetry in general. Cowboy movies weren't being made much, but there were a few key ones in the 1980s: *Heaven's Gate, The Long Riders,* and *Bronco Billy* in 1980; *Cattle Annie and Little Britches* in 1981; *Rustlers' Rhapsody* and *Silverado* in 1985. Then *Dances with Wolves,* starring Kevin Costner, came out in 1991—and won the Academy Award for Best Picture. The following year *Unforgiven,* starring Clint Eastwood, came out and also won awards from the Motion Picture Academy.

On television, the 1980–81 season saw *Little House on the Prairie, Father Murphey, Bret Maverick,* and *Best of the West* in prime time; during the 1981–82 season there was *Seven Brides for Seven Brothers*. In 1988 there was *Paradise* (later renamed *Guns of Paradise*) and the following year *Young Riders*.

Lonesome Dove, which had been a Pulitzer Prize–winning novel in 1984, aired as a TV miniseries February 5–8, 1989, and many consider it the best western ever made. In 1992 came the debut of *Dr. Quinn, Medicine Woman*, which soon became popular with TV audiences.

In 1991 Michael Martin Murphey released his landmark album, *Cowboy Songs*, which went gold and ushered in a whole era of western singers. Murphey's record label, Warner Brothers, created Warner Western, a label devoted exclusively to western music, and they signed Don Edwards, Sons of the San Joaquin, and Waddy Mitchell—bringing these excellent artists to the forefront. Joey Miskulin produced a number of these albums, establishing himself as a major producer in western music. An explosion of western music occurred during this period, with many groups and singers beginning careers as western singers.

In terms of demographics, a number of people who grew up watching Gene Autry and Roy Rogers began to reach retirement age. For their retirement years, many elected to try and recapture those golden moments of their youth—and play the western music they had first heard on the silver screen from Gene and Roy. And so a lot of these retired, semiretired, and soon-to-be-retired folks joined a crowd of western singers.

It is interesting to note that, when a number of these people jumped into western music, they sang the songs that Riders In The Sky had been singing. Many tried to incorporate humor in their shows like the Riders and openly copied the Riders' basic musical line-up.

By this point, the Riders, along with Michael Martin Murphey, were certainly at the forefront of western music. The Riders had been on TNN's *Tumbleweed Theater* 1983–85; on public radio with *Riders Radio Theater* 1988–95, then continued this show on TNN; and on CBS TV Saturday morning with a children's show 1991–92. In addition, there were TNN specials featuring the Riders, as well as numerous appearances on such other TNN shows as *Nashville Now*, *Star Search*, *Backstage at the Opry*, *Country Cooking*, and *Tennessee Outdoors*.

By 1992, the Riders had become the most influential group in western music, inspiring others to follow their example—as well as their song set list—as western entertainers. Western music was not exactly sweeping the nation, but it had become an important niche market in America, and the Cowboy Way was a popular way to go. It would not have happened the way it did if the Riders In The Sky hadn't been laying the groundwork for western entertainment during the previous fifteen years.

Chapter 33

On January 27 the Riders were at Ray Benson's Bismeaux Studios in Austin, Texas, where they recorded the old Cindy Walker song, "Dusty Skies," with Asleep at the Wheel for a tribute to Bob Wills album.

"That album was nominated for a CMA Award, so we got to go to the CMA Awards," said Slim. "We didn't win—the Eagles Tribute did. But it felt like prom night. Bert had never gone to a prom, so I got her a corsage, and we posed for a picture outside Ranger Doug's house by the bush."

On January 30 they were back in Elko for the annual Cowboy Poetry Gathering. On February 4 and March 12 they appeared on *Crook and Chase* on TNN; on February 10 and 11 and March 22, 23, and 24 they were in Cincinnati for more radio show tapings. On May 20 the Riders were on *Nashville Now,* then on May 25 they were in Hollywood, where they appeared on CNN.

On June 8, the Riders were at the White House, where they performed for President Bill Clinton. "That was a congressional barbecue in a big tent on a hot steamy night," said Slim. "Bill and Hillary loved it, and we took pictures. One was with him in my cowboy hat—which *never* appeared. I tried to get a copy of that picture, but they must've burnt the negative. Maybe it was too much like Dukakis in the army helmet. We watched Bill work the room all night—that guy never stopped! He was incredible at working a room. That was his strength!"

On September 21, the Riders were in Burbank, where they appeared on television with Tom Snyder. "That was hilarious—

we just cut up," said Slim. "Woody was always a big Tom Snyder fan, and he brought him a toy train. I took an ashtray with his picture on it from the set. We met Robert Stack there."

On October 5 the Riders taped their Christmas special, "Merry Christmas from Harmony Ranch," at the TNN Studios in Nashville.

"That was our highest-rated TNN show ever—mainly because of Reba," said Slim. "I had an idea I'd written for her and called her up and pitched it over the phone. There was no laughter—I thought it was dead. When I finished she said 'I'll talk to Narvel.' She called back and said 'Yeah, I'd love to do it.' She wasn't doing much TV at the time. Reba sang 'O Holy Night.' There was a runaway stagecoach, and Reba was the schoolmarm who saved the day."

On November 11, the Riders were in Tucson, where they were inducted into the Western Music Association's Hall of Fame. "Woody didn't go—it didn't pay," remembers LaBour.

 ON THE ROAD WITH RIDERS BY BILLY MAXWELL

December 2, 1993: We were on an Emmylou Harris tour, opening for her. The first show was in Green Bay, Wisconsin, on the third. Her lights and sound people were traveling in a closed-box straight-bed truck. I couldn't understand how anybody could do that for eight to ten hours at a time. Nobody is supposed to be in there. But the people had lawn chairs in there and sat in them and rode down the road. No light, no way to see out. That's how the sound and light people traveled.

In Washington Slim and I went to the Holocaust Museum and then did the Jim Bohannan radio show. The Riders did the first hour, and Oliver North did the second hour. That's how I met Oliver North. The guy's name with the radio show is Jim Bohannan, but Slim always thought his name was Jimbeau Hannon till he actually met him.

In New York we went to CBS to do the morning show. Afterwards, we came back to the Essex Hotel to take a shower. Slim was the only one who checked in the hotel—the rest of us slept in the bus. The hotel rooms were about three hundred dollars a night, and nobody wanted to pay that much. Also, we were afraid to leave the bus unprotected on the street. So we all went up to Slim's room and took a shower the next day before we headed out.

The next morning, December 11, we were on the New Jersey Turnpike, and I was sitting in the passenger seat in the bus when all of a sudden we hear this terrible thump on the side of the bus. I thought we'd just picked up a rock or something, but somebody had thrown a brick at us. You could see the imprint where it had struck the side of the bus. It just kinda crunched in that fiberglass. We had the lights on in the bus, and you could see there was people in there. That's one of the great things about New York City—you just never know.

At Augusta, Maine, on December 13 we got stiffed. The promoter took the money and left, but the show went on anyway. The acts didn't get their money. Too Slim said to not pay the venue the percentage for the mercantile. But they were two different groups of people doing that show—one promoted the show, and one was running the venue. So these big muscle-bound guys came up to us and blocked the door to the bus and wanted their money. I asked Too Slim what we should do. Slim said we can either pay 'em or fight it out, and he recommended we pay 'em.

In 1993 Joey rejoined the Riders, performing with them full time. Playing with Michael Martin Murphey was wonderful," said Joey. "I was well rewarded financially for what I did. But Michael is a recording artist, and you have to recreate on stage what was on the record. And even though it was me who was playing on the record, I would have to play the same things over and over again. But with the Riders, you can play whatever you want to play. You can work around and improvise, have fun. I am and always have been a team player. There is nothing more musically satisfying than performing with a group of musicians who are mentally in tune in terms of direction, commitment, enjoyment, and respect, not only with the music but with each other. Ranger Doug, Too Slim, and Woody Paul have given me the opportunity to experience that kind of satisfaction. It's a pleasure to produce and mix our recordings, but the real rush is standing on stage and looking over my left shoulder at the three other people who make up this team. Woody does something different every time—and so do Slim and Ranger Doug. It's just fun—four guys having a ball playing."

On February 3, 1994, the Riders entered Nightingale Studios and recorded "Early Autumn," "The Yellow Rose of Texas," "One Has My Name (The Other Has My Heart)," "La Malaguena," and

"You're Wearing Out Your Welcome, Matt." This would be the beginning of a new album for Columbia, and Joey Miskulin would be producing; it would be the first in a long line of Riders albums with Joey at the production helm.

The original version of "The Yellow Rose of Texas" dates back to the Texas Revolution and is supposedly about an indentured servant, Emily D. West, who served Col. James Morgan, a plantation owner who fought for the Texas army. Emily was with Santa Ana in his tent the afternoon of April 21, 1836, when Sam Houston's forces attacked the Mexican army at San Jacinto; her favors had distracted the Mexican general, who ran out into the battle in his underwear and red slippers. This lack of preparation and resultant chaos caused the defeat of the Mexicans. Emily's story was told to British ethnologist William Bollaert by Colonel Morgan in 1842, who conveyed the idea that the charms of the "yellow rose" were responsible for Texas independence. The song achieved its greatest national fame in 1955 when Mitch Miller and his group recorded it and performed it on TV and in concerts.

Husband-and-wife team Eddie and Dearest Dean composed "One Has My Name (The Other Has My Heart)," and Eddie recorded the first version in 1948 for a small label. However, the big hit came from Jimmy Wakely, who reached number-one with the song that same year. The next year Bob Eberly reached the charts with this song, and in 1969 Jerry Lee Lewis's version reached number-three on the country charts.

Eddie Dean was born Eddie Glossup in 1910 in Texas. After stints on the radio in Tulsa and then in Chicago at the National Barn Dance, Dean came to Hollywood as a singing cowboy. His first major movie was *The Harmony Trail* in 1944; during the next four years he starred in eighteen films. He appeared on *The Beverly Hillbillies* TV show during the 1960s.

Ranger Doug had known Eddie and Dearest Dean since his days at the Country Music Foundation; later the Riders met the couple and became friends as well. Dean had also written "Hillbilly Heaven," which Slim had adapted to "Sidekick Heaven."

Ranger Doug wrote "Early Autumn" while traveling on the Riders' bus to Cincinnati to tape some *Riders Radio Theater* shows. "I got the idea for the chorus, with the melody jumping an octave, from Tim Spencer's 'Cowboy Country,'" said Green, who confesses that the song expressed his "conscious grieving over the very painful ending of a love affair."

> The past like grains of sand slips through my fingers
> The future waits like the empty wastes I roam
> And the memory of her smile is all that lingers
> Early autumn, just a cowboy riding home

"La Malaguena," an old song adapted by Ranger Doug, is sung in Spanish by him. "You're Wearing Out Your Welcome, Matt" was pitched to the Riders by songwriters David Kent and Joey Scott. Slim remembers riding around in his car with the cassette in the player "laughing my head off. So I called Woody and said, 'Drywall should do this.' Woody listened and said, 'Yeah, I'll give it the treatment.'" And he did.

On February 5 they went back into the studio and recorded "Along the Santa Fe Trail" and "Farr Away Stomp."

Will Grosz and Al Dubin, along with Edwina Coolidge, wrote "Along the Santa Fe Trail," which was published in 1940. Dr. Wilhelp Grosz escaped from Hitler's Germany before World War II and settled in England, then the United States, where he wrote songs. Grosz, born in Vienna in 1894, began as a classical pianist; in England, where he moved in 1934, he wrote "Red Sails in the Sunset" and "Harbor Lights" with Jimmy Kennedy. Grosz wrote the music to those songs under the name "Hugh Williams." In April 1939, Grosz came to the United States and signed with Warner Brothers Pictures to write songs for their movies; in December of that year he died of a heart attack.

Al Dubin, born in Zurich, Switzerland, in 1891, came to the United States in 1896. A popular lyricist for Broadway shows in New York, Dubin moved to Hollywood in 1929. Edwina Coolidge, who receives partial credit for the lyrics, was Dubin's nurse and girlfriend; since they could not marry (Dubin was already married), he gave Edwina songwriting credit in order to financially provide for her. Later, after the relationship had ended, Dubin gave Edwina a sum of money in exchange for future royalties, although her name continues to appear as a cowriter.

"Along the Santa Fe Trail" was written for the movie of that

title, starring Errol Flynn and Ronald Reagan. It was an assignment from the studio to the professional songwriters, who wrote
songs on demand. It is ironic that the song was written by European immigrants whose backgrounds were far removed from the
real Santa Fe trail, which was a commercial trade route between
Missouri and the Southwest from 1821 to 1880.

Karl and Hugh Farr were the musicians with the Sons of the
Pioneers; Hugh played fiddle, while Karl played guitar. This instrumental, "Farr Away Stomp," was composed by the two brothers, who performed it with the group.

On February 8 and 9 the Riders were in Cincinnati taping their
radio show, then on February 11 were in Jackson Hole, Wyoming,
for the "Cowboy Ski Challenge." "We played a concert there,"
said Slim. "It was the week of the ice storm in Nashville. We had
done *Riders Radio Theater* in Cincinnati and gotten iced in—had to
stay there for four days. Finally we got home and barely got out
of town on the plane before the town was frozen in. There was no
electrical current in the house."

On February 16 they were in Austin at Ray Benson's Bismeaux
Studios, where they recorded "Hang Your Head in Shame" and
"I'm a Ding Dong Daddy (From Dumas)."

"I'm a Ding Dong Daddy" is a western swing number, originally recorded by Bob Wills and his Texas Playboys, and Asleep
at the Wheel's bandleader Ray Benson takes a verse; so does
Sidemeat. "Hang Your Head in Shame," written by New York pop
songwriters Ed and Steve Nelson with Fred Rose, was a hit in
1945 for both Bob Wills and Red Foley.

"For some time Riders In The Sky had contemplated an album of love songs, which Too Slim always jokingly referred to as
'Ranger Doug Sings for Western Lovers,'" said Green, who added
that it was their fifteenth album and "time to do something a little
different. . . it was time to sing some of those codependent, dys-
functional love songs you hear on the radio all the time." They
had already recorded the first group of songs for the album earlier in the month.

On February 21 the Riders came back to Nightingale Studios
and recorded "The Cowboy's in Love," "Wimmen . . . Who Needs
'Em?," "The Ballad of Palindrome," "Sweet Señorita Teresa," and
"The Running Gun."

"Slim came up with the album title," continued Doug, "but we had no title song to go with it. I saw an opening and went for it."

Why does the sun shine so much brighter today?
Why does the stream sing a song in its play?
Why does the breeze add harmony on the way?
Why? 'Cause the cowboy's in love

The song was easy for Ranger Doug to write, because that cowboy was indeed in love with a young lady named Dianne, whom he would marry.

"Wimmen . . . Who Needs 'Em!" was written by Ranger Doug for Slim's "Sidemeat" character. The song is a joy to listen to as Slim really gets into his character. Sidemeat lays out his message early, "I got some words of wisdom you whippersnappers ought to hear:"

Now I've been around the block a time or four
When it comes to wimmen, boys, I know the score
They're fickle
They're ungrateful
They'll bite the hand that feeds them
Wimmen . . . who needs 'em!

Sidemeat observes that he's done some courtin' and "each little chickadee turned out to be a tough old hen" and then warns, "Boys, there's two places you can learn about this—in this song or in court. Which do you think is cheaper?"

You think that breakin' broncs is rough?
Well, I'll tell you this for certain
Sign up with a woman for a Ph.D. in hurtin'.
They'll chew you up and spit you out
And leave you there to bleed some
Wimmen—who needs 'em?

Woody Paul's "Sweet Señorita Teresa," a beautiful waltz in three-four time, is a song of love for Woody's new love, and soon-

The Columbia years. 1991 from the *Harmony Ranch* photo shoot. *Photo courtesy of Columbia Records. Photo by Jim McGuire. Photo provided by the author and Riders In The Sky.*

1992 Macy's Thanksgiving Day Parade. (CBS Saturday morning TV show year.) *Photo provided by the author and Riders In The Sky.*

Riders and their doubles in the CBS Saturday morning show. Episode of "Mail Order Brides," 1992. *Photo provided by the author and Riders In The Sky.*

Boomer Esiason (Cincinnati Bengal) backstage at Riders Radio Theater with his new offensive line, 1993. *Photo provided by the author and Riders In The Sky.*

The Riders with President Bill Clinton. Left to right: Too Slim, Woody Paul, President Clinton, and Ranger Doug. *Photo provided by the author and Riders In The Sky.*

Always Drink Upstream from the Herd, 1995. Photo courtesy of Rounder Records. Photo by Jim McGuire. Photo provided by the author and Riders In The Sky.

Merry Christmas from Harmony Ranch, 1992. Photo courtesy of Columbia Records. Photo by Frank Ockenels 3. Photo provided by the author and Riders In The Sky.

Riders In The Sky with their longtime hero, the legendary Gene Autry. Riders In The Sky were performing a tribute to Gene Autry, and the evening gave rise to their new release, *Public Cowboy #1: The Music of Gene Autry*. Left to right: Woody Paul, Ranger Doug, Gene Autry, Too Slim, and Joey the Cowpolka King. *Photo provided by the author and Riders In The Sky.*

Riders In The Sky during Woody's Roundup video shoot. *Photo courtesy of New Frontier Management. Photo by Mark Lowrie.*

Riders at Melody Ranch for an IMAX movie that never saw the light of day, September 2000. *Photo courtesy of New Frontier Management. Photo provided by the author and Riders In The Sky. Photo by Michael N. Marks.*

Riders In The Sky with tour manager, Brandon Taylor, at Opry's seventy-fifth anniversary. *Photo courtesy of New Frontier Management. Photo by Nicole Lester.*

Riders In The Sky with their awards at the Grammys in 2001. *Photo courtesy of New Frontier Management.*

Riders In The Sky twenty-fifth anniversary photo. *Photo courtesy of New Frontier Management. Photo by Jim McGuire.*

The Riders with Paul Lohr at Melody Ranch. *Photo courtesy of New Frontier Management. Photo by Michael N. Marks.*

Riders In The Sky twenty-fifth anniversary photo. *Photo courtesy of New Frontier Management. Photo by Jim McGuire.*

(Above) Hank Peterson, Ranger Doug's uncle, 1930s. *(Below)* Arvid Peterson, Ranger Doug's uncle, 1930s. *Photos provided by the author and Riders In The Sky.*

to-be wife, Teresa. Woody sang this song to his bride on their wedding day.

> Sweet Señorita Teresa
> Laughter and love are your face
> Echoes of joy ring inside me
> The melody of your embrace
> Forever charmed by your magic
> Always I'm longing for you
> Sweet Señorita Teresa
> You are my love deep and true

"The Running Gun" was written by Jim Glaser, youngest of the three Glaser brothers, who had a string of hits beginning in the 1960s as Tompall and the Glaser Brothers. Jim Glaser wrote the 1960s hit "Woman, Woman" for Gary Puckett and the Union Gap and also had a solo career that extended into the 1980s. The Glaser brothers began their professional career singing backup harmonies for Marty Robbins. Robbins recorded an album, *Gunfighter Ballads and Trail Songs*, that contained "Running Gun" as well as "Big Iron," "El Paso," and "Cool Water."

There were several movie projects about Davy Crockett in production or preproduction, so Rhino Records decided to put together an album of songs about Davy Crockett to capitalize on these movies. There seemed to be a resurgence of interest in Davy Crockett, who was the star of young Baby Boomers' lives back in 1955 when Walt Disney broadcast several shows on Crockett on Sunday nights. "The Ballad of Davy Crockett" was a huge hit, and many young Baby Boomers remember wearing coonskin caps during the mid-1950s. Rhino wanted to be ready for a resurgence of interest in ole Davy.

On March 8 the Riders went to the Mark Howard Studio to record a group of songs associated with Davy Crockett. On that day they recorded "King of the River," "Heading for Texas," "Old Betsy," and "The Ballad of Davy Crockett." The next day they recorded "Remember the Alamo," "Farewell," and "Be Sure You're Right (And Then Go Ahead)." On March 10 they recorded "Colonel Crockett's Speech to Congress" and "The Grinning Tale."

"There were about three Davy Crockett movies in development, so Rhino wanted a Davy Crockett set to compete with that when they came out," said Slim. "But all the movies were dropped. Never came out." The Riders tried to purchase the recordings to release them, but Rhino wouldn't sell. That album has never appeared—a major disappointment for the Riders, who poured a lot of creative energy into the project.

On March 30, 1994, the Riders played in Winston-Salem, North Carolina, and Ranger Doug lost his voice. "I could hardly talk," said Green. "It was frustrating, and I did think that maybe I should be planning for another career."

"It was nerve-wracking," said Slim. "Scared us all. He went to the Vanderbilt Voice Clinic, and they put a little light down his throat but never could find anything."

"They never could figure it out," said Doug. "They thought later that it was Bell's palsy, which usually affects your face, but can affect your vocal cords. It's a virus that attacks the nerves. In retrospect, it didn't last that long—eight or nine months—but I never did get back those last three or four high notes. They're just gone. I got back to where I could yodel up to an E flat, but I used to hit a G way up there. As it was healing, I gradually found my range. It was six notes, then eight, then twelve, then fifteen. But I never stopped singing, because I didn't have an alternative, really. I had to make a living. When you're self-employed, you can't just stop."

"We shifted our vocals around," said Slim. "Woody did the yodeling." "We made adjustments," said Green. "Both of the guys showed that they could yodel. We came up with a new arrangement of 'That's How the Yodel Was Born' and ended up keeping it because it was fun. I didn't have any volume, but I could work the mike. If I had a solo, I just picked one with a fairly limited range or let them do the solos while I did the harmony."

Ranger Doug has always been fascinated by harmony. "I remember liking 'Mr. Sandman' by the Chordettes," he said. "That may have been the first forty-five I ever bought. When real rock and roll came in I was not particularly interested, although I thought Buddy Holly had a kind of cool energy—until I heard the Everly Brothers. They blew me away, and I bought everything by them I could. I used to harmonize along with them. Musically they touched me the most because of my obsession with harmony, yet they sang the music of my generation."

In high school Douglas Green "fell in love with the sinuous harmonies of Peter, Paul, and Mary and learned to play some of their songs. I enjoyed the Kingston Trio as well but never bought their records or learned their songs.

"My lifelong fascination with harmony singing prepared me for singing with the Riders," said Ranger Doug. "Singing along with duets like the Everly Brothers or Louvin Brothers and picking out the third part helped train my ear. But I honestly had no idea how hard singing western music would be, how difficult it is to sing that harmony in good tune, with precision and feeling. It has been a continuing education, and one of the most enjoyable things about being in this group is that we are still trying to improve our blend, our stacking, our arrangements. We do have our own sound and we have worked really hard to get it.

"In general we hear the outline of our parts fairly well, and when it comes time within a line to switch parts up or down we fall into it pretty easily as a rule," continued Green. "Having Joey and his ears of gold helps enormously—he can pick out all the parts on accordion. The outline comes fairly easily, but the devil is in the details—the little pickup notes, the transition notes between chords—these are sometimes hard to hear and harder to sing in tune.

"The easy part is hearing, in a general sense, where the part will go. The hard part is hearing my part while everyone else is learning theirs at the same time, especially if my part is not the melody. That is one reason I love to sing with the Reinsmen at western get-togethers. They have their parts honed to a razor's edge, and it's hard to make a mistake when the other two parts are so clear. When we are all learning at once it's hard to get a note to sing to, and we all get frustrated.

"Another very difficult and frustrating part is if the monitors are not adjusted well or if there is a 'swell' on some note or another coming back at us on stage, or if there is a resonance in the room which the sound guys can't eliminate. We each or all spend the evening fighting, fighting to sing in tune, and it really makes it a job to act like you're having the time of your life while you know you are singing flatter than crap. The audience knows when it's sour, and, while I have no fears that we'll entertain them, we all want the music to be the best it can be. And its maddening to all of us if one or more of us can't hear the pitch correctly. I would venture to say that more than the traveling or lack of sleep or any other discomfort associated with this job, that the nights we can't hear well onstage are the most physically and emotionally trying. You hate to disappoint an audience. You hate to disappoint yourself.

"I've had a lot of influences through the years. For yodeling surely it is Elton Britt, who set the bar so high none of us have reached it yet. For solo western singing I think probably Jimmy Wakely would be the most influential. I think my voice may be more like his in tone than many of the other western singers of the past. I love the relaxed and easy way he had with solos. Ken Curtis was very influential on the way I sing. I didn't always love his phrasing, but his tone and feel were incomparable. I always wished I could sing like Lloyd Perryman, but God only gives gifts like that very rarely. As a harmony singer I am always amazed by the subtle baritone of Jesus 'Chucho' Navarro, who sang that part with Trio Los Panchos, and of course Tommy Doss."

Too Slim learned harmony singing by ear. "I started with my sister when I was little," he said. "I never took any formal training, which I probably should have, but I never sang in a choir, never sang in any choral group, I just sang along with records and then sang at gigs. With Dickey Lee, singing harmony with Bill Collins was a big part of our sound. Collins had a real good ear for harmony and a real high voice. I would generally sing one above Dickey, and Collins would sing a really high—as we say, a high baritone—above that. So I knew the fundamentals of harmony, but I didn't know a lot of the nuances of it, and this is something that I endlessly strive and work on to this day—trying to improve the Riders' sound or my own contribution to the sound.

"To do the parts right is endlessly difficult and an incredible challenge and something we work on to this day," continued LaBour. "My voice has changed through the years—it's lower. I've found I'm more comfortable in the lower register these days, so the blend, which has changed many times for Riders In The Sky, is generally me on the bottom, Ranger Doug in the middle, and Woody on top. So I've had to learn bass parts, and it's been wonderful for me to learn what works at the bottom of the chord as opposed to working at the top of the chord, which is what I worked at before.

"The easy part is that I have a natural affinity for it—I hear a more basic part. I think Woody hears a more sophisticated jazz-oriented part to a chord, but I hear a very basic gospel-country-type chord, a folk chord. I hear the one, the three, and the five really clearly in a chord, so that makes it easy; I have a good shot at the basic note. The hard part is discovering phrasing—what moves a song in terms of phrasing, what phrasing does with the emotional content of the song as well as the dynamics and learning to sing with two or three other people so that there is a blend happening. Where does my voice fit in that blend? How can I make my voice disappear in the blend so that it just becomes one voice? That's the great challenge of what we do. We're not brothers—except we've sort of become brothers in a way—but we say our vowels differently. We've got one guy from deep middle Tennessee who says his vowels one way. Ranger Doug has sort of a polyglot of influences and voices, and then I've got a sort of upper Midwest accent with flat A's and certain ways of doing things. I've had to listen to myself, listen to people talk, listen to the other guys talk, so I can sing my vowels the same, the phrasing, the dynamics. It's easy to do it in a cursory way. It's tough to do it in the ultimate smooth, relaxed, effortless pleasing way that we strive for."

Woody states, "I didn't have any trouble with harmony because I actually knew it better than they did—how to figure out what the parts were. I wasn't always exactly right at the beginning because I worked under the principle that when the lead moved the other two guys moved too, and that was better than church singing when the lead moved but the other guys stayed with the same note. I liked moving them all together. It was pretty easy to pick out harmony—we didn't do anything super hard back when we started. Not a lot of weird modulations. But the hard part for us is that we all have voices in the same range, so it's got an interesting sound. It's harder to do harmony that way, with no two- or three-range octave. You've got to sing all your songs in the same range. You don't hear us jumping octaves very much, except maybe on a yodel."

Woody said that phrasing was not a problem for him "because I never paid any attention to it. I don't really have a good ear for pitch or for where the beat is or where the stress is, where the consonant ends or where it starts. Joey does. Joey knows that stuff really well and knows where it can be corrected and, like all the studio guys these days, takes the computer and corrects it. Having studied music theory, Joey seems to have a deeper understanding of what harmony should be."

"Sometimes we do one-three-fives; sometimes it works in a lateral method," Joey said. "Say you're doing a one-three-five of a moving chord and you go to a two minor chord, it would be a two-four-six together. And instead of resolving back to the three-five-eight you would go back to three-five-seven, which is very cowboy. Everyone following a uniform part. Cowboy music is just a little bit of a different voice. They're not perfect harmonies, and that's what makes it different.

"Let's just say a lead passage goes one-two-three," continued Joey. "The second voice will go three-four-five and the third voice in perfect harmony will go five-six-eight. But in cowboy music, a lot of times it will go five-six-seven. It follows everything else—everything is following the same pattern the lead is following. If you listen to cowboy music—that's the style you do. It's more difficult—a little trickier.

"We all feel sorry for Woody because he's singing the tenor part," said Joey. "And he's not really a true tenor. Sometimes he sings falsetto. The good thing about Slim is he's found his niche in singing bass. Early on, at least when I started with them, Slim used to sing lead a lot, and Doug would sing the baritone part. But now Slim sings baritone—and he's got a great baritone voice that blends in very, very well. It's just a good blending voice. So Ranger Doug sings a strong lead, and then Woody is on the top—he just knows how to do it. He knows how not to accentuate his falsetto. You know, you can get three great singers on the street corner to sing any part you want, but to get people who have created a style—and they're really great stylists—you've got that in Riders In The Sky. Many times I'll sing a sixth. Sometimes it'll allow Ranger Doug to yodel where before they had to go to two parts. I'll sing the third part. So it works out great.

"Four-part is not cowboy harmony. Listen to the Sons of the Pioneers. If they had a fourth guy singing, generally it would be Hugh Farr singing bass. But just to sing four-part harmony can be a clash in cultures. It isn't true cowboy music. It doesn't sound right—it sounds too modern."

On April 25, right after Ranger Doug lost his voice, the Riders went into the studio to film an instructional video on harmony singing. On September 13 the Riders entered the Mark Howard Studio and recorded songs for Rabbit Ears Radio with Roy Rogers. That first day they recorded the traditional western songs "Whoopie Ti Yi Yo" and "Home on the Range." The next day they recorded "I Ride an Old Paint," "The Yellow Rose of Texas," "The Streets of Laredo," and "The Old Chisholm Trail."

On September 15 they recorded "Home on the Range"; Roy and Dale's theme song, "Happy Trails"; and "The Buckaroo's Life." The next day, September 16, was their last day of recording, and they only did one song: "Night-riding Song."

The Rabbit Ears folks wanted traditional songs but told the Riders they could add a couple of songs if they sounded traditional. Ranger Doug composed "The Buckaroo's Life" and "Night-riding Song."

> Lie still, little dogies, lie still
> The moon's rising over the hill
> Don't you get restless, you've eaten your fill
> Lie still, little dogies, lie still

"Woody calls them 'Elko-type songs,'" states Green. "It's a true trail song, portraying not the grandeur of the West but the hot (or cold), dusty, gritty, difficult ordeal of the trail hand."

"The shows were broadcast," said Slim. "But then the company went bankrupt, so it's never come out as an album." This has been another major disappointment for the Riders—having an album recorded with one of their heroes, Roy Rogers, and then it not be available. "It's stuck in a warehouse in New Jersey somewhere, I think," said Ranger Doug.

Another major frustration that year came with the release of the movie *The Cowboy Way*. Producer Brian Grazer, a successful Hollywood veteran who had produced movies like *Splash, Spies Like Us, The Burbs, Parenthood, Kindergarten Cop,* and *Far and Away,* and who would go on to produce *Apollo 13, The Nutty Professor, Liar Liar, Dr. Seuss's How the Grinch Stole Christmas,* the award-winning *A Beautiful Mind,* and *Stealing Harvard* had stolen a title from the Riders long-used phrase in their live show ("that would be the easy way, but it wouldn't be *the cowboy way"*) that was also the title of one of their albums. Grazer apparently heard the phrase after he and/or some of his staff had seen the Riders perform in California.

The Riders received no acknowledgment, did not get to perform a song in the movie, or even "a handshake, a thank-you, or a kiss my ass," said Ranger Doug. In strictly legal terms, Glazer didn't have to acknowledge the Riders, but common courtesy and a sense of ethics would have led him to include the Riders in some form or fashion with the movie. But apparently that ain't the way Hollywood works.

 ON THE ROAD WITH RIDERS BY BILLY MAXWELL

December 8, 1994: We were going to Green Bay, Wisconsin, but somewhere in Kentucky we discovered that Woody had left his fiddle at home. So we called David Skepner, who called the promoter, who borrowed Woody a fiddle in Green Bay from a lady who played in the symphony. You would think a man would not leave his tools. But Woody did. After the show, we spent the night in Green Bay and the next day drove to Wausau. We stopped on the way there and bought some cheese and sausage. Then we drove back to Nashville, and the Riders played the Opry.

Chapter 34

On January 16–20 the Riders were in Oklahoma City at the National Cowboy Hall of Fame.

 ON THE ROAD WITH RIDERS BY BILLY MAXWELL

January 16, 1995: We were going to the Cowboy Hall of Fame in Oklahoma City to do a one-hour TV special for TNN. And of course it took us four days—Monday through Thursday—to film the one-hour show. We did the Opry just before we left, loaded up the stuff, and went to Houston, where we did a show at Rockefeller's. After that show we drove north and arrived in Oklahoma City at ten-thirty in the morning, took a nap, took a shower, and met Skepner at the hotel. After dinner we came back to the hotel for a production meeting.

We taped all day and got to go into the vaults at the Cowboy Hall of Fame to see stuff they don't have out on display. Some of their Remingtons, saddles that belonged to famous cowboys—we got to see a lot of the behind-the-scenes stuff.

We'd get to the Cowboy Hall of Fame at nine in the morning and lots of times go till after dark. The last night we had a big show in the big meeting hall where they had an invitation-only audience for this TV show. Waddy Mitchell was there. So was Michael Martin Murphey. They were the guests on the show.

I'd drive over there from the hotel twice a day—over there and back—for four days. The last night, Slim said for me to drive because he'd had a little too much to drink. But he told me every single turn—like I'd never been there before. The next day I drove to Phoenix by myself, and they flew to Columbia, Missouri. I got to Phoenix about 5 o'clock on the 21st. They flew into Phoenix. There was a foot of snow in Flagstaff when I drove through and then when I got to Phoenix it was seventy degrees. Sun was shining, not a cloud in the sky. Stuff like that amazes me.

January 26, 1995: We were going across the Donner Pass from California over to Reno, and when we come out of the west side of Donner Pass I'm hearing on the radio that chains are required to go over the top because it's snowing on top of the mountain. 'Course we didn't have chains. Everybody in the bus was asleep so I thought, "I'll see what I can do here." And so we got stopped at an exit because we didn't have chains.

I got fuel and they opened up the roads, so I went on to the next exit, where they stopped us again. This time we sat for two hours, and it got worse. So we had to buy some chains, which cost $180. It started to really snow again, and the guy said, "You can't stay here." But we couldn't go back down either because they closed the mountain back down behind us. That's why we didn't have any alternative but to buy the chains.

This ole guy we bought 'em from was just a crook out there by the side of the road—selling you chains, putting 'em on, and charging you an arm and a leg. But we bought 'em and went across the top of the mountain and then took 'em off. Grace, Doug's daughter, was due to be born the next morning, so there's nobody on the bus but Woody and Slim and me. And so we stopped at the Nuggett in Reno for just a little while, but we didn't want to stay there long—just for one hour. Woody was asleep. This was like eight or nine o'clock, and we go to get something to eat because we were ready to leave. Well, a couple of minutes before we were going to leave, Woody wakes up and comes in and says he's going to get himself something to eat. I told him we were leaving in fifteen minutes, and he said it wouldn't take him long.

When I got back to the bus, Slim was there, but Woody wasn't. We sat there and waited an hour and a half. I went back in the casino but couldn't find him. Slim got real mad and said he was flying home. But when he went into the casino to call the airport, he found Woody, and they came back to the bus. Turns out Woody was in the men's room, sitting on the toilet, writing a letter to the owner of the Nuggett. Slim was very mad. Woody is totally oblivious to everybody else—he was just in there fooling around, doing nothing. Slim got so mad again, and they got into a big shouting match right in each other's face right in the lobby of the place. Woody was threatening to fly home then.

We drove on for a couple of hours and then we stopped at a truck stop outside Winnemucka, and Woody got the oil changed in the bus.

We drove on to Nashville and got back to Slim's house at 5:30 A.M. on Wednesday the twenty-eighth, and Slim was getting ready to get out so I could turn the bus around. Bert came out and said Dianne had gone to the hospital the night before and had the baby that morning. Then Woody and I drove to his house, took a shower, and Woody cooked breakfast.

On March 6 they went into the Mark Howard Studio and recorded "Rawhide." The next day they recorded "Desert Serenade," "The Running Gun," "Cattle Call," and "Texas Polka."

"Rawhide" was the theme song to the popular TV show that starred Clint Eastwood from 1959 to 1965. It was sung by Frankie Laine; in the 1980s it was resurrected by John Belushi and Dan Ackroyd in the movie *The Blues Brothers*. The song was written by two veteran Hollywood writers, Dimitri Tiomkin and Ned Washington, who also wrote the theme song to the movie *High Noon* ("Do No Forsake Me, Oh, My Darling").

Tiomkin was born in 1899 in St. Petersburg, Russia; he left after the 1917 revolution that brought communists to power and toured Europe as a concert pianist. In 1925 he emigrated to the United States and moved to Hollywood in 1930 to choreograph screen musicals. Tiomkin soon found work composing scores for movies (he would eventually compose the scores for over 160 movies, be nominated for twenty-four Academy Awards, and win four). In addition to scoring the theme song for *High Noon*, which won two Oscars—one for best score and another for theme song— Tiomkin also scored *Duel in the Sun, Gunfight at the O.K. Corral, The Alamo,* and *Giant.*

Lyricist Ned Washington was born in 1901 in Pennsylvania. In addition to writing the *High Noon* theme, he also wrote the lyrics to the themes for *The Marshal of Wichita, The Man from Laramie, Gunfight at the O.K. Corral, The 3:10 to Yuma,* and *Broken Arrow.*

The original version of "Cattle Call" was written by Tex Owens and published by Forster Music in 1934. Owens was born in 1892 and raised in Bell County, Texas, and worked on ranches as a youth, but he was more interested in show business and worked in a number of shows in the area. In 1928 he worked as an entertainer on KMBC in Kansas City, and one day while watching snow fall outside his window composed "The Cattle Call" to the tune of "The Morning Star Waltz." Publisher Fred Forster felt the lyrics needed rewriting and assigned the job to Fred Rose, who created the lyrics that became a hit song for Eddy Arnold. Rose never received credit for his extensive contributions; one version is that Owens was so upset with Rose's changes that he wouldn't let Rose's name appear on the song or share in the royalties.

Discussing "Desert Serenade," Ranger Doug states, "I was doing a yodeling workshop at the western music festival in Tucson when it occurred to me that no one, to my knowledge, had tried to yodel over a diminished chord, so I determined then and there to write such a tune," adding, "I wrote 'Desert Serenade' with the great cowboy balladeer Don Edwards in mind."

The moon is high, the fire is low
A million stars outshine the embers' glow
A lonesome yodel soft and low . . .

On March 8 they recorded "The First Cowboy Song" and "The Wayward Wind."

"The Wayward Wind" was a number-one pop hit for Gogi Grant in 1956; that same year Tex Ritter also reached the pop charts with it. It charted again for Grant in 1961. "The First Cowboy Song" featured a verse sung by former Asleep at the Wheel vocalist Chris O'Connell.

On the ninth they recorded "The Trail Tip Song," "I Still Do," and "After You've Gone."

"The Trail Tip Song," written by Too Slim, offers up such gems as

Always drink upstream from the herd
Never look straight up at a bird
When you get bucked off, get back on
And, son, don't squat with your spurs on.

This recording would become the basis of their first video.

On March 10 they finished up recording, doing "Boots and Saddle," "Riding the Winds of the West," "Idaho," and "The Whispering Wind."

The idea for "Boots and Saddle," also known as "Take Me Back to My Boots and Saddle," came to Walter Samuels on the rooftop garden of a New York City hotel. Samuels took the partial song to Teddy Powell and Lenny Whitcup, and the three finished it. The three took the song around to a number of publishers, who weren't interested; finally, they tried one last publisher—Bob Miller of Schuster & Miller. Miller took the song immediately, and soon there were ten recordings of the song made. The three songwriters were longtime friends. Walter Samuels was born in 1908, studied law at New York University, and eventually wrote musical scores for twenty Gene Autry and Roy Rogers movies. Teddy Powell, born Alfred Paoella, was born in 1906 and became a bandleader after serving as violinist and guitarist in the Abe Lyman Orchestra. Leonard Whitcup, born in 1903, was a native New Yorker and graduated from New York University. "Boots and Saddle" first hit the charts in November 1935; later it was the name of a movie starring Gene Autry. "Riding the Winds of the West," written by Ranger Doug, came about after Woody and Slim had both observed they had "no new up-tempo yodeling songs in the 'Texas Plains' / 'When Payday Rolls Around' style." And so the Ranger decided to compose one.

You'll greet the day with coffee bitter and strong
You'll ride away with a heart full of song

Dogies may stray, but for not very long
When you're riding the winds of the west

"The Whispering Wind" is a song written by Ranger Doug
that has beautiful three-part harmony throughout the entire song.

In the dawning's grey
I hear her sigh
When the twilight fades
I hear her cry
And I know that I will heed to her plea
For her song makes my yearning heart
Long once again to be free
On a winding trail
By the light of the moon
She whispers a tale
Of that sweet sad old tune
And I know that soon
I'll be riding again
A wanderer called by the sigh and the cry
Of the whispering wind

On March 30 they were at Melody Ranch in California. "That
was the Santa Clarita Festival," said Slim. "It was a thrill to be on
Gene Autry's old ranch and the movie lot where they'd filmed so
many cowboy shows."

Their last *Riders Radio Theater* in Cincinnati occurred on August 18, 1995. "It had run its course," said Slim. "I was tired of
writing it. I loved it, and it was a great generator of material, but
I was tired. It presented us in a way that played to our strengths."

After the radio show ended, David Skepner negotiated a contract for the Riders to do their *Riders Radio Theater* as a series of
television specials for TNN. On September 26, 27, and 28 the Riders were in the TNN Studios recording "Riders Radio Theater:
Christmas Special."

On October 13 and 15 the Riders performed at the "Country
Gold Festival" in Kumamoto, Japan. "We were over there with
Marty Stuart, Rhonda Vincent, Boy Howdy, and a bluegrass group,
the Laural Canyon Ramblers—Herb Peterson's group," said Slim.

"We played in a big volcanic crater. Went to the fish market at 4 A.M. and saw them bid on a giant tuna. Then we got to eat the tuna raw and drank saki at 6 A.M. We went over in a bus, and Woody was late coming out from the hotel. And when he came out he was wearing his red long johns with cutoffs, and on his head was an orange aviator cap with the wool ear flaps pulled down. It was a sight. Came out of the hotel and turned the wrong way—and everybody on the bus was watching and cracking up laughing. Fortunately, he'd remembered his fiddle."

"The fish market is huge in that town," said Ranger Doug. "And they had the tuna out there for bidding so restaurateurs and wholesalers could come in and bid on the stuff. The Japanese are so orderly anyway—12 tuna in a row, 150 octopus in a row, just laid out perfectly. It was interesting to see these people running around taking bids. Then they had a very formal ceremony where they invited us to drink beer and saki and eat raw fish first thing in the morning. I said 'No thank you!' but Skepner ate about six pounds of it. He could really put away food, and sushi was his favorite. 'This is $600 worth of tuna here if you bought it in a restaurant,' he said. Huge slabs of raw tuna. I tried to be polite, but I didn't eat any of that stuff."

 ON THE ROAD WITH RIDERS BY BILLY MAXWELL

October 31, 1995: Halloween. We were at Fred's sister's in Tucson, and Slim and Bert and little Alice all went out trick-or-treating. Slim dressed up as himself—Too Slim—and nobody recognized him. Ranger Doug was going to take Dianne down to Nogales the next day, and he asked me if I'd like to go and so I went. We got there about 1 P.M., parked the bus on the U.S. side, and walked across the border. I bought an armadillo there, and we were coming back across the border, and of course you've got to declare what you got. I didn't know you couldn't bring an armadillo across the border, so I declared my armadillo, and they said you can't bring an armadillo across the border. So we went back and sold it to the guy we bought it from for ten dollars less than what we gave for it. No animals dead or alive. That's what they said, so I asked them, "What about a belt? A belt is a dead animal." But it was no dice.

We drove back to Tucson, and the next morning I had to go back to Phoenix to pick up Woody at the airport. We stopped at the ostrich farm on the way back and looked at them. We did two shows at the Western Music Association that night, went back to the hotel for a short time, then headed for Los Angeles.

November 3, 1995: We went to L.A. to do a Harvest Festival in the downtown area and stayed on Hill Street. It was only a block and a half from where the O.J. Simpson trial had been held, and I walked down there and saw the Criminal Justice Center and saw all the places I'd seen on TV just weeks before that. We did two shows at the Harvest Festival, came back to the hotel, and went right to sleep. Next morning I got Woody out about ten-thirty, and we walked around and went to a cutlery shop, where Woody bought a pair of scissors to cut his hair with. While we were paying I said, "I bet this is where O.J. bought his knife," and they said it was. They showed us the kind of knife he bought, and the guy said, "My brother had to go testify, but he's not here today." Then we went down to another store and Woody bought some shirts and some Christmas presents. From L.A. the next date was in North Carolina.

Chapter 35

The Riders appeared on a TNN special, "An Evening of Country Greats," in February 1996, which led to them recording a tribute album to Gene Autry, *Public Cowboy #1: The Music of Gene Autry.* "We did a medley of five songs of Autry's with him in the audience," said Slim. "And that's what led to this album."

On June 17–20, the Riders were in the studio recording songs for that album. On June 17 they recorded "Mexicali Rose," "Lonely River," and "Blue Canadian Rockies"; on June 18 they recorded "Be Honest with Me," "That Silver-Haired Daddy of Mine," "South of the Border," and "Riding Down the Canyon." On June 19 they recorded "You Are My Sunshine" and "Have I Told You Lately That I Love You." They finished recording on June 20, doing three final songs: "Back in the Saddle Again," "Can't Shake the Sands of Texas from My Shoes," and "Sioux City Sue."

The next month the Riders recorded "Hoop Dee Doo" with Frank Yankovic. The month before the Autry sessions, the Riders recorded, through the miracle of technology, a duet with Marty Robbins on "Rudolph the Red-Nosed Reindeer." "Joey produced it," said Slim. "They found some old tapes and put on some new instrumentals. It was on a Sony compilation album."

At the beginning of the year the Riders had appeared in Elko at the annual Cowboy Poetry Gathering and taped another *Riders Radio Theater* for television. In March they received two more Wrangler Awards from the Western Heritage Association.

On August 23, the Riders entered cyberspace with the launch of their website, thanks to the volunteer efforts of Kate Henne, affectionately known at "Dakota Kate."

 ON THE ROAD WITH RIDERS BY BILLY MAXWELL

November 7, 1996: The Riders had just gotten a brand-new bus, and this was the first time I'd been in it. We went out to Woodward, Oklahoma, to do a show. We did the sound check and we're just hanging out at the theater before the show—we didn't have hotel rooms—and Ranger Doug is laying on a couch, had his hat over his face and was taking a little nap. Everybody was just taking it easy. This guy came into the dressing room and said, "You sure are taking it easy, Ranger Doug." And Ranger Doug looks up at the man, real serious, and says, "What do you want us to do—push-ups?"

During 1996 the Riders had launched their web site and joined the revolution in cyberspace. The next year, Ranger Doug's solo album *Songs of the Sage* on Warner Western was released. The idea of Ranger Doug doing a solo album had been born several years earlier. "An engineer-turned-producer named Bill Halverson approached me out of the blue one day," said Green. "I'd known him for several years through one thing and another. He was a friend of Robby Adcock's, who had produced some of those early albums. That's what put the germ of the idea in his mind, and I talked it over with the guys and everybody said that would be great—there were no ego or band problems. But nothing came of it and it receded into the background, and I never heard from him again.

"Then, when Warner Western opened their office in Nashville and wanted to go beyond Don Edwards and Michael Martin Murphey and Sons of the San Joaquin and Waddy Mitchell, they called me," continued Ranger Doug. "Their offer was not connected to Bill, so I didn't feel obligated to use him as a producer. By then, we were such good friends with Joey and he's such a good producer that I knew he could produce something that would be musically exciting and as different as we could make it from the Riders and still make it 'western.' Skepner and I went round and round about this. He wanted me to put on old, tattered cowboy clothes and look like a range rider from right off the prairies. I just said, 'That's not Ranger Doug.' I don't know what his thinking was, really—but he had some very definite and strong opinions about certain things. But that's how that album came about. Joey and I selected the songs. I chose six old ones that the Riders had never done for one reason or another but I believed in, and then I wrote six new ones for the project. I'm so proud of that record."

The album, *Songs of the Sage*, is perhaps the finest truly western album produced in the last quarter of the twentieth century. It certainly represents Ranger Doug's vision of western songwriting —what it should be and how it should be presented. The addition of horns and an orchestra shows his debt to the big-band era when the original singing cowboys were doing their filming.

The album never tires on the listener—it is beautiful and moving through and through. Unlike Riders albums, which always attempt to capture various aspects of the Riders—their humor, the visions and personalities of each member, and the demand that each song be one that can be performed live for an audience— this album offers no compromises. Ranger Doug is, at heart, a romantic, and this album is saturated with his romantic visions of the West, singing cowboys, lovers past and current, and himself. It is, quite simply, an autobiography of feelings, dreams, and self-image.

"Singing in the Saddle" is a phrase Ranger Doug loves—it was the name of a song by the Reinsmen, but he uses the same title for his own song. And it seems to encapsulate the singing-cowboy image for Ranger Doug. He also tells listeners that he's going to be a spokesman—in song—for the West.

As my days unravel I'll be singing in the saddle
'Cause this is where I'm gonna stay
For the coyote and the breeze and the wind in the trees

And the bawling of the cattle as they graze
Is a song they've sung since time begun
That I'm singing in the saddle all day

"Hurry Sunrise" is a song of lost love—and the singer wants desperately to forget her. Sleepless nights—or nights with very little sleep—are not uncommon for a heartbroken soul. In this song, Ranger Doug makes it obvious that he's had a few of those.

Hurry sunrise
I've been waitin' all night
Endless hours go past as I lie here
And wait for the light
Hurry sunrise
I've done all I can do
To forget her sweet song
As I wait for the dawn to break through

"Riding on the Rio" is about a lover living down on the border between Texas and Mexico. This is probably about a real-life lover that Ranger Doug had an affair with, then put the story into a song.

So I started for the Rio
Lips are parted on the Rio
She holds all I ever wanted in her hand
Where slowly flows the Rio
Grows my Rose along the Rio
Blooming by the silver Rio Grande

"Virgen Maria (Why Are You Weeping?)" is a song about the young Mary, mother of Jesus, crying with joy over the birth of the baby savior. One verse is in Spanish; the final verse translates that verse into English:

Oh Mary, Mary, why are you weeping?
They're tears of joy upon the birth
Of the promise God is keeping
To bring mankind his peace on earth

"Amber Eyes" was written for Doug's third wife, Dianne, whom he was very much in love with at the time he recorded this album. The later divorce, which was unpleasant and hurtful, has caused him to dislike this song because of the memories it brings.

Though the miles stretch for ever
Like the river I'm flowing back home
And I promise that never will you ever
Be so far from my song
The soft sunrise can't disguise
The love light in your amber eyes
And hoof beats fly as I ride for the dawn

"Night-riding Song" was also recorded on the Rabbit Ears project with Roy Rogers. It is a lullaby song—sung to cattle. Still, it could easily be a lullaby to Ranger Doug's children as well.

Lie still, little dogies, lie still
The moon's rising over the hill
Don't you get restless
You've eaten your fill
Lie still, little dogies, lie still

"Welcome to the West" has a sprightly tune with Woody's fiddling accenting Rich O'Brien's tasteful guitar. Ranger Doug adds some yodeling, reminiscent of Roy Rogers's work. The lyrics have Green as an emcee for the West, offering a "mighty fine and a great big howdy" to those looking toward the setting sun. It could easily be the theme song for a documentary of the West.

When she breaks the gentle twilight
With an eerie coyote's wail
When she soars on wild wings lightly to her nest
When she winks her eye as moonbeams dance
Upon a sleeping trail
That's Mother Nature's way of saying:
Welcome to the West
Wings in flight, moon's delight, a perfect night
Welcome to the West

"Jesse" is the story of a "stove-up" cowboy who couldn't work. He'd worked at the singer's ranch for thirty years—but they hadn't seen him in a dozen years.

> He said the saddest thing to me
> Said "Don't matter where you roam—
> When the time comes to cash 'em in,
> A man ought to die at home."
> And when I brought his supper to the barn,
> Jess was cold and still and I
> Knew that somewhere he was satisfied
> For he just came home to die.

The song takes Robert Frost's poem, "The Hired Hand," and sets it in the West.

The melody of "River of Mystery" is like a winding trail. This is an allegory of Ranger Doug's own dreams—tying them and his life to a river flowing.

> Wild in the wintertime, cold as the snow
> Mild in the sunshine, in summer she flows
> River of mystery, river of dreams
> Flowing like history to futures unseen

"Bells" is an alliterative poem by Edgar Allen Poe. Green's song barely touches this poem, but there is an "echo" of the tragic poet's work in this song. There's also a touch of the Beatle's song, "Do You Want to Know a Secret" in the opening line of each verse. In this song, the singer has given his heart away—totally—and wonders if his lover's heart is as deep and wide as his own.

> Listen (listen!) to the echo of bells
> They call me on to the one who waits
> For me to fly to her side
> I beg of you Echo,
> Is her heart true as mine?
> "She waits for you by the wishing well"
> Rings the reply

"Idaho Moon" paints that state in a rosy, romantic light. Green also seems to see Idaho as a way to get away from the cares and worries of life as Ranger Doug with Riders In The Sky.

Down a trail through a vale I'm hurrying
To where the mountains kiss the sky
At the top I'll stop my worrying
And throw my cares to the Idaho moon on high

"Where the Wild Winds Blow" is an up-tempo song that races forward with several messages. The first is part of Ranger Doug's personality—the desire to be alone—and be left alone—while, at the same time, wanting the public spotlight.

I'm going to ride where the wild winds blow me
I'm going to go where nobody knows me
I'm going to gallop 'cross the plains to a wide-open range
Where no fences grow to enclose me

In real life, Ranger Doug is a worrier and some of the lyrics of this song express his desire to shed that characteristic:

Cast my worries to the wind and watch them scatter
Toss the troubles from my shoulders, they don't matter

This song, painted in the romantic images of the freedom-loving cowboy of the West, seems intensely autobiographical in terms of the inner Douglas Green.

Chapter 36

 ON THE ROAD WITH RIDERS BY BILLY MAXWELL

February 7, 1997: Show number 3,500 was in Tucson at the Temple of Music and Art. We had come from Los Angeles to Tucson. In L.A. Woody, Joey, and I went to Universal Studios Theme Park and played all day and had a good time. Then they did a *Crook and Chase* show. On *Crook*

and Chase they also had a fashion show with Frederick's of Hollywood, and everybody was joking about sharing a dressing room with the models. Turned out the models took all the dressing rooms, and we had to get ready in the hall. From L.A. we drove down to Tucson. Slim's two sisters came to the show. The next day we took Joey to the airport, and then we drove on and stopped at a little feed store restaurant. And the guy in there recognized Riders In The Sky and they signed autographs, and there was no charge when we got ready to leave.

The Riders had been doing well with their performances with symphony dates, and a letter from Alan Burdick, conductor of the Lawton Philharmonic, confirmed this. Commenting on a recent Riders performance with his orchestra, the letter states: "Orchestra arrangements of timeless western classics such as 'Cool Water,' 'Red River Valley' and '(Ghost) Riders in the Sky' had symphonic depth, sophistication and made for a very enjoyable experience for our musicians. As always, the off-beat, campy humor of America's Favorite Cowboys kept the audience in stitches and provided a quick-paced evening. What a pleasure these days to work with true professionals who are friendly, thoroughly prepared, superb musicians."

On September 23 the Riders were in a Nashville studio recording "Wah Hoo," "Song of the Trail," "Autumn on the Trail," "Cimarron Moon," "A Border Romance," and "One More Ride."

"Wah Hoo" was a song the Riders had been singing since their earliest performances but did not record until 1997. It was written by Cliff Friend, the same man who wrote the music to "Lovesick Blues," which was the first hit for Hank Williams. Unfortunately, Friend only had forty cents in his pocket after he wrote that song, so he sold all rights for five hundred dollars.

Friend was born in 1893, one of ten children of a fiddle-playing father. He studied at the Cincinnati Conservatory of Music and in 1929 went to Hollywood to write for Fox Films. In 1936 he wrote "Wah Hoo," based on a common expression of exclamation in the West, and the song was a national hit. It was sung by the Andrews Sisters in the 1944 movie *Moonlight and Cactus.*

"Cimarron Moon," written by Ranger Doug, begins with some clever three-part yodeling.

Wish I could join that cimarron moon
Way up in the sky
And scatter moonbeams 'cross the prairies
From on high
Cimarron moon are you waitin' for me
I'm comin' you see
When I'm ready to roam
Cimarron moon I won't be far away
I'll be there any day
Then I'll be comin' back home

"A Border Romance," written by Ranger Doug, is a story song with a mariachi feel that tells of a couple's early escape for love:

She was a nobleman's daughter
He was a dirt-poor cowhand
On the Mexican border
By the old Rio Grande
How he courted and won her
No one ever knew
But they fled in the night
By the quarter moon's light
When he asked for her hand
They fled from her family
And their hot angry gun
They fled through the desert
The two hunted ones
They fled to the future
That neither could see
But their young love was strong
And it carried them on
To their destiny

The song concludes:

In the hills of Montana
Where the broad rivers flow
In a snug little cabin
Quite a few years ago
My grandma and grandpa
Holding hands by the fire

Told of danger and chance
Of a border romance
And the love that still glows

"The Sidekick Jig," written by Ranger Doug for the character of Sidemeat, is a Celtic fiddle tune with humorous lyrics about a man who struck it rich but then turned off everyone when he danced.

Returning to town it was drinks all around
Yes I was rich for life
I felt like a king and it seemed a good thing
To cast about for a wife
Pie Faced Nelly she rubbed my belly
and so did Slew Foot Sue
and Jenny McDuff she showed me some stuff
I never dreamed you could do
Life was a pearl, on top of the world
I never felt so durned big
But they screamed in shame and cursed my name
When I did the sidekick jig
I lost my chance at real romance
When I did the sidekick jig
Love might have lingered
But it slipped through my fingers
When I did the sidekick jig

"One More Ride," by Bob Nolan, featured a guest performance by Marty Stuart, who had been a frequent guest on *Riders Radio Theater*. Stuart also played a hot mandolin break in the song as the group of talented musicians obviously had fun in the studio.

The following day they recorded "A Hundred and Sixty Acres," "The Ballad of Palindrome," "Trail Dust," and "The Arms of My Love."

"The Arms of My Love" had begun as an instrumental, but Woody Paul later put lyrics to it:

Silver moon sailing high
'Cross the wide prairie sky

Lead me home to the arms of my love
Why did I ever go
Chasing cattle and rainbows
Far away from the arms of my love
Does she wait by the firelight
Cry through the long night
Does she dream of the cowboy
Who rode through her heart
Dusty trail lead me on
And I'll never roam
Nevermore from the arms of my love

During the final two days of sessions the Riders recorded "Cherokee" and two songs from the Sons of the Pioneers: Bob Nolan's "He Walks with the Wild and the Lonely" and "Cowboy Camp Meetin'" by Tim Spencer.

Chapter 37

In 1995 and 1996, Nashville's tourism numbers went up, although attendance at Opryland had begun to decline. By 1994 the theme park was ranked twenty-sixth nationally. The development of downtown Nashville, particularly Second Avenue, was partially responsible. But Opryland had failed to install new rides as fast as other theme parks and had failed to develop a water park—although there was a very successful Wave Pool a few miles down the road from Opryland.

The whiz kids on Wall Street got to the smart guys at Gaylord and demanded that stock prices soar higher and higher each quarter and profits increase exponentially. Opryland was making a profit, but that wasn't good enough for the Wall Street analysts, who demanded even bigger profits.

In February 1997, Gaylord sold TNN and CMT to Westinghouse/ CBS for $1.5 billion to generate cash. In October 1997, Gaylord announced it was going to bulldoze Opryland and build a shopping mall. Some of the genius Gaylord executives announced "there was no economic connection between the marginally successful theme park and the highly successful hotel and convention center next door to it."

After E.W. "Bud" Wendell retired as CEO from Gaylord, the company named Terry London, formerly the chief financial officer, to head the company. During Wendell's tenure, there had never been any discussion of razing Opryland; a few months after he left the executive suite, his successor announced the death of Opryland. Wendell had always seen that the success of the company was dependent on its unique mix—the success of the Opryland Hotel and Convention Center depended on the success of the theme park, the TV networks, and the Grand Ole Opry.

The following years would see the dismantling of a formerly successful entertainment company in order to structure a "hotel and hospitality" company. The results were a disaster for Nashville's tourism industry, the country music industry, and the company itself. It was also a disaster for the talented youngsters who came to Nashville and received their first exposure and training as performers at Opryland. The theme park had been a training ground for talent in Nashville; after this the talented newcomers would have to make the best of it in bars and clubs.

But the smart guys at Gaylord had made their decision, spurred on by the geniuses on Wall Street, so there was no turning back. Those who thought there was too much irrational exuberance in the stock market were considered fools.

In 1998 the Riders' annual Hospital Hospitality House concert netted sixty-seven thousand dollars, a far cry from the amounts they had collected twenty years before when they started this tradition. Their album *A Great Big Western Howdy! from Riders In The Sky* was released, and they appeared on the *Barney & Friends* TV show teaching Barney to yodel. That segment would appear on a Barney videotape that was marketed to children who loved the purple dinosaur.

In February the Riders went into the studio to record a Christmas album. On the first session they recorded "Corn, Water, and Wood," "Let It Snow, Let It Snow, Let It Snow," "The Christmas Yodel," "Sidemeat's Christmas Stew," and "The Prairie Dog's Christmas Ball." Ranger Doug wrote "The Christmas Yodel," "Sidemeat's Christmas Stew," and "The Prairie Dog's Christmas Ball."

"The Christmas Yodel" has a lot of show-off yodeling as well as a chorus where the Ranger holds a note while Slim and Woody sing beneath him.

So ride . . .
Through stormy clouds that gather high on the hills above
Along . . .
To where my open arms will hold the one I love
So ride . . .
Don't step slow, pal you know it won't be long
Along . . .
She waits for the wind that brings
My yodeling Christmas song

"Sidemeat's Christmas Stew" again makes light of their sidekick's cooking abilities. In this song, Sidemeat gives his special recipe for his Christmas signature dish:

You grab some bone, you grab some fat
A leg of this, a leg of that
That's the study point if you must know what's true
Then you toss 'em in a pot
That ain't been washed a lot
Now you're cookin' with the super-lative brew
Toss in a can of coffee grounds if you can get 'em
Why the boys are never gonna know what hit 'em
A motor oil, a splash of wine
Mingle for a taste divine
A base on which to build a fine burgoo

"The Prairie Dog Christmas Ball" is a cute children's song with a bouncy melody:

What happens to the notes from the little bitty fiddle
It's a great big riddle
It's the riddle of the fiddle
What happens to the notes from the little bitty fiddle
When they roll and tumble and roll all around
Down the hole in the ground

Where the prairie dogs go
And what do the prairie dogs do with 'em all
With all of them notes that they gather in the fall
Well they have a big prairie dog Christmas ball
And they roll and tumble and waltz all around
In a great big ball down deep in the ground
Way down in the hole where the prairie dogs go

 ON THE ROAD WITH RIDERS BY BILLY MAXWELL

March 7, 1998: We had just played the Ingersoll Dinner Theater in Des Moines. They were calling for snow, and somebody said maybe we should leave right away instead of the morning. But we already had hotel rooms and they were comped, so we said "No, let's just wait and leave in the morning." Next morning we got up, and it was snowing so hard you couldn't see the building across the street. I mean we got down to the bus, and the snow was already up past the door of the bus. You had to break the snow back off the door.

Joey had to get back to Nashville to work on their album. He was able to get to the airport and got the last plane out before they closed the airport.

We had to go about 250 miles to Bassett, Nebraska, so we leave at six-thirty in the morning. Blizzard conditions. Ranger Doug was driving, and it was only about 250 miles to Bassett, Nebraska, but it took us all day to get there. We drove from six-thirty in the morning till five o'clock that afternoon to go 250 miles. We got to Bassett, and they were playing in a stock sale barn in the ring and the seating was up around the deal. And they had a sign up behind them where they sold cattle and it said "Number of head and average weight." Up on the sign while the Riders were playing it said, "Number of head: 3" and "Total weight: 422 pounds" and "Average weight" was whatever it was. They had the whole deal like they was selling them.

Some little guy who was very wealthy owned the only hotel in town, and he took us there for dinner. We was going to stay but decided to check out and leave that night. Slim had got a new pair of snowshoes for Christmas, but he hadn't been anywhere where there'd been some real snow, so he hadn't had a chance to use 'em. But he had them on the bus. So Slim was sitting in the bus while we were waiting for Woody to come out of the hotel, and Slim said, "This would be a good time for me to try out my snowshoes." So he straps them on his feet and starts off down the road—he knew which way we were going. He said, "I don't know how far I'll walk but ya'll pick me up."

So he walks down the middle of the street where there's snow piled up three feet deep. You could see him in the street lights. In a few minutes Woody comes out and we start to leave, and I said, "Let's pretend that we forgot Slim and just drive on by him." We had the light on in the bus so he could see us both sitting up there in the front. Woody was driving, so I said, "Let's pretend we're really talking hard and just totally ignore him when we drive by him," and we did it.

Now, there's a lot of snow on the ground and he's just stomping around in those snowshoes. So here we come up the road and we got about even with him and he stops like he's waiting for us to open the door, and we don't even look at him. We just slowly drive on by and look in the rearview mirror, and he's standing in the middle of the road with both arms waving over his head. He thinks we've totally forgotten him. It was so funny. When he got on he said, "Gawd, I didn't know what I was going to do. Thought I was going to be stranded in this God-forsaken place."

We arrived in Laramie around 7 A.M. and did a show there. After the show this guy came up and said, "What are you guys doing tomorrow?" And we actually had a day off. He said, "I'm having a little breakfast for my employees, and I'd like to hire you to come over and play for them." So Slim says, "If you've got the dough, we've got the show." So they arrived at a price, and we went over there early the next morning. This guy had just sold a computer software business he'd started to some Japanese guys for like nine million dollars, and this was the end of the road for them employees.

I didn't bring the mercantile in because I didn't think anybody would be buying. But we got over there, and the guy says, "Where's the mercantile?" Then he said, "At least bring the CDs in." So I brought all the CDs in, and he told the employees to go pick them out one, and he wrote me out a check for all of them. That was the easiest mercantile I ever did. It was like 150 people each picking out a CD.

In May, an article by John Brown appeared in *American Cowboy Magazine*. It stated: "These guys could not be further from the glitz and hype that currently grips country music's capital. . . . Matter of fact, these boys aren't even country. They're 'western' . . . [they make a] solemn pledge: 'We will send out no newsletter before it's written' . . . Asked once to say exactly what it took to be a cowboy, Too Slim replied, "You had to be fourteen years old and possibly deranged and live between 1865 and 1882."

The Riders continued recording their Christmas album in May, doing "The Friendly Beasts," "Virgen Maria (Why Are You Weeping?)," "I'll Be Home for Christmas," and "Old-Fashioned Christmas Polka."

"Old-Fashioned Christmas Polka" is written by Joey and shows his polka roots as well as his musical genius. Who'd have thought a Christmas polka could be so appealing?

> Let's have an old-fashioned Christmas polka
> On this happy holiday
> Let's have an old-fashioned Christmas polka
> And throw our cares away
> We'll gather round the old piano
> And sing all the songs we know
> Woody: I'll play fiddle
> Slim: I'll play my bass
> Ranger: My guitar will set the pace
> All: Let it snow, let it snow, here we go

The next day they recorded "The Twelve Days of Cowboy Christmas" and "Just Put a Ribbon in Your Hair." Too Slim wrote "The Twelve Days of Cowboy Christmas" and adapts an old Christmas chestnut for the group:

> On the twelfth day of Christmas the Riders gave to me
> no drummers drummin',
> eleven dogies lowin',
> ten coyotes howlin',
> nine weeds a-tumblin',
> eight spurs a jinglin',
> seven Joeys squeezin,
> six sidekicks singing,
> five golden notes,
> four fiddling kings,
> three bass thumps,
> two manly strums,
> and a yodel-oh-doo-lay-dee-dee

The Riders split with their longtime manager, David Skepner, in 1997. The reason was that the Riders found evidence of major financial malfeasance by Skepner, who'd taken checks for the Riders and deposited them in his own personal account. Although this was a breach of trust, the relationship between Skepner and the Riders had started to unravel in other areas as well.

"The thing had kind of run its course," said Ranger Doug. "It was time for us to find someone else. Maybe time for him, too. It was winding down, and we were going separate ways. When he first took us over, he was still riding pretty high and had quite a bit of influence. That's why a lot of stuff really popped for us in a hurry when he first started managing us. But I think his influence in the industry diminished through the years, and not as much stuff was happening."

"He did a lot of great things for us as a manager," added Slim. "And I'd rather dwell on the positive. He had a good run, and then he did something really stupid."

Management duties were taken over by Paul Lohr, who had been their booking agent since 1985.

They celebrated their twentieth anniversary as Riders In The Sky with a one-hour TV special broadcast during prime time on TNN. In an article in *Billboard* discussing their newest album, *A Great Big Western Howdy! from Riders In The Sky*, Rounder's vice president of national promotion and publicity, Brad Paul, is quoted saying, "We have a saying here coined by their new manager, Paul Lohr, that everybody is a Riders fan—they just don't know it yet." The article adds that "Rounder is putting new comedic bits in between cuts on the September edition of their 'Frontiers of Country' sampler promo discs it mails to country radio." And Brad Paul notes, "We're showing what these guys have accomplished in twenty years by not playing the latest flavor-of-the-month country music but by staying true to their western music roots."

More national press came from an article in *Country Music Weekly* by Larry Holden, who notes, "The Riders are on a constant crusade to preserve western music. All the Riders live near Nashville. But they aren't really cowboys." Ranger Doug is quoted saying, "We live and breathe the western lifestyle in our hearts and heads, but none of us have any horses or cattle. And we

don't go out and do branding in the fall. I do, however, think Too
Slim wears his chaps around the house. He may even sleep in those
things."

Too Slim added, "We'd love to do a Riders In The Sky movie.
It would pay homage to the B-western, while including our gentle
brand of comedy. It would be a fine, exciting, singing western."

Chapter 38

The Riders would feature Joey and Woody on their next recordings. The songs delve into their jazz roots and showcase the musical virtuosity of the Riders. On their first day of recording they
did "Texas Sand," "Dizzy Fingers," "Clarinet Polka," a medley
that comprised "Annie Laurie," "Scotland the Brave," and "Haste
to the Wedding," and "Jesusita En Chihuahua." The next day they
recorded "We're Burning Moonlight," "Never Go to Church on
Sunday," "Katherine's Waltz," "You Stole My Wife, You Horse
Thief," and "I'm an Old Cowhand."

Written by Joey, "We're Burning Moonlight" features him singing lead and shows him to have a nice, smooth voice.

> I got my fiddle, got my bow
> Got my squeeze box set to go
> Let's put on a cowboy show
> We're burnin' moonlight
> A desert stage is all we need
> A cactus and some tumbleweed
> A swingin' swayin' trusty steed
> We're burnin' moonlight
> At the end of every day
> Folks come round to hear us play
> Hot licks keep the blues away
> Fiddles, keys, and moonlight

On "Never Go to Church on Sunday," written by Woody, the
song has a "Turkey in the Straw" type of fiddle and melody as he
sings,

Well I asked my ole grandpappy
Pap, how do you stay so happy
He said, never go to school and never get a job
And never go to church on Sunday
Dip a little snuff and play a little fiddle
And never go to church on Sunday
So if you wanna be happy
Like me an' my ole grandpappy
Never take a bath and never get a job
And never go to church on Sunday

"I'm an Old Cowhand" was written by Johnny Mercer, who began his songwriting career as a Tin Pan Alley songwriter in New York. He moved to Hollywood in 1935 as a songwriter and singer after serving as a big-band vocalist with the Paul Whiteman Orchestra. On a trip from California to Georgia by car to visit relatives, Mercer and his wife drove through Texas, where cowboys dressed in hats and boots with spurs drove cars; this inspired Mercer to write "I'm an Old Cowhand." The song was first sung by Bing Crosby in the 1936 movie *Rhythm on the Range*. In 1941 Gene Autry performed this song for his movie *Back in the Saddle*, and Roy Rogers did it in 1943 in his movie *King of the Cowboys*. Johnny Mercer also wrote "On the Atchison, Topeka, and the Santa Fe," "Lazybones," "In the Cool, Cool, Cool of the Evening," "Moon River," and "Days of Wine and Roses." He was one of the founders of Capitol Records.

Their third day of recording saw them do the jazz classic, "How High the Moon," which had been a pop hit for Les Paul and Mary Ford in 1950, and "Don't Sweetheart Me."

The Walt Disney studio was working on *Toy Story 2*, a follow-up to their successful animated film, *Toy Story*. They were tossing around ideas about Woody, the wooden "dummy" who was a singing-cowboy star, being stolen by a toy collector. The creators wanted to make the toy "valuable," so they researched the 1950s black-and-white cowboy kiddie TV shows and made the doll and packaging as accurate as possible. They wanted an authentic sounding theme song for "Woody's Roundup," and Ash Brannon, a co-director on the project, had seen Riders In The Sky some years before. He suggested the group, and the creative team went out and bought a Riders In The Sky album. When they played it, they knew that the Riders would be perfect for the project.

On August 24, director John Lasseter walked into the O'Henry Studio in Burbank, and there were the Riders dressed in their stage costumes—full cowboy regalia. During the introductions, Woody Paul thanked Lasseter for naming the lead character after him. In response to comments on their clothing, the Riders told Lasseter that the outfits "make us sound better." Lasseter tried on Slim's furry chaps—and so did Randy Newman, the composer of the score.

Soon after this session, Randy Newman and Lasseter went into the studio with an orchestra and finished the soundtrack. Lasseter and Executive Music Producer Chris Montan then met with Jay Landers, the senior vice president of A&R (Artists and Repertoire) for Disney Records, and Landers had an idea to do an entire album based on characters in the *Toy Story 2* movie and soundtrack. Landers then contacted the Riders about the project, and they readily agreed. They would write some more songs for the album, use some songs they'd done in the past, add "Woody's Roundup," and, at Landers' suggestion, the old country song "Act Naturally," which had been recorded by Buck Owens and the Beatles.

In November the Riders went into the studio and recorded "Woody's Roundup," "Jessie, the Yodeling Cowgirl," "How Does She Yodel?" "The Ballad of Bullseye," and "Act Naturally." The next day they recorded "'One, Two, Three,' Said the Prospector," "You've Got a Friend in Me," "The Prospector Polka," "My Favorite Toys," and "Two Roads." On their final day of recording they did "Home on the Range" and "Hey, Howdy, Hey."

On November 9 the *Toy Story 2* movie soundtrack was released, and on November 24—Thanksgiving—the movie opened in theaters nationwide. It was successful right from the start—the opening gross of $80.8 million was the biggest opening in the history of Walt Disney Pictures and Pixar Animation Studio. The Riders were in Hollywood to take part in the opening. They also shot a video that had some animated clips as well as a live performance.

That Christmas season their album *Christmas: The Cowboy Way* was released.

Chapter 39

The highlight of the Riders' professional performing career came on Friday, August 11, and Saturday, August 12, 2000, when they performed at the Hollywood Bowl. On the Friday evening there were thirteen thousand in the audience; on Saturday evening there were seventeen thousand. The Riders performed with the Hollywood Bowl Orchestra, "the finest musicians we've ever played with," said Ranger Doug.

"I'm not really sure how that came about, but it was from the Toy Story thing," continued Green. "Disney wrote a beautiful chart of a medley we'd put together. It was a beautiful score. It just worked. It was a big night of Americana—they had folk songs, a lot of different things. But we did thirty to forty-five minutes. The announcer for the Lone Ranger came out—'Out of the west with a cloud of dust and the hearty Hi Ho Silver, the Lone Ranger!' They got him for that. Tommy Smothers came to the show. Jackie Autry came to the show. To me, that's the highlight of anything we've ever done. It was just so wonderful."

"It was a great thrill," added Slim. "I remember when I was a little kid we had records 'Live at the Hollywood Bowl.' That was like the classiest thing you could do. And I got to play there! Even though my parents are not living, I felt like they were there emotionally. I could look up and say, 'I'll bet my folks are tuned in tonight!'"

On August 29, *Woody's Roundup Featuring Riders In The Sky* was released on Walt Disney Records. A full-scale marketing campaign for the Riders was under way by the Disney folks. An article in *Billboard* by Deborah Evans Price noted that "consumer ads, ads on the nationally syndicated Radio Disney" along with tie-ins with "Johnson & Johnson, which will be selling shampoo based on the Woody and Buzz Lightyear characters" would be part of the campaign. The song "Act Naturally" was on a cassette single in the shampoo packaging, and the video of the Riders performing a medley of their *Toy Story 2* songs would be "aired in Disney theme parks, in Disney stores, on United Airlines, on the Disney web site and at other retail outlets."

On October 9, the *Toy Story 2* video and DVD were released to video outlets. At the end of the movie was a video clip of the Riders performing a medley of five songs from their *Woody's Roundup* album. This video clip was shown to 41 million households through airings on CMT and the Disney Channel and played on the big screen in 600 Disney stores, Target stores, and other retail outlets. The Riders were getting the biggest and widest exposure of their career. As Ranger Doug observed at the time, "We vacillate between being living legends and the hot new thing."

By this point, *Toy Story 2* was the second-highest-grossing animated film of all time, bringing in $245 million at the box office.

The boys had really hit the big time.

The success of the Riders in *Toy Story 2* led to their recording "The Big High Wire Hop," an instrumental for an animated cartoon that would be shown before the *Monsters, Inc.* feature movie. In April the Riders had recorded the song, which was composed by all of the Riders in a collaborative effort. "We'd actually been playing that song when we warmed up at sound checks," said Ranger Doug.

Taking advantage of the Rider's success on Disney, Rounder re-released their *Saddle Pals* album.

 ON THE ROAD WITH RIDERS BY BILLY MAXWELL

January 22, 2001: We were coming from Las Vegas to Reno, and we got to a place called Hawthorne, Nevada, which is an old military base. It's an ammunition plant, and they've got all these bunkers out in the desert—it's really a remote, desolate place. Around midnight, the bus just quits. Everything goes out—lights, everything—so we pulled off the side of the road and finally got a wrecker to come from Fallon, which is about seventy miles away. The law says you can't ride in a towed vehicle, but we had five people in the bus and there's no way five people can fit in the wrecker. So the plan was for everybody to stay quiet in the bus and don't let this guy pulling us know there's anybody in here. Slim was driving, and he did the talking. He never told the guy with the wrecker that there was anybody else with him—but the guy never asked either. The rest of us just stayed in the bus and got towed for seventy miles. When we got to Fallon it was three or four in the morning, and a repair guy opened the chain-link fence around his shop and we put the bus inside there. 'Course we were all still in it.

Next morning we wake up and we're all locked inside a chain-link fence. They couldn't fix the bus right then, so we had to rent a vehicle in Fallon and go on to Reno. The next day Woody and I went back to pick up the bus and drive to Denver. The other guys all flew home because there were three days off. Woody and I were going to pick them up in Denver and drive to a show in northern Colorado. When we got back to Fallon, they were still working on the bus—they weren't quite finished with it. The bus was parked inside the shop, and all the doors were open; they were working on it inside and out. The guy at the repair shop had a couple of dogs.

Finally they get the bus fixed, and Woody goes in and pays. We were looking for a place to have lunch, and this guy told us about this really good Mexican restaurant in Lovelock, Nevada, which was about sixty or seventy miles away, and we would have to go through it. So we drive up there and find the Mexican restaurant. But you can't park that bus just anywhere, so we pulled in a big truck stop beside the restaurant. We locked up the bus and walked over to the Mexican restaurant, but when we got there we saw a sign on the door, "Closed for vacation, be back Monday" or something like that. So we go back to the bus and, just as Woody unlocks the door to the bus, here comes this mechanic's dog down the steps—whoosh!—right by us. That dog had gotten in at that mechanic's shop and gone in the back and gone to sleep. Anyway, the dog doesn't recognize either one of us, and he doesn't recognize his surroundings. He's acting like something wild, and we couldn't catch him. He was just running through that truck stop parking lot.

So Woody found a pay a phone, called back to the repair shop, and told the guy what had happened. The guy says, "I've got some friends up there, and I'll get them to check on him." Six months later, Woody told me he'd talked to the guy and said he'd gotten the dog back. We'd driven an hour or hour and a half with that dog.

On Wednesday evening, February 21, 2001, in Los Angeles, the Grammy Awards were held at the Staples Center in Los Angeles. The headlines that dominated the Grammy news concerned Eminem, the rap performer who'd said on record that he didn't care about Grammys. He was known for his strident anti-gay remarks—but on the telecast agreed to perform with the openly gay Elton John.

"We flew out the day before and checked in the big fancy hotel," said Ranger Doug. "Ann Marie Flores and I were getting serious at that time, so she came with me and I spent most of my time with her. She's loved music all her life, and to be at the Grammys was really huge for her. We went to that party the night before, and I remember seeing Les Paul and they did some kind of tribute to him."

The Riders had been nominated for two Grammys: the first one announced was their nomination in the Country category for "Best Country Vocal Performance." The Riders sat and watched Asleep at the Wheel collect that award. But in the "Musical Album for Children" category the presenter in the pre-telecast portion of the show called the Riders to the stage to award them a Grammy for their *Woody's Roundup Featuring Riders In The Sky* album. To put it mildly, the Riders were ecstatic.

"It was an explosive release of emotion," said Slim. "My daughter said, 'I saw sparks flying out of your ears.'"

Accepting the award, Ranger Doug told the audience, "As Gene Autry often said, 'I don't think I deserve this award, but I've got tendinitis and I don't feel like I deserve that either.'"

Backstage, Too Slim almost knocked over Paul Simon on the way to get the award. "I didn't even see him," said Slim. "Woody told me, 'Hey, man, you just knocked over Paul Simon!'—and I love Paul Simon. I would never knock him over!"

After the awards show, the Riders attended the big party where Doug saw "this little Django style group, a five-piece, three guitars, fiddle, and bass line-up. They had a dozen groups playing at this party, and this group was the Johnny Crawford Quintet. It was Johnny Crawford, the former child star on *The Rifleman*. He's a fifty-five to sixty-year-old man now. I just sat and watched those guys, and then they realized who I was.

"We saw a lot of people backstage," noted Green. "We saw Tony Bennett and Les Paul and a lot of extremely tacky dresses. I talked with Johnny Crawford for a while. Then we went Latin dancing, which I can't do, but Ann Marie is very forgiving."

Too Slim took his wife, Bert; daughters, Lily and Alice; and son, George, to the party after the awards show. "After Bert and Lily went upstairs," said Slim, "my young daughter Alice and I went back to the party and we danced to Jack Mack and the Heart Attack."

The Riders appeared on the Grand Ole Opry on Friday and Saturday evenings, September 7 and 8; on September 9 they performed in Brentwood, a suburb of Nashville, at the Eddy Arnold Amphitheater, an outdoor park, on a Sunday evening. The Riders started their show with "Texas Plains," then introduced the band members before Ranger Doug sang "How Does He Yodel." This was followed by a jazzy version of "Wah Hoo," where Slim played his face. "Cool Water" came next, then they sang "Happy Birthday" to an audience member before Woody Paul played a jazzy fiddle and sang "Buffalo Gals."

Ranger Doug sang "Molly Darling," an old Eddy Arnold hit, in honor of playing the Eddy Arnold Amphitheater. The Riders then did their "Woody's Round-Up Medley," which consists of excerpts from the songs "Woody's Roundup," "Jessie, the Yodeling Cowgirl," "Bullseye," "Act Naturally," "Prospector Polka," "To Infinity and Beyond," and finally "You've Got a Friend in Me."

The Riders then gathered all the children in the audience on stage as Slim led them in singing "I'm Gonna Leave Old Texas Now." Slim added verses to give a pitch for the mercantile, and the kids dutifully sang along. This was followed by Joey doing "Burning Moonlight," the group singing "Rawhide," and then Joey doing "Hoop De Doo," with some audience participation clapping. Ranger Doug then sang a ballad in Spanish, followed by the group doing "Sioux City Sue." Woody Paul got his rope and did some rope tricks, accompanied by Joey on the accordion. Too Slim sang "The Trail Tip Song," the group did their instrumental from *Monsters Inc.*, "Big High Wire Hop," and the Riders finished with "Happy Trails."

The audience stood and clapped until the Riders came back and did an encore performance of "Turkey in the Straw." The show lasted about an hour.

On September 11, 2001, the Riders were home when they received the news about the twin Trade Center towers in New York "and were in shock like the rest of the nation," said Slim.

The question immediately arose: Should the upcoming dates be canceled? On September 14, the Riders were scheduled to play at Playhouse Square in Cleveland, Ohio; the next night they were scheduled for the Woodstock Opera House in Woodstock, Illinois; and the night after that they were booked in Lake Delton, Wisconsin, for the Wisconsin Opry. Their schedule showed them appearing on September 20 in Dawson, Minnesota; on September 21 in Fergus Falls, Minnesota; on September 22 in Fish Creek, Wisconsin; and the following night in Hartford, Wisconsin.

"At first, we thought we should cancel," said Ranger Doug. "But then the concert promoter in Cleveland called and said our performance would be a good way to show that 'life still goes on' and that we were needed. It turned out that he was right. We added some patriotic numbers—we began those shows with 'The Star-Spangled Banner' but mostly did our regular shows."

On September 28 the Riders recorded "There's a Star-Spangled Banner Waving Somewhere," which had been a major hit in World War II for Elton Britt and which they had performed whenever they played on Memorial Day. That song was part of a compilation album put together by Steve Popovich in Cleveland to raise funds for the victims of September 11.

Ironically, the Riders' former manager, David Skepner, died on the evening of September 11; he had a massive heart attack while gassing up his car. At a special memorial service held several months later, the Riders—Ranger Doug, Too Slim, and Joey—performed "This Ain't the Same Old Range." Woody wasn't there—it didn't pay.

Chapter 40

In November 2002 the Riders celebrated their twenty-fifth anniversary, so they wanted to record a double CD of their best, most enduring songs as well as some new ones for this milestone. On October 29, 2001, they began recording for this project, doing "Here Comes the Santa Fe," "Way Out There," "Woody's Roundup," and "How Does He Yodel." The next day they did "Texas Plains," "Cool Water," "That's How the Yodel Was Born," "Blue Bonnet Lady," and "Ride, Cowboy, Ride."

On Halloween, the Riders recorded "Lonely Yukon Stars," "The Line Rider," "Ringo," "Reincarnation," "Tumbling Tumbleweeds," and "The Arms of My Love."

On November 15 the Riders returned to the studio and did "Thomas Timberwolf," "Riders in the Sky," "My Oklahoma," and

"La Malaguena." The next day they recorded "Sidekick Heaven," "Phantom of the Chuckwagon," "Sundown in Santa Fe," and "Compadres in the Old Sierra Madres."

The Riders also decided to do an album of train songs, based on the Tweetsie Railroad park, a western-theme park in Blowing Rock, North Carolina, where they had appeared a number of times. "The Tweetsie Railroad album was my idea," said Slim. "We had an association with Tweetsie going back to our earliest years. We loved Tweetsie Railroad—had taken our kids there. And last year as we were going up to do our show there I thought, 'We should do an album of train songs and sell it at Tweetsie Railroad.' We talked to the guy who's the head of Tweetsie Railroad, and he said, 'I could get behind this.' And so we made some phone calls. And Joey produced the album, where we had fun doing trains songs in Riders In The Sky style. We did it so that people would have a CD to pop into their car player on their way out of Tweetsie railroad and relive the great memories they had there with their kids."

On January 29, 2002, they recorded "Railroad Corral" and "The Great Northern."

"Great Northern," written by Ranger Doug, contains plenty of yodeling.

> All aboard and ride that northern railway
> Grab a seat and settle down to ride
> To that land beyond where the sun has gone
> Behind the purple hills to hide
> Across the rolling plains of old Montana
> To the wide Pacific sea
> Let's ride that northern railroad line
> Come on it waits for you and me

The next day they recorded "Tweetsie Railroad Line," "Wabash Cannonball," and "Orange Blossom Special." Ranger Doug also wrote "Tweetsie Railroad Line."

> Way up in the Carolina hills
> Whistle echoing across the rocks and rills
> Calls me to a better place and time
> And you get there on the Tweetsie Railroad line

You're in the heart of the wild wild west
Woo-woo . . . wooo . . . woo-woo . . .
It's the place I love the best
Leave your worries and your problems far behind
All aboard, let's ride that Tweetsie Railroad line

The following day they recorded "New River Train," "Rock Island Line," and "I've Been Working on the Railroad." Their fourth consecutive day of recording consisted of them recording "Casey Jones," "Tweetsie Junction," and "Ghost Train."

"Tweetsie Junction" was written by Joey and tells a brief history of the famous railroad engine:

Way up in the Carolinas
Where the mountains meet the sky
Big and shiny in the sunlight
Number twelve comes rolling by
Built back in the 1860s
Built to tough the rough terrain
Hear her happy whistle echo
That's how Tweetsie got her name

"Ghost Train," written by Too Slim, sounds like it could have come from a Boris Karloff movie:

The train slides into the station at midnight
Just a couple of shadowy shapes a-waitin' there
A conductor beckons a bony finger
Says "All aboard if you dare"
Ride the ghost train
Igor takes your suitcase
And Dracula shows you to your seat
Right between Frankenstein and the Wolfman
Here's a couple of my friends I'd like you to meet
On the ghost train
On the ghost train
Goblins ghosts and ghouls
All ridin' next to you
On the ghost train

Because of the success of *Toy Story 2*, the Riders were asked about doing an album based on the characters of the *Monsters Inc.* movie. On April 18 they recorded "I Only Have Eye for You," "The Perfect Roar," and "Under the Bed."

On April 22 they recorded "Monster Inc. March," "Doo-Wah Diddy (Mike's Song)," "Lullaby for Boo," "Monster's A-B-Cs," "If I Didn't Have You (vocal version)," "If I Didn't Have You (instrumental version)," "It's Our Job," "Paperwork (Roz's Song)," and "The Monsters' Jubilee."

Musically, the *Scream Factory Favorites* album is their most diverse album by far. If anyone had doubts about the musical talents and abilities of Riders In The Sky, those doubts would be put to rest after listening to this album.

The album begins with "If I Didn't Have You," a song written by Randy Newman where each of the four Riders takes a verse, punctuated by some repartee. "Doo-Wah Diddy Diddy," the 1963 hit by Manfred Mann, written by Jeff Barry and Ellie Greenwich, follows with Too Slim singing lead. The lyrics are altered, and the production sounds like it came right out of 1960s pop radio.

"I Only Have Eye for You," written by Ranger Doug, is a Dixieland-sounding song that adds a semi-yodel over a banjo-playing rhythm and cornet wailing. "Monster Inc. March," written by Too Slim, sounds like a marching song written for an old black-and-white movie. "Monster's ABCs," also written by Too Slim, is a song that has the Riders sounding like a doo-wop group off a 1950s Philadelphia street. If you didn't know better, you'd expect to find this in a K-Tel package of "Greatest Hits of the '50s."

"Lullaby for Boo," written by Woody Paul and Too Slim, with vocals by Sonya Isaacs, is a sensitive lullaby ballad, just lush enough to make a listener drowsy. "It's Our Job," written by Joey Miskulin, is a campy, jazzy song with cute lyrics from a monster's perspective that announce that scaring people is "our job." "Paperwork (Roz's Song)" is written by Ranger Doug and has a Carribean feel with Ranger Doug singing with a pinched throat through his nose. The message is the bane of all those who work in an office: The paperwork must get done!

"Monsters' Jubilee" is written by Woody Paul and Ranger Doug and sounds like a square dance fiddle number, complete with Woody Paul calling the steps. "Under the Bed," written by

Ranger Doug, features a Boris Karloff–sounding track with lyrics about monsters lurking under the furniture where you sleep. "Perfect Roar," written by Woody Paul and Joshua Archibalt-Sieffer, has a march-like tempo with a melody that goes up a staircase and then down again.

The *Scream Factory Favorites* album is an absolutely astounding work, a true surprise to all except the most dedicated Riders In The Sky fans. The group proves they can write lyrics in the voice of movie characters—monsters, no less!—and musically can go way beyond the western music they'd cut their teeth on. At the same time, this album serves as a reminder that the music of the singing cowboys was written by guys writing songs for the movies. The songs were mostly written on demand—the songwriter was given a situation or scene and had to write a song to fit—and that's exactly what the Riders did on this album. Still, having said all that, *Scream Factory Favorites* is a long, long way from the Sons of the Pioneers doing "Cool Water" and "Tumbling Tumbleweeds."

By 2000, most of the tourist-related businesses near Opryland reported revenue drops of about a third, while most of the tourist attractions near Music Row had closed down. But the brilliant minds had not finished wreaking havoc in their pursuit of upward spiraling profits and stock prices.

In 1999 most of the televised entertainment shows based in Nashville went off the air; in 2000 the New York–based owners of TNN announced that it would no longer be The Nashville Network; from thence forward it would be The National Network. The brilliant minds in television concluded that running professional wrestling and reruns of shows like *Starsky and Hutch* was a sound investment.

In January 2001, Viacom severed most of TNN's ties with Nashville; in October it cut the last thread when it eliminated local sports and outdoor programming.

Meanwhile, across the state in Pigeon Forge, Tennessee, there was a reality check for those who said there was no market for a theme park: Dollywood was pulling in record numbers, and the small town was developing venues for live entertainment as tourists flocked to the area.

By 2002 many Nashville residents were sick of Gaylord and just wished it would go away.

This had a major effect on the careers of those trying to follow in the boot steps of Riders In The Sky. No longer would they have regular and ongoing access to a national audience. Gone were shows such as *Nashville Now* and *Crook and Chase*. CMT remained—but it showed videos, then gradually developed some other locally based shows.

But the geniuses of television programming are slaves to the advertising agencies, who demand a young demographic—18 to 34. Not satisfied to gather an older audience—even in huge numbers—the ad agencies can only figure out how to sell to young demographics, and so they demand TV shows that attract these young people or else they won't buy advertising. It makes you wonder if those guys are all as brilliant as they claim to be.

By this time the Riders had firmly established themselves as a major entertainment act; the year 2001 would be their best so far financially. They were heard in the movies, had won a Grammy, and were touring extensively. Still, they did not have TNN shows to give them a national audience and keep them in front of the eyes of the public.

Chapter 41

In the fall of 2002, *Singing in the Saddle: The History of the Singing Cowboy* by Douglas B. Green was published by the Vanderbilt University Press and the Country Music Foundation. This scholarly work will be the standard in its field for years to come and shows a side of Ranger Doug the public hadn't seen in many, many years: the historian and scholar.

The seeds for the book were planted before Riders In The Sky was formed. "When I was working for the Country Music Foundation I did interviews with these old-time cowboys and fell in love with the music back then," said Green. "There are books on some of these guys, but so many are full of errors and bad press releases endlessly repeated. It just seemed like the film community didn't take the singing cowboy too seriously; they thought it was all too silly, I suppose. Perhaps fantastic, dopey, or juvenile. That community has always looked down on the singing cowboys as a sub-genre. And the music community has always thought it was all much too slick, too Hollywood and duded up. Lomax and those people thought they were not the authentic cowboys of the plains. The whole field had really kind of fallen into a crack. And the whole style at the time I was doing those interviews—the mid-70s—had fallen into a crack. That was part of the impetus for starting the band. So I wrote this long piece for the *Journal of Country Music*, which was probably the first real academic look at the phenomenon. When Bill Malone and Judith McCullough put out their book, *Stars of Country Music*, I wrote a chapter on Gene Autry. So I was interested in the West and western singers and western movies. I'd been going to some of those film festivals, and the books that were coming out of there were gee-whiz fan books. The authors of those books were trying to get information together, but there was no substance to the causation of why this all happened. So it seemed to me that somebody ought to write something serious about it, and I did.

"The original piece was a fifty-six-page article in the *Journal of Country Music*," continued Green. "I had a couple of university presses interested in it at the time, but they wanted a completed manuscript and that was around the time I left the foundation and started Riders and didn't have the time to sit down and write that kind of a book. So I just put it on the shelf. I never stopped collecting articles—when I'd see something I'd clip it, and I collected a lot of pictures. Whenever I went somewhere and found an old picture, I'd just save it for the files. A new book would come out, and I'd always pick it up and read it—as long as it was about western films or cowboy singers. So that was the genesis of it.

"But I think the biggest impetus of all was the invention of the laptop computer and the fact that there is a lot of time on the road. When we played places like Cactus Pete's or the Nugget in Reno, we'd do two weeks at a time, so I had a lot of time to myself. And number three was that I was pretty distressed at things going on in my personal life and was waking up early. So I took that old article and started expanding and expanding and expanding. I put out a couple of feelers. The Country Music Foundation and Vanderbilt took about two weeks to respond that 'Yes, we'd love to do it.'"

Green admits that the book "was a long and laborious process. The publisher was very, very slow in getting things back to me for corrections. And given my erratic schedule, I must admit that I couldn't spend four or five hours a day working on it. So sometimes I was slow in getting things back to them. It really took a long, long time."

Noted rhythm guitarist John Parrott once told Ranger Doug, "You're the most visible rhythm guitarist in the country." That made Green reevaluate his guitar playing, and he worked harder at his rhythm playing. "I had several jazz friends who taught me a lot—David Sebring and Ron Hillis—when I had just gotten to Nashville," said Green. "I quickly gravitated to old swing music when I was surrounded by players who knew it. At Michigan, where I went to college, there was a lot of interest in old-time folk music, but there wasn't much interest in jazz. The jazz guitar players there seemed ancient—just old guys—and I couldn't relate to them at all then. But in Nashville I really discovered the charms of old swing music and discovered that it was learnable, and a thirteenth chord wasn't impossible or pretentious, it was just a good chord in the right spot.

"I fell in love with western swing," he continued. "I used to go see Asleep at the Wheel every time they came to town. Also, being around Bob Pinson, who's the western swing expert of all time, I came to appreciate it even more. I guess not being an instrumentalist and thinking with a songwriter's hat on, I got into western music because the lyrics are so beautiful. What Bob Nolan and Tim Spencer were doing with their songs was marvelous to me. The fact that people could take such a poetic approach and not sound pretentious or fake was wonderful. The music still had a folk and real feel, but it was just so beautiful. So I veered off from western swing into the Sons of the Pioneers, because of the vision they presented, which was better than country songs about drinking beer and feeling sorry for yourself."

When he's home in Nashville on a Monday night, Ranger Doug goes down to the Station Inn and plays rhythm guitar with a western swing group, The Time Jumpers. "The Time Jumpers are all friends of mine. I went down to the Station Inn to see them and they invited me on stage and I sang a song or two," said Green. "That happened a time or two. Johnny Cox especially but also Hoot Hester said, 'Why don't you sit in and play guitar.' They just kept saying it and saying it, but I said, 'This is your thing and I don't want to push myself on it.' I didn't want to shove my way in. But they kept asking, so I started bringing my guitar and sitting in with them and singing maybe one song. I wasn't there to be their vocalist—they have plenty of vocalists. And I sing plenty somewhere else. It was a great place for me to just work on guitar, work on new positions. You play a song like "The Kind of Love I Can't Forget" which is just G and D, but you can play those chords all up and down the neck. And it really gave me a great chance to work on that stuff. And it's great western swing.

"I'm still learning new chords, and it's still the same old mechanics I used when I was nineteen of going from this one to this one and I'll play that for an hour," he added. "Pretty soon your fingers get used to it. We play a lot—we do 180 to 200 shows a year—and I don't play every song the same way every night. I'm always finding a new way to jump to this or that. Joey is so musical—he just hears these chords, and he'll give me lots of ideas.

"I practice in the bus some, and we practice a lot at sound checks. Before the show there's usually fifteen to twenty minutes or maybe half an hour that we're just sitting there, dressed, with not a lot to do. And Slim and I will always go to Joey and say, 'Let's play a jazz tune like 'Lullaby of Birdland' or 'Avalon' or 'Tangerine' or some of the other tunes—like 'Polka Dots and Moonbeams' or 'Stomping at the Savoy.' Standards with really great chords.

"I've really tried to do something that I don't think has been done in western music," observed Green. "And that's to bring that Freddie Green pulse—he's the guy who played rhythm guitar for Count Basie who's just my total hero in terms of guitar playing—to western music. There's a lot of people who play a lot of chords. Karl Farr played fantastic chords, but his were more inspired off the Django Rhinehart mold of melody and half chords. But I'm all in the middle strings—the A and D strings—and bringing that certain mid-range sound to it. Which is exactly what Freddie Green did with Count Basie. If you listen to our later albums—the Tweetsie album or the Monsters album or the Woody's Round-Up album—you can hear the guitar making a different kind of statement, and it's giving a different kind of pulse than anyone else has done. We always go out and see all these other groups out there and there's all these people who play good guitar, but they're still playing the big six note chords and that's not what I do.

"Most of the time I'm just playing two or three notes, maybe four. That's all you need—you just need the leading tones in the right range because if you get too high you're in the fiddle range and if you get too low you're fighting the bass. So I'm just providing the middle sonic range and the pulse, which is an important part.

"I don't think in terms of this is the name and number and the separation of fifths—I just play what sounds good and the form that I think will work. It's much more visceral. I don't play tons of chords—there's a lot of guys out there who play a million chords around me. I play six or eight really good ones a night, just in different locations, and again that's very much a Freddie Green thing. I owe that to him—he wasn't a genius as far as doing incredible chord solos like Joe Pass or people like that. He was a genius at keeping the beat of the band and playing the right notes.

"Freddie Green played forty-three years with Count Basie and never took a solo," noted Ranger Doug. "You really start to hear Freddie come out in the fifties. If you get that *April in Paris* album, every time you hear a piano solo, that guitar is just so clear and so right. And it's nothing fancy, it's just the perfect pulse of the group."

Along the way, Douglas Green developed a love for Stromberg guitars. "When I started Riders I had a really nice 1939 Gibson L-5 Cutaway and a Martin flattop that had been refinished in sunburst," said Green. "My son, James, is playing that one now. The L-5 got stolen, unfortunately. I had another L-5 as a backup, and I used that for awhile. Jim Triggs first made me a Gibson, when he worked at Gibson, to replace the one that had been stolen, and then he made me a beautiful Triggs guitar. I played that for a number of years—played that up until the Stromberg.

"I didn't get my first Stromberg until pretty late," continued Green. "I had a chance to get one when I worked for Gruhn's for eight hundred dollars and then there was one down there when we were with Riders for eight thousand dollars. But I just couldn't afford it at the time—either one. Then about six years ago George

Gruhn called and said, 'I've got two Strombergs down here, if you're interested.' By the time I got down there the Master 400 was sold but the Deluxe was still there. I played it and said, 'This is the best guitar I've ever played. I've got to have this.' So I traded a whole lot of stuff. That had to be in the middle-nineties. Since then the Strombergs have become my passion.

"Stromberg died in '54," continued Ranger Doug. "The guitars are valuable because they're so rare. There aren't that many people playing the style the Stromberg excels at. So they're just incredibly rare—he only made about 336, I think. And of those, the really good ones—actually, they're all good—but they were a good guitar in the thirties and a great guitar in the forties. For that big-band style—if you want to sound like Freddie Green or any of those guys that played in the top swing bands—that's the only guitar that'll give you that sound. Epiphones are good, some Gibsons are really good, but the Stromberg just has that cutting quality that rises above an entire orchestra. Just listen to any Count Basie recording and you'll hear it."

Chapter 42

"Ever since practically day one with the Riders," said Woody, "I've felt that we were successful. To me, those things that happened—like the TV shows and *Riders Radio Theater* and the Grammy—are just icing on the cake. I always knew that we could entertain and we were good musically and had fun on stage. I've always been very positive and felt successful from the first day with the group."

Talking about their performances, Woody states, "A whole lot of our material is developed on stage—the seed will be thrown and then it germinates until you get really sick of it, so you get something else. One of the bad things about the kinds of shows we do most of the time—they're only an hour or an hour and ten minutes long—so you try to do your most tried and true material even though it's not always the best. I used to always, between every couple of songs, try to come up with something—stupid or off the wall—to get Slim or Doug going on it so they could create something."

That's what led Woody to learn some rope tricks. "We needed a rope on stage, and I worked real hard learning to do it," said Woody. "I wouldn't have had to work so hard if I'd just gotten somebody who knew what they were doing to show me. Like playing the fiddle or anything else. I never had a teacher—always been teaching myself, whatever it was.

"I practiced a lot when I started, but then it developed into a comedy routine better than a roping routine," continued Woody. "What I do with that rope is very hard because I don't use a hoop. I've had a few rope artists say, 'How in the hell do you swing this thing anyway?' 'Cause they have a heavy metal honda on their rope. But I can't spin those kinds of ropes at all. So what I do is really my own style. I bought a Will Rogers 'How to' book, and I'd practice in a hotel room with a heavy honda on the rope and I would hit myself in the nuts with that damn thing, and it was bad. Real bad. I'm serious. You try to jump through that rope with a metal honda and you don't make it, you're gone."

In terms of songwriting, Woody notes that "I kind of lost a lot of motivational energy writing songs after the *New Trails* album. It had some really good potential radio air play cuts on it, but it never got played." Woody has always wanted a hit song on country radio, and that's one dream the Riders haven't fulfilled. When their big attempt at that failed with the *New Trails* album, Woody lost a lot of impetus to continue writing, although he adds songs to the group now and then.

"I'm prolific on melodies," said Woody. "That's what I love to do now. I've got tape after tape of good little melodies. I can't hardly throw any of them away. I started putting some down in Joey's studio, and I've been giving them to Slim and Doug to try and put lyrics to."

The Riders have been careful with their expenses, never letting themselves get overextended. They've watched where their money goes and have never bought into the Big Star lifestyle—custom-built buses, huge homes, big road crews and staff to cater to every whim, and elaborate stage effects. That's why they've remained a profitable act. They set aside money from each paycheck for bus maintenance and other expenses so they won't have to go deeply in debt if they need expensive repairs or a new vehicle. In this way, they're the envy of many other country artists, who wake up each day deeply in debt, convinced they must live an expensive, high-profile life in order to keep up appearances.

Woody said, "You don't notice the big jumps in income with a band. You notice the big jumps in expenses—like the bus, music charts for symphonies, instruments, divorces—those are the things you notice. The big jumps in income tend to wash out."

As for their outfits, "We've all worn so much different stuff," said Woody. "That's part of the fun of having a band that dresses up to play. I didn't realize it at first, but then all of a sudden it was like a door opened and I could see where all these guys who were in professional bands wore flashy clothes. Now I'm in a band where I can wear clothes as flashy as I want. That's part of the fun. There's a lot of people who play music just so they can wear those kinds of clothes.

"It is expensive but you learn how to make deals," added Woody. "I've figured out how to clean 'em—use paint thinner. Just pour a gallon in a bucket and it'll do two shirts.

"I don't know what I'd do if I lost either Doug or Slim," Woody reflected. "I've contemplated a lot about what if there were no more Riders. Sometimes I think the Riders would go on without any of us. Some other guys or our kids might come in and keep it going. If they lost me they'd just hire another fiddle player. But if we lost Doug or Slim—that would be it. That's the Riders.

"They don't pay me to play in this band," observed Woody as he drove down a dark highway in the early morning hours. "I do that for free. They pay me to drive this bus." He then added, "I like tinkering with the bus. That's my job with the Riders."

Woody still thinks and talks about physics. "Physics is still in bad shape in the sense that there's more to be figured out now than there ever has been," he said. "Problems are apparent, there are many many explanations to lots of phenomena that we've got, but we really don't know what's going on. We really don't know what's going on in the small and we don't know what's going on in the large. On the earth here, we know what's going on—it's all part of electrodynamics. But the problems are really too complicated to work out in detail analytically. Within a few hundred miles high and a half a mile deep we know what's going on, but we don't know what's going on under us as deep as a mile."

He continues to read books on physics "because I love it and I can do it—like I do music. I still play in it as a hobby. I like to play and ponder. I don't have to sit there and deal with a bunch of graduate students, figure out how can we get this guy through the program and then on top of that explain to him what he's going to write a thesis about. I don't have to deal with teaching or university academic politics. The only thing I have to deal with is my wife."

Woody has been married three times. "I am just so intensely emotionally and physically wrapped up in physics and playing music that I think they really get tired of that," he said. "Wives," he observed, "are awfully unhappy with musicians. It's my experience that a woman is going to get mad and upset no matter what the hell you do. They ain't gonna like it. They get mad and upset for whatever reasons and you're the reason. I think that when you do what we do—spend a lot of time on the road—they're upset because you're not there and they have to raise the kids. But they don't know that half the guys making any decent income are on the road too. They don't realize that and they don't realize how many guys are in the military and not home; and they don't realize that a lot of guys that come home after working eight or ten hours and if they're not industrious or aggressive they're dead tired and they sit and drink their beer. So they're mad at you for being gone and when you're home they want to let you have it for being gone. So you can't win for losing, whether you bring 'em money or you don't—it's always your fault. They're unhappy and you're the reason. I just get tired of that."

Woody's current wife is Teresa, and the couple has two young children. Woody's "home" now is Boise, Idaho, although he points out that, "I haven't really moved. My wife moved back there because that's where she was from. She wanted to move back there several years ago, so I just moved her back. My little kids are growing up there. I don't get to see 'em near as much as I did when they lived with me in Nashville, of course. It's sure frustrating, but it's just the way it is."

Still, he goes back to Idaho whenever he gets the chance.

Chapter 43

"There were never any low spots with me and Riders In The Sky concerning the three guys," said Joey. "They have always been wonderful to me in every way. What most impresses me about each of the Riders is that each one is not only a fine musician but also a fine stylist. Too Slim has developed a style of bass playing that's all his own. Ranger Doug has developed a style of playing rhythm guitar that is all his own. Woody Paul has a bluegrassy-be-bop style of playing fiddle, his banjo-esque fiddle solos are wonderful. The amazing thing is that you can put two or three or four fine stylists together and it doesn't jell as a band. But with Riders In The Sky the end result is what's on everybody's mind—how does this work? Not how does it work for Woody or Joey or Doug or Slim—but how does it work for Riders In The Sky? Everyone is looking out for the whole. When a new piece of material is brought in, the question is always, 'How does this work with the band?' It's a wonderful organization and everything is thought of in an organizational type of way. So you have the three guys plus myself, each having done our own thing through the years—Slim with his rock 'n' roll and folk music and other things, Ranger Doug with his bluegrass music, and Woody Paul with bluegrass and fiddle, and then me with polka music. And by bringing all these elements in from not only a unique individual but a unique group perspective, it all works so well.

"It's never difficult for me when the curtain goes up—it's something I look forward to, charging out on stage, ready to have fun," Joey continued. "That's a great thing. There's never been a day with Riders In The Sky through all the years I've been with them that I wished I wasn't playing. In fact, I can say the music has really helped me out in times when things were not going well in other areas of my life. I knew I could always count on getting on stage for that hour and a half or two hours and have a great time and have it be a big release.

"The crowds are very, very important, because an enthusiastic crowd can spur you on to play very well and you enjoy yourself even more. In my time with the Riders, I don't remember crowds ever being less than enthusiastic. I would say that would be the other side of the coin—a crowd that just didn't care about what you were doing would be very distracting, and you certainly wouldn't do the same job as with a very happy crowd.

"The sound in the auditorium is also very important, and we try to present the music in a very natural way. We all take pride in owning wonderful acoustic instruments and want the audience to hear the sound with minimal coloration. Little or no effects are used in our shows. Lately, on stage, we have created a kind of tight semi-circle around one monitor. Sound technicians are amazed at both the simplicity of our set-up and how well it works.

"Instrumentally, I always think of the four of us as sections of an orchestra. Ranger Doug and Too Slim are the rhythm section— the foundation of the band. Woody solos and backs up with counterpoint. I solo and play the part of the strings and stinging horn sections."

Joey loves performing with the Riders. "There were so many times in my life, especially with Frank Yankovic during the golden years when everyone in the band was a great musician and we learned from each other. Especially me; I learned from them. It was unbelievable the amount of knowledge I gained from those guys. But it got to the point where I was the best musician in the band. The other guys were pick-up musicians, and it became no fun at all. And that's when I said I was tired of the road. I also didn't like to just play what I played on the record."

Reflecting on life off the road with the Riders, Joey notes, "The problem with us is that everyone has such different schedules. You have a band that's doing 200 engagements a year, so you have just 165 days to stay with your family and do other things. And that's really not a lot of time. So Woody will go to Idaho, Ranger Doug's got children, Slim's got children and a family here. Fortunately, my kids are grown, and they've got their own thing.

"That's why I have a studio in my home—because we can do overdubs here. It's a turnkey studio. Although I can do full sessions—overdubs and things—it's not for rent, not for hire. It's just our own studio. So if Woody comes into town, I'll just sit him down and let him play."

Discussing the other Riders, Joey states, "I give Ranger Doug all the credit in the world. Ranger Doug really really studied western music. He devoted his life to studying it. I've never really known a person like that. With me, my gift was that everything came so easily.

"With the Time Jumpers, Doug just sits in a chair and plays music—he doesn't have to worry about emceeing or being Ranger Doug. He's just Douglas Green, the guitar player. I still do lots of recording session work because I get to do things I don't normally do. That's a good thing. It's a great balance because I've got Riders on one hand, but I still produce and I still do sessions. It's everything I want to do.

"Woody's a natural too," observes Joey. "But look at all the hours he's spent dissecting Charlie Parker solos and Lester Young solos. And I'm talking hours and hours he's spent doing that stuff. Woody is dedicated to the point of being obsessive with something. Thank God it is something with music because he does things that nobody else will do. And why would he do them? I mean, Charlie Parker solos on fiddle! But he'll do it. With me I did things I really loved but mainly I did things I had to do because I was thrust into performing them. I always say thank God I was getting paid to practice—thirty-five dollars a night when I started out in 1962. I didn't sit in my bedroom and practice on my own— I was practicing on the bandstand four hours every single night.

"Woody has always got his fiddle in his hand. He practices so much that we've got him on mute. That's one of the secrets of Riders In The Sky. Everybody has their own life—even in music. That's what makes it work.

"Slim knows everything chronologically," said Joey. "To me, life just goes by. It's like when I do a recording session—I play the chart, I do it as well as I can. People say it's great, and when it's over, it's done. I forget about it. But Slim's memory is incredible. We'll say, 'Slim, do you remember when we played on October 10th of 1989? It was a little club in Eureka, California.' And he'll say, 'Yea, it was so and so. And so and so was there. Remember that?' Nah, I don't remember that. But he's incredible."

Talking about producing the Riders recordings, Joey states, "Sometimes we work up a song in the studio, but usually we'll sit in the kitchen at my house and work up a song. When we have a recording session we won't go in the studio and work 'em up— we'll do it before. So when we get to the studio we don't waste time—we're ready to record.

"That's why we've got the studio in my home. Ranger Doug can come in here, and in fifteen minutes the mike is all set up and he can lay down his demo. He prepares it at home. Same thing with Slim. For the Disney record, we worked out all the songs here. That's what's so great about it. You don't have to put it on a little tape recorder. You can come in here in the studio and get something that's a little better.

"Since I've been in music virtually all my life I can't imagine myself doing anything different than playing with Riders In The Sky," states Joey. "I can't think of any other profession that would please me. I just can't. I've often said that when I was twelve or thirteen, I wished I could do this for twenty or thirty years. Well, it's been going on forty years now and hopefully I can do this another twenty. I'd sure like that—there's no finer and no more satisfying feeling than standing up there with three of your friends and playing the music that you love for people that you love.

"The performing instrumentalist who impressed me the most was Frank Yankovic for his showmanship, his charisma, his stylistic playing, and for giving me a chance to go on the road at such a young age and learn my craft. Others would be Benny Goodman and Artie Shaw, because I've drawn so much from how they executed their solos in my own playing—the cleanliness, their choice of notes. Also the fine musicians who made up the Sons of the Pioneers, from Hugh Farr to Karl Farr, all the way down the line to folks who recorded with the Sons to give them that great western feel. Art Van Damm was also influential for me, because he is the guy who did the most to introduce the world to jazz accordion. Art recorded on Columbia Records for many years with a quintet at the same time I was recording with Yankovic in the same recording studios in Chicago. I met Art and was just bowled over by the way he played. He won the *Playboy* Jazz Poll for miscellaneous keyboard for years and years until the seventies when people like Keith Emerson started winning on miscellaneous instruments.

"In the end," concludes Joey, "what is most important is the music. We approach each new song or project with the full intention of doing our best. We give a hundred percent, whether we're at the Bar-D Chuckwagon in Durango, Colorado, or at a sold-out performance at The Hollywood Bowl with the Hollywood Bowl Orchestra."

Chapter 44

"When I try to sum up Riders In The Sky, I think that one thing we've done that separates us from other groups is that there were precious few people doing what we did when we started," said Slim. "We've made it fun for people. I think that with our show, with the good time we have playing the music, that it's a fun experience for people to come and hear us. It's entertainment, and it happens to be western music. We can rope 'em in the door and then they realize there's this whole body of great western music which they will then go and check out. We've had so many people say, 'I heard you guys and then I heard some records by the Sons of the Pioneers—have you heard those?' And we say, 'Yes we have.' So people have become aware of this whole cowboy music renaissance that's going on.

"The high spots are many—the chance to get paid for doing what I wanted to do," continued Slim. "But I'd do it anyway. And to this very day, I still feel that incredible satisfaction that I got when I was bringing home five bucks from the first show. It's just a sense that I'm doing what I love to do, that I'm giving it everything I have. Plus it's something I can make a living with—it gives me money that I can take home. The lows with the group were generally financial in character, although money was never a big deal to me. It's a bigger deal when you don't have any of it, and we had so little of it when we started.

"Part of our appeal is that we're accessible," Slim reflected. "We're enough of a show biz tradition so that we get people in and entertain 'em and expose them to this wonderful heritage of western music. Then, hopefully, they'll continue this heritage and kick it down the trail a couple of more feet. We stand on the shoulders of the giants of the past like Bob Nolan and Tim Spencer and Roy Rogers and the Farr brothers and Foy Willing and Andy Parker and all the great musicians who have worked in this genre as well as those who continue to work in it today—like the Sons of the San Joaquin and Don Edwards. We owe a great debt to those folks from the past. Patsy Montana, Gene Autry—the list goes on and on. Those are the people who invented what we do and made it possible for us to go on and do what we love to do.

"We used to hand out a big book that Ranger Doug had for people to write down their names and addresses so we could stay in touch, and that's how we built our first mailing list. We'd just pass that book around and people would write comments, their names and addresses, so we could keep track of them. That's what we did at the early shows. We were traveling around for about three hundred bucks a night and doing that.

"I contribute a lot of comedy and showmanship to the group, and one of the acts who influenced me comedically along the line were the Smothers Brothers," continued Slim. "Those first Smothers Brothers albums were real important to me, and I saw them live when I was a kid in Grand Rapids and that was always a big deal to me. The Kingston Trio too—the way they incorporated comedy in their act. I also saw them when I was a kid. I used to go see the Grand Ole Opry Shower of Stars, and the first time I heard the Grand Ole Opry I was listening to WSM and heard Minnie Pearl say 'How-deee,' and the way the audience responded was just magic to me. It was a thrilling moment—the hair stood up on my neck. I heard her comic routine, and it just blew me away. She was certainly one of my early influences. The Marx Brothers, W.C. Fields, Charlie Chaplin—I studied all those guys in college. Then there was the Firesign Theater. When humor got a little more hip, those guys had a big influence on what we were doing.

"The way we split up our responsibilities is that Ranger Doug does the promotional-type considerations—interviews, that type of deal—and a lot of the schmoozing. He's sort of the ace schmoozer—we call it 'laying on the cheese.' I'm in charge of the mercantile, which is selling stuff at the show, maintaining an office, and maintaining a mail order business. Which is an important part of our income. Woody's in charge of keeping the bus going down the road, and he also did the books for awhile, but now we've hired an accountant. Now he just gets the bus down the road, and if you've ever crawled under a bus in a screaming blizzard in Colorado when it's twenty-four below with newspapers on fire to get the diesel line unclogged, you'll know the contribution that Woody makes is enormous. There's also Texas 'Bix' Bender—his real name is Steve Arwood—who has collaborated with us for about twenty years, creating shows for Riders In The

Sky. He and I have collaborated on about two hundred public radio shows and half a dozen or so 'Riders Radio Theater Specials' for TNN. We've continued to work together—in fact we've developed a musical comedy which will hopefully be in production soon. Between him and me, we generate 90 to 95 percent of the comedic material. I tend to do more of the stuff that winds up on stage, although everyone contributes. A lot of our best stuff has been ad-libbed off the cuff. Ranger Doug is a wonderful wit, a quick wit, and we've got a wonderful chemistry together. Woody will surprise you with absolutely the finest capper you can think of. He doesn't do it all the time, but every now and then he'll really nail it.

"Joey has become an integral part of the band and has helped us tremendously with his musicality and with his production know-how. He's produced our last six or eight records and he knows us intimately, probably far more than he would ever need to or care to. He knows what we can do and is never satisfied with what we do—he always wants us to do better and tries to pull out the best performances. Plus he's great on the road. He's dependable to the nth degree and always goes the extra mile. He's been on the road his whole life, beginning with Frankie Yankovic, when he was twelve or thirteen years old, so he's the ultimate complement to us. When we thought that three was it, we had not met Joey. Joey knows where to step out, where to stay back, where to add the pad, where to put the dramatic fill, and he's just a great musician and it's great to learn from him and play with him every night and learn about music from him."

Chapter 45

Discussing the Riders, Ranger Doug states, "Slim is the linchpin of the group. The audience might be laughing at us, not with us, if it wasn't for his particular comic genius. Musically the audience probably has little appreciation for the depths of his talent and contribution, because he is the driving heart of the band. He is steady as a rock, yet fluid enough to go with the unexpected as a player, and is always eager to learn and stretch on his instrument. As a singer, like all of us, he has worked very hard to become good and develop a good ear.

"There's sort of two types of audiences—the people who come to see you and the people who are subscribers to a concert series," said Ranger Doug. "And they're there because they have the ticket and don't want to waste the money. You've got to reach those people if you can. We've fished through a lot of different kinds of comedy and approaches to songs to try to get them amused. I think it taught us a lot about stagecraft—what we do on stage came out of those early years. A lot of the funny stuff came out of those clubs where people were being real goofy and we were being real goofy. But a lot of reacting to audiences or relating to audiences came out of those concert shows."

Pacing the show "was trial and errors," said Green. "We have very much of a formula now, which we sometimes step out of because we get tired of it. But usually you want a yodel song up early, an instrumental up fairly early, got to do a classic up near the top, hit 'em with a couple of originals and funny stuff. Go back to a classic. That was worked out in those early years. We've never had a set list, per se. We've always winged it, like when it's time for Woody's song, Woody picks one. Time for Joey to do one, so Joey picks one. I get a slow solo, and I can pick from a dozen or more, although if the instrumental before it is in B flat, then I'm probably not going to do a song in B flat."

On his own contributions to the group, Ranger Doug states, "Along the way I discovered that my baritone voice was far better suited to big-band standards and classic country and cowboy tunes than it was to the high lonesome sound of bluegrass. And more and more I found cowboy music drifting into my repertoire: 'Back in the Saddle Again,' 'South of the Border,' 'Big Iron,' 'Little Joe, the Wrangler,' and others. Because I could yodel I was a big fan of Elton Britt in those years and knew several of his songs: 'There's a Star-Spangled Banner Waving Somewhere,' 'Someday,' and 'Chime Bells.' And so I practiced yodeling because I loved it and began to do it well.

"I just always loved to play rhythm guitar with that swingy, moving, changing chord-on-every-beat style," continued Green. "That's the pulse and heart of the band. I think it's one thing that really distinguishes western music, in addition to the poetic lyrics and lush melodies. That driving, loping beat on the rhythm guitar, first perfected by Lloyd Perryman and Karl Farr, gives western music a unique feel unlike any other. Try it with open chords and a country beat and the feel is gone, the music is something else. Go back to the old-style chunka chunka chords, and the music comes back to life. Get a strong, subtle bassist like Too Slim and you have a rhythmic bed just made for the songs of the West. It swings, but it's not dance music. It has its own lope and feel, and I never stopped loving it from the first day I heard it.

"After all these years of performing on the road, I've had more than enough applause to last a lifetime," said Ranger Doug. "My ego has long been gratified, and if I never perform again I wouldn't miss the applause. But I would miss the music. What drove that twenty-one-year-old guy so hard—well that's hard to remember. I guess, as I try to reconstruct the past, that I was eager to prove that I could more or less do the impossible and found a place I could shine, a place so unlikely and so completely different from my sheltered suburban upbringing that it was like stepping into another world. To take on this other world and succeed in it seems like the grandest twist of fate I could ever pull off. I rejoiced in every little perceived success and draped myself in fatalistic gloom over every blunder. It still seems like a great scam to have pulled off, to have been successful as a cowboy singer, given my raising and my limits as a singer and a musician. I couldn't ever have been happier if I had done anything else, although in some ways it's been a difficult life.

"The low spots were what you'd expect—minuscule pay, traveling in a van with no air-conditioning, replacing three guys within the first eighteen months. There were the inevitable ego clashes and hurt feelings and different musical visions. We worked through them all, since we were all so committed to each other and to this style.

"The high spots, generally, were two. First, we kept having good things happen to us, measures of success which surprised us, delighted us, and gave us courage to go on through the hard times. Things like the *Austin City Limits* appearance, the guest spots on the Grand Ole Opry, the first recordings for Rounder. Second was the reaction of the audiences. What a delight to take this precious music, which was a passion for us, and make a contemporary audience enjoy it. And of course to have them appreciate our twisted sense of humor was as delightful. It made for fun shows, fulfilling for us and for the audience."

Chapter 46

In November of 2002, the Riders went to the annual Western Music Association gathering in Las Vegas, where they were feted with a special "roast" honoring their twenty-fifth year as Riders In The Sky. The roast began with a video that ended with the heads of the Riders on Mount Rushmore. The roasters included John Sandidge, Alan Sacks, Johnny Western, Fred Goodwin, Hal Cannon, John Lasseter, former Dixie Chick Laura Lynch, and Ray Benson, with a special, surprise roast by Tommy Smothers. Video clips of Baxter Black, the Osborne Brothers, Connie Smith, Clint Black, Little Jimmy Dickens, The Whites, Billy Walker, Rebecca Lynn Howard, Jack Greene, Jeannie Seeley, Porter Wagoner, Pete Fischer, Waddie Mitchell, and others were interspersed throughout the evening. The Roast ran long—almost three hours—but the laughter and fun was genuine and real.

The previous night the Western Music Association Awards Show was held, and the Riders won the top award, "Entertainer of the Year," as well as the award for "Traditional Western Album" for their *Pair of Kings* album. In addition, Joey won the "Instrumentalist of the Year" honor.

On Saturday night, the Riders presented a concert after opening act Brenn Hill performed. The Riders were sharp, and Woody was on, but Slim's voice gave out about a third of the way through the set. Joey had to step in and do Slim's harmony part, while Woody and Doug took over Slim's lead vocal chores within the songs. Slim characterized the evening as a "long, hard day's work," but the crowd loved them. For the dedicated fan who knows how the vocals are usually handled, it was an impressive display of the versatility of the Riders as well as their professionalism when they handled this difficult situation effortlessly.

The next day the Riders boarded a ship for a cruise to the Hawaiian islands. Hawaii was the only state where the Riders had never performed—after this two-week cruise they could lay claim to performances in all fifty states of the union.

The Riders had come a long way from the days of Herr Harry's and the Blue Hole of Death, but, then again, they hadn't come so far at all. They still sang western music, and they still dressed the part.

They continue to tour extensively. Most nights on stage are high moments as they entertain full houses who come to see them. But there are some low moments as well. Branson, Missouri, which had once bragged about leaving Nashville in the dust, is now a shadow of its former self. The city was greedy and did not invest in the necessary infrastructure when the boom years hit; short-sighted financial gains took precedence over long-range planning. The result is that the tourist industry is drying up. At the Mel Tillis Theater, which seats 2,800, only about 150 showed up for the Riders' show in the summer of 2002. It was that way all over town with other shows as well.

That doesn't mean the Riders put on a bad show—they perform as hard for 150 as they do for 1,500 or 15,000. That's because first and foremost the Riders are entertainers. This is their love, their passion, and their life. The fact that they play western music in their show and promote "The Cowboy Way" makes them Ambassadors of the West and all things western.

Although the Riders love what they do—individually and collectively—and none wants to trade his life for anything else, their success has come at a price. The years on the road have brought them fame and a comfortable income but have cost them on the personal side. Between the four Riders there have been eleven wives and nineteen children; Ranger Doug has been married four times, Woody Paul has been married three times, while Joey and Slim have each been married twice. Woody Paul has six children, Ranger Doug has five, Too Slim and Joey each have four.

The Riders seem to have all settled down at this point and are happy in their personal lives. Slim is married to "the fair Roberta," Joey is married to Patti, Woody is with Teresa, and Ranger Doug married Ann Marie Flores on May 5, 2002, in a Mexican-flavored ceremony in the backyard of his home in Nashville. They seem to be happy together, and Ranger Doug insists "this is it." Those who know him believe it.

Good things continued to happen for the Riders as the year

2003 unfolded. On February 23 they were called to the stage at Madison Square Garden and received their second Grammy Award. It was for their *Monsters, Inc. Scream Factory Favorites* album in the "Children's" category. On March 28 they were inducted into the Walk of Western Stars at the Santa Clarita Festival in California. Their work with cartoons was continuing to grow. They sang the theme song as well as some other songs for "Jasper," a cartoon developed by Meredith Hodges (daughter of Peanuts creator Charles Shultz). For the Disney cartoon "Stanley" they also sang the theme song and some other tunes. And for the Warner Brothers cartoon "Duck Dodgers" the Riders became animated characters for their songs in that feature.

The Riders began as individual musicians with a common bond of western music but have grown into a group where the sum is greater than the parts. They have endured personality clashes, ego bruises, new and ex-wives, children, and the rigors of life on the road. They have grown very close, personally as well as professionally, and each has a tremendous respect for the others as musicians as well as individuals.

Life on the road has settled into a comfortable pattern for them, taking turns driving, pitching in to help set up and then break down the stage set, jamming during and after their sound checks, and discussing their business affairs and career moves in open, unguarded discussions. Woody Paul is still eccentric—he generally sleeps during daylight and is most active between midnight and sunup, while the other Riders operate on a more normal schedule.

The deep conflict that once almost split them apart—Woody's substance abuse problem—has been resolved, although Woody continues his pattern of obsessive behavior. "Right now I play the mandolin a lot. It's a lot better than drinking and irritates the other guys twice as much," said Woody with a sly grin. "But I really love those guys," he continued. "We've really grown close together, and I wish we could start all over and could wipe out those early years."

For a number of years, the cowboy fell out of favor with American popular culture. There were still cowboys in the West—through their work or through their dress—but the cowboy in the

world of entertainment was hard to find. And the singing cowboy was impossible to find.

Not that there weren't people dressed up as cowboys singing.
Country music singers regularly wore cowboy hats, boots, and
jeans—although country singers before Waylon and Willie tended
to dress in sports coats, slacks, and even tuxedoes. But there's a
difference between singers dressed as cowboys, cowboys who
sing, and the singing cowboys. There are a lot of singers dressed
as cowboys and a good number of cowboys who sing—but the
singing cowboys in their fancy, flashy clothes singing songs of
the beauty and romance of the West were gone from the American musical landscape until Riders In The Sky came along.

So was the idea of the cowboy as a white-hatted hero, "the
idol of American Youth." That concept had given way to the black-
hatted antihero, the snarling loner totally immersed in himself.

For many Baby Boomers, the cowboy—particularly the TV
cowboy—was one of the biggest influences in their lives. They
grew up dreaming of being a cowboy, being a hero, righting
wrongs, and riding off into the sunset, carefree and easy. The following years jaded them; Vietnam, Watergate, and the antiheroes
in movies and on TV all planted a deep cynicism in their souls
and hardened their hearts to the good man with pure motives
who did what is right not because of financial rewards, career
incentives, or any of that—but simply because it was right. Riders In The Sky came along at a time when Baby Boomers were
ready to remember those thrilling days of yesteryear when there
were cowboy heroes in white hats doing good simply because it
was the right thing to do.

That's the debt that America owes Riders In The Sky. After
Americans had made cowboys antiheroes in the movies and lonesome, onry, and mean cusses in song, relegated to the dust bins of
history in everyday life, the Riders walked on stage in white hats
and made the cowboy hero come alive again. Before Riders In
The Sky came along, America had forgotten all about her singing-cowboy hero. Riders In The Sky brought him back and reminded Americans what a source of joy, hope, inspiration, humor,
and beauty the singing cowboy and his songs can be.

Not many young kids today dream of growing up to be a cowboy; certainly not as many as during the 1950s. But there are a

few. And there's a whole huge group of aging Baby Boomers who have been reconnected to their cowboy past because of Riders In The Sky. It is a connection that is treasured by this audience who, sometimes late at night in a dark den, slips a CD into a nice stereo system and listen to "Cool Water," "Tumbling Tumbleweeds," "Back in the Saddle Again," or maybe "Lonely Yukon Stars," "Blue Bonnet Lady," "Here Comes the Santa Fe," or "Ride With Me, Gringo."

Life is good when you can spend an evening with Riders In The Sky.

Discography

Three on the Trail
(Rounder 0102, 1980)

Producers: Russ Miller and Riders In The Sky
Associate Producer: Paul Worley
Studio: Audio-Media, Nashville, Tenn.
Engineer: Marshall Morgan
Ranger Doug: Guitar, vocals
Too Slim: Bunkhouse bass, vocals
Woody Paul: Fiddle, guitar, banjo, vocals
Additional musicians:
Percussion: Eddie Bayers
Guitar: Paul Worley
Steel guitar: Weldon Myrick
Accordion: John Probst
Vibes: Dennis Burnside
1. Three on the Trail (Douglas B. Green)
2. (Ghost) Riders in the Sky (Stan Jones)
3. That's How the Yodel Was Born (Douglas B. Green)
4. Don't Fence Me In (Cole Porter)
5. Blue Montana Skies (Douglas B. Green)
6. When Payday Rolls Around (Bob Nolan)
7. Cowboy Song (Woody Paul)
8. Skyball Paint (Bob Nolan)
9. Blue Bonnet Lady (Woody Paul)
10. Cielito Lindo (P.D. arr: Fred LaBour)
11. Here Comes the Santa Fe (Douglas B. Green)
12. So Long, Saddle Pals (Woody Paul)

Cowboy Jubilee
(Rounder 0147, 1981)

Producers: Fred LaBour and Woody Paul
Studio: Creative Workshop, Nashville, Tenn.
Engineer: Todd Cerney
Mastered by Denny Purcell
Ranger Doug: Guitar, vocals
Too Slim: Bunkhouse bass, guitar, accordion, vocals
Woody Paul: Fiddle, gut string guitar, accordion, harmonica,
    vocals
Additional Musicians:
Horns: Louis Brown
Electric and acoustic lead guitar: Tommy Goldsmith
Percussion: Kenny Malone
Steel guitar: Kayton Roberts
1. Cowboy Jubilee (Fred LaBour–Woody Paul)
2. Ol' Cowpoke (Gary McMahan)
3. Compadres in the Old Sierra Madres (Woody Paul)
4. Back in the Saddle Again (Ray Whitley–Gene Autry)
5. Desperado Trail (Woody Paul)
6. Red River Valley (P.D.)
7. Ride with the Wind (Douglas B. Green)
8. Soon As the Roundup's Through (Woody Paul)
9. On the Rhythm Range (Bob Nolan)
10. Riding Alone (Douglas B. Green)
11. Ojo Caliente (Tommy Goldsmith)
12. At the End of the Rainbow Trail (Douglas B. Green)

Prairie Serenade
(Rounder 0170, 1982)

Producers: Fred LaBour and Woody Paul
Studio: Quadraphonic, Nashville, Tenn.
Engineer: Todd Cerney
Ranger Doug: Guitar, vocals
Too Slim: Bunkhouse bass, guitar, accordion, vocals
Woody Paul: Fiddle, gut string guitar, accordion, harmonica, mandolin, vocals
Additional musicians:
Horns: Louis Brown
Percussion: Kenny Malone
Steel guitar: Kayton Roberts
1. Prairie Serenade (Douglas B. Green)
2. Jingle Jangle Jingle (Joseph J. Lilley–Frank Loesser)
3. Blue Shadows on the Trail (Johnny Lange–Eliot Daniel)
4. Pretty Prairie Princess (Woody Paul)
5. Cowpoke (Stan Jones)
6. Nevada (Woody Paul–Karen Ritter)
7. Down the Trail to San Antone (Deuce Spriggins)
8. I Ride an Old Paint (P.D.)
9. Utah Trail (Woody Paul)
10. Old El Paso (Douglas B. Green)
11. Chasing the Sun (Douglas B. Green)
12. Home on the Range (P.D.)

Weeds and Water
(Rounder 1038, 1983)

Producers: Jim Sutton and Riders In The Sky
Studios: Audio Innovators, Pittsburgh, Pa. and Woodland
    Sound, Nashville, Tenn.
Engineers: Norm Cleary, David Markovitz, and Steve Ham
Ranger Doug: Guitar, vocals
Too Slim: Bunkhouse bass, vocals
Woody Paul: Fiddle, vocals
Additional musicians:
Drums: Bob Mater
Steel guitar: Kayton Roberts
1. Cool Water (Bob Nolan)
2. West Texas Cowboy (Woody Paul)
3. La Cucaracha (P.D.)
4. Streets of Laredo (The Cowboy's Lament) (P.D.)
5. Singing a Song to the Sky (Douglas B. Green)
6. Tumbling Tumbleweeds (Bob Nolan)
7. Pecos Bill (Johnny Lange–Eliot Daniel)
8. That's How the Yodel Was Born (Douglas B. Green)
9. Wasteland (Douglas B. Green)
10. Bound to Hit the Trail (Woody Paul)

Live
(Rounder 0186, 1984)

Producer: Riders In The Sky
Recorded live at The Birchmere, Alexandria, Va.
Recorded by Bias Recorders, Springfield, Va.
Engineer: Bill McElroy
Mixing Engineer: Todd Cerney
Mixed at Creative Workshop, Nashville
Ranger Doug: Guitar, vocals
Too Slim: Bunkhouse bass, vocals
Woody Paul: Fiddle, vocals
1. Cowboy Jubilee (Fred LaBour–Woody Paul)
2. Yodel Blues (Robert E. Dolan–Johnny Mercer)
3. When the Bloom Is on the Sage (Fred Howard Wright–Nat Vincent)
4. After You've Gone (Turner Layton–Henry Creamer)
5. Cowboy Song (Woody Paul)
6. Hold That Critter Down (Bob Nolan)
7. Cielito Lindo (P.D.)
8. The Last Roundup (Billy Hill)
9. I Grab My Saddle Horn and Blow (Bob Nolan)
10. Blue Bonnet Lady (Woody Paul)
11. When Payday Rolls Around (Bob Nolan)
12. So Long, Saddle Pals (Woody Paul)

New Trails
(Rounder 0220, 1986)

Producers: Robby Adcock and Riders In The Sky
Studios: Studio 19 and Audio Media, Nashville, Tenn.
Engineers: Todd Cerney, Bill Halverson and Larry Rogers,
    Hollis Halford and Marshall Morgan
Second Engineers: Tom Der, John Kelton, and E.J. Walsh
Mixing Engineers: Hollis Halford, Bill Halverson, and Robby
    Adcock
Ranger Doug: Vocals
Too Slim: Vocals
Woody Paul: Vocals
Additional musicians:
Acoustic guitar: Steve Gibson, Paul Worley
Bass: Joe Osborn
Electric Guitar: Gary Burnette, Steve Gibson, Paul Worley
Drums and Percussion: Eddie Bayers
Keyboards: Dennis Burnside
Steel Guitar: Bruce Bouton, Sonny Garrish, Larry Sasser
Harmonica: Buddy Green
Piano Solo: Buck White
String Arrangements: Dennis Burnside
Additional Vocals: Robby Adcock, Mike Black, and Scott Jarrett
1. Cimarron (Johnny Bond)
2. Trail of Tears (Lee Domann–Pete Sebert–Ralph Whiteway)
3. I'm Satisfied with You (Fred Rose)
4. Even Texas Isn't Big Enough (Kerry Chater–Patti Dahlstrom)
5. Slowpoke (Frank "Peewee" King–Chilton Price–Redd Stewart)
6. Blue Bonnet Lady (Woody Paul)
7. Cowboy of the Highway (Woody Paul)
8. Any Time (Herbert "Happy" Lawson)
9. All Those Years (Douglas B. Green)
10. Soon As the Roundup's Through (Woody Paul)

Best of the West
(Rounder 11517, 1987)

Compiled from previous Rounder albums
1. Cowboy Jubilee (Fred LaBour–Woody Paul)
2. That's How the Yodel Was Born (Douglas B. Green)
3. (Ghost) Riders in the Sky (Stan Jones)
4. Don't Fence Me In (Cole Porter)
5. Ol' Cowpoke (Gary McMahan)
6. Wasteland (Douglas B. Green)
7. Blue Bonnet Lady (Woody Paul)
8. Blue Montana Skies (Douglas B. Green)
9. After You've Gone (Turner Layton–Henry Creamer)
10. Here Comes the Santa Fe (Douglas B. Green)
11. Tumbling Tumbleweeds (Bob Nolan)
12. La Cucaracha (P.D.)
13. Soon As the Roundup's Through (Woody Paul)
14. I Ride an Old Paint (P.D.)
15. Riding Alone (Douglas B. Green)
16. Hold That Critter Down (Bob Nolan)
17. Ride with the Wind (Douglas B. Green)
18. Cowboy Song (Woody Paul)
19. Prairie Serenade (Douglas B. Green)
20. Nevada (Woody Paul and Karen Ritter)
21. Home on the Range (P.D.)
22. So Long, Saddle Pals (Woody Paul)

Best of the West Rides Again
(Rounder 11524, 1987)

Compiled from previous Rounder albums
1. Three on the Trail (Douglas B. Green)
2. Back in the Saddle Again (Ray Whitley–Gene Autry)
3. Cool Water (Bob Nolan)
4. Desperado Trail (Woody Paul)
5. At the End of the Rainbow Trail (Douglas B. Green)
6. Down the Trail to San Antone (Deuce Spriggins)
7. Blue Shadows on the Trail (Johnny Lange–Eliot Daniel)
8. Jingle Jangle Jingle (Joseph J. Lilley–Frank Loesser)
9. Pecos Bill (Johnny Lange–Eliot Daniel)
10. Streets of Laredo (The Cowboy's Lament) (P.D.)
11. West Texas Cowboy (Woody Paul)
12. Cowpoke (Stan Jones)
13. Old El Paso (Douglas B. Green)
14. Skyball Paint (Bob Nolan)
15. Compadres in the Old Sierra Madres (Woody Paul)
16. Bound to Hit the Trail (Woody Paul)
17. Ojo Caliente (Tommy Goldsmith)
18. The Yodel Blues (Robert E. Dolan–Johnny Mercer)
19. Pretty Prairie Princess (Woody Paul)
20. Chasin' the Sun (Douglas B. Green)
21. When the Bloom is on the Sage (Fred Howard–Nat Vincent)
22. Singing a Song to the Sky (Douglas B. Green)
23. On the Rhythm Range (Bob Nolan)
24. Red River Valley (P.D.)
25. When Payday Rolls Around (Bob Nolan)

Saddle Pals
(Rounder 8011, 1987)

Producers: Robby Adcock and Riders In The Sky
Studio: Studio 19, Nashville, Tenn.
Engineers: Todd Cerney, Hollis Halford, Bill Halverson, Larry
 Rogers, Skip Shimmin, and E.J. Walsh
Mixing Studio: Audio Media, Nashville, Tenn.
Mixing Engineers: Hollis Halford and Robby Adcock
Ranger Doug: Guitar, banjo, percussion, vocals
Too Slim: Bunkhouse bass, guitar, percussion, vocals
Woody Paul: Fiddle, banjo, percussion, vocals
Additional musicians:
Guitar: Gary Burnette, Steve Gibson
Bass: Joe Osborn
Keyboards: Dennis Burnside
Drums: Eddie Bayers, Darren Osborn
Harmonica: Buddy Green
Mandolin: Gary Burnette
Percussion: Robby Adcock
1. Yippie-Yi-Yo and Away We Go (Woody Paul)
2. The Old Chisholm Trail (P.D.)
3. Get Along, Little Dogies (P.D.)
4. Biscuit Blues (Bob Nolan)
5. Sweet Betsy from Pike (P.D.)
6. There's a Great Big Candy Roundup (Louis Robino–Joe
 Estella–Dick Manning)
7. I'm Going to Leave Old Texas Now (P.D.)
8. The Cowboy's A-B-Cs (Douglas B. Green)
9. Clementine (P.D.)
10. "One, Two, Three" Said the Miner (Douglas B. Green)
11. Fiddle Medley (arr: Woody Paul)
12. Down the Lullabye Trail (Douglas B. Green)

The Cowboy Way
(MCA 31244, 1987)

Produced by Emory Gordy
Studio: Emerald, Nashville, Tenn.
Engineer: Steve Tillisch
Mixing Engineer: Ron Treat
Second Engineers: Russ Martin, Tim Kish, Mark J. Coddington,
    Keith Odle
Ranger Doug: Guitar, vocals
Too Slim: Bunkhouse bass, vocals
Woody Paul: Fiddle, vocals
Additional Musician:
Lead guitar and mandolin: Mark O'Connor
1. Texas Plains (Stuart Hamblen)
2. Back in the Saddle Again (Ray Whitley–Gene Autry)
3. (Ghost) Riders in the Sky (Stan Jones)
4. Carry Me Back to the Lone Prairie (Carson J. Robison)
5. Mr. Sincere (State Fair Burnout) (Fred LaBour–Douglas B.
    Green–Woody Paul)
6. Concerto for Violin and Longhorns (Woody Paul)
7. Lonely Yukon Stars (Douglas B. Green)
8. The Salting of the Slug (Fred LaBour)
9. When Payday Rolls Around (Bob Nolan)
10. My Oklahoma (Terrye Newkirk)
11. Reincarnation (Wallace McRae)
12. Miss Molly (Cindy Walker)
13. Ridin' Down the Canyon (Gene Autry–Smiley Burnette)
14. That's How the Yodel Was Born (Douglas B. Green)
15. Happy Trails (Dale Evans)

Riders Radio Theater
(MCA 42180, 1988)

Producers: Bruce Hinton and Chip Hardy
Studio: Emerald, Nashville, Tenn.
Engineer: Willie Pevear
Second Engineers: Tim Kish, Russ Martin
Ranger Doug: Guitar, vocals
Too Slim: Bass, vocals
Woody Paul: Fiddle, vocals
Additional Musicians:
Accordion: Joey Miskulin
Temple blocks: Bronco Stroud
Announcer: Texas "Bix" Bender
1. The Scene (Riders In The Sky and Steve Arwood)
2. Riders Radio Theme (Fred LaBour)
3. Chant of the Wanderer (Bob Nolan)
4. Udder Butter on a Rope (Riders In The Sky)
5. Trail Traffic Report (Riders In The Sky and Steve Arwood)
6. Sagebrush Sports Report (Riders In The Sky and Steve Arwood)
7. Cattle Call (Tex Owens)
8. Bio Feedbag (Riders In The Sky)
9. Trail Traffic Update (Riders In The Sky and Steve Arwood)
10. Call of the Wild (Riders In The Sky and Steve Arwood)
11. Triple X Stock Report (Riders In The Sky and Steve Arwood)
12. Sundown Blues (Douglas B. Green)
13. Riders Radio Theme (Reprise) (Fred LaBour)
14. Pops (Riders In The Sky)
15. Saddle Whiz (Riders In The Sky)
16. Meltdown on the Mesa (Riders In The Sky and Steve Arwood)
17. So Long, Saddle Pals (Woody Paul)
18. The Long Show (Riders In The Sky and Steve Arwood)

Riders Go Commercial
(MCA 42305, 1989)

Producers: Bruce Hinton and Buzz Stone
Studio: Emerald, Nashville, Tenn.
Ranger Doug: Guitar, requinto, vocals
Too Slim: Bunkhouse bass, vocals
Woody Paul: Fiddle, guitar, vocals
Additional musicians:
Accordion: Joey Miskulin
Announcer: Texas "Bix" Bender
Additional effects: Carl Pederson–Henry Fennell
1. The Board Room (Riders In The Sky–Steve Arwood)
2. Accordion Repair Course (Riders In The Sky–Steve Arwood)
3. Studebaker (Riders In The Sky–Steve Arwood)
4. Udder Fantastic (Riders In The Sky–Steve Arwood)
5. A Side of Opera (Riders In The Sky–Steve Arwood)
6. Perfume, Passion, and Polka (Riders In The Sky–Steve
     Arwood)
7. The Queen Elizabeth Trio (Riders In The Sky–Steve
     Arwood)
8. Polkaholism (PSA) (Riders In The Sky–Steve Arwood)
9. Cow Paint and Body Shop (Riders In The Sky–Steve
     Arwood)
10. Along the Navajo Trail (Larry Markes–Eddie DeLange–Dick
     Charles)
11. There's a Blue Sky Way Out Yonder (Arthur Fields–Fred
     Hall–Bert Van Cleve)
12. Geezer Training Course (Riders In The Sky–Steve Arwood)
13. No Rodeo Dough (John Jacob Loeb–Lewis Harris–Cy Coben)
14. Riding the Old Front Range (Douglas B. Green)
15. Ride with Me, Gringo (Fred LaBour)
16. Toolkit in a Holster (Riders In The Sky–Steve Arwood)

Horse Opera
(MCA 42338, 1990)

Producer: Buzz Stone
Studio: 16th Avenue Sound and Treasure Isle and Hummingbird
Engineer: Russ Martin
Mixing Engineer: Tim Kish at The Castle Studio
Second Engineers: Jim Demain and Dave Parker
Ranger Doug: Guitar, vocals
Too Slim: Bunkhouse bass, vocals
Woody Paul: Fiddle, vocals
Additional musicians:
Accordion: Joey Miskulin
Percussion: Kenny Malone
Guitar: John Willis
1. Ride, Cowboy, Ride (Rex Allen Jr.–Curtis Allen–Denny DeMarco)
2. Maybe I'll Cry over You (Elton Britt)
3. Texas Echo (David Ball)
4. Slocum Intro (Riders In The Sky)
5. What Would I Do without You? (Woody Paul)
6. The Arms of My Love (Woody Paul)
7. Homecoming Yodel (Douglas B. Green)
8. Call of the Canyon (Billy Hill)
9. Drywall Intro (Riders In The Sky)
10. Livin' in a Mobile Home (Ronny Scaife–Rory Michael Bourke)
11. The Line Rider (Douglas B. Green)
12. Sidemeat Intro (Riders In The Sky)
13. Sidekick Heaven (Eddie Dean–Hal Sothern–Fred LaBour)
14. Someone's Got to Do It (Douglas B. Green)

Harmony Ranch
(Columbia, 48589 1991)

Producer: Steve Gibson and Steve Buckingham
Studio: Nightingale Studio and The Doghouse
Engineers: Marshall Morgan, Brad Jones, Rich Schirmer, Gary
    Paczosa, Chrissy Follmar
Mixing Engineer: Marshall Morgan
Ranger Doug: Vocals, guitar
Too Slim: Vocals, bass
Woody Paul: Vocals, fiddle
Additional musicians:
Accordion: Joey Miskulin
Drums & percussion: Kenny Malone
Acoustic guitar, banjo, harmonica, and jaw harp: Mark Casstevens
Acoustic guitar, mandolin, Spanish dobro: Steve Gibson
Steel Guitar: Paul Franklin
Violin: David Davidson and David Angell
Viola: Kris Wilkinson
Cello: Grace Bahng
String arrangements: Kris Wilkinson
Additional vocal arrangements: Dennis Wilson
1. Harmony Ranch (Woody Paul)
2. How Does He Yodel (Douglas B. Green)
3. Great Grand-Dad (Frank Luther)
4. The Big Corral (Romaine Lowdermilk)
5. Pecos Bill (Johnny Lange–Eliot Daniel)
6. I Always Do (Douglas B. Green)
7. One Little Coyote (Douglas B. Green)
8. Come and Get It (Tim Spencer–Glenn Spencer)
9. The Cowboy's A-B-Cs (Douglas B. Green)
10. Face: The Music (Fred LaBour)
11. Cody of the Pony Express (Bob Nolan)
12. Prairie Lullabye (Woody Paul)

Saturday Morning with Riders In The Sky
(MCA 10495, 1992)

Compiled from previous MCA albums
Producer: Emory Gordy Jr., Bruce Hinton, Buzz Stone
1. Texas Plains (Stuart Hamblen)
2. Back in the Saddle Again (Ray Whitley–Gene Autry)
3. Riders in the Sky (Stan Jones)
4. That's How the Yodel Was Born (Douglas B. Green)
5. Someone's Got to Do It (Douglas B. Green)
6. Ride, Cowboy, Ride (Rex Allen Jr.–Curtis Allen–Denny DeMarco)
7. The Queen Elizabeth Trio (Riders In The Sky)
8. There's a Blue Sky Way Out Yonder (Fred Hall–Arthur Fields–Bert Van Cleve)
9. Cattle Call (Tex Owens)
10. So Long, Saddle Pals (Woody Paul)

Merry Christmas from Harmony Ranch
(Columbia 52778, 1992)

Producers: Steve Gibson and Steve Buckingham
Studio: Nightingale, Omnisound, Imagine Sound, and The
    Doghouse, Nashville, Tenn.
Engineers: Marshall Morgan and Rich Schirmer
Second Engineers: Toby Seay and John Kunz
Mixing Engineer: Marshall Morgan
Ranger Doug: Guitar, vocals
Too Slim: Bunkhouse bass, vocals
Woody Paul: Fiddle, vocals
Additional musicians:
Drums and percussion: Kenny Malone
Accordion: Joey Miskulin
Percussion: Farrell Morris
Guest Artist: Kathy Mattea
1. Here Comes Santa Claus (Gene Autry–Oakley Haldeman)
2. Silver Bells (Jay Livingston–Ray Evans)
3. Rudolph the Red-Nosed Reindeer (Johnny Marks)
4. White Christmas (Irving Berlin)
5. Navidad Y Año Nuevo (J.J. Chucho Navarro)
6. Christmas Time's a Comin' (Tex Logan)
7. Deck the Bunkhouse Walls (arr: Riders In The Sky)
8. Sidemeat's Christmas Goose (Douglas B. Green)
9. Riding Home on Christmas Eve (Douglas B. Green)
10. Merry Christmas from Harmony Ranch/Jingle Bells (Woody
    Paul and Karen Ritter/arr.: Riders In The Sky)
11. Christmas Carol Medley/The Greatest Gifts (Douglas B.
    Green/arr: Riders In The Sky)

Cowboys in Love
(Columbia 64268, 1994)

Producer: Joey Miskulin
Studio: Nightingale and The Reflections, Nashville, Tenn.
Engineers: Gary Paczosa, Mark Howard, and Ed Simonton
Ranger Doug: Guitar, vocals
Too Slim: Bunkhouse bass, vocals
Woody Paul: Fiddle, vocals
Additional Musicians:
Drums: Tommy Wells
Accordion and organ: Joey Miskulin
Percussion: Kenny Malone
Acoustic and electric guitars, mandolin: Mark Howard
Steel string and nylon string guitars: Gregg Galbraith
Violin: Barbara Lamb
String arrangements: Dennis Burnside and Joey Miskulin
1. The Cowboy's in Love (Douglas B. Green)
2. Along the Santa Fe Trail (Al Dubin–Wilhelm Grosz–Edwina Coolidge)
3. One Has My Name, the Other Has My Heart (Eddie Dean–Dearest Dean–Hal Blair)
4. Wimmen . . . Who Needs 'Em! (Douglas B. Green)
5. Sweet Señorita Teresa (Woody Paul)
6. Farr Away Stomp (A Tribute to Our Four-Legged Friends) (Karl Farr–Hugh Farr)
7. The Yellow Rose of Texas (P.D. arr.: Douglas B. Green)
8. La Malaguena (P.D. arr.: Douglas B. Green)
9. I'm a Ding Dong Daddy (Phil Baxter)
10. Early Autumn (Douglas B. Green)
11. You're Wearin' Out Your Welcome, Matt (David Kent–Joey Scott)

Always Drink Upstream from the Herd
(Rounder 0360, 1995)

Producer: Joey Miskulin
Studio: Mark Howard Studio
Engineers: Mark Howard, David Ferguson, and Hank Tilbury
Mixing Engineers: Gary Paczosa and Joey Miskulin
Ranger Doug: Guitar, vocals
Too Slim: Bunkhouse bass, vocals
Woody Paul: Fiddle, vocals
Additional musicians:
Accordion: Joey Miskulin
Acoustic guitar: Mark Howard, Richard O'Brien, Gregg Galbraith
Drums: Tommy Wells
Clarinet: Denis Solee
Violin: Carl Gorodetsky, Lee Larrison, Andrea Zonn, Pamela
      Sixfin
Percussion: Kenny Malone
Trumpet: George Tidwell
Viola: Kris Wilkinson
String arrangements: Charles Cochran and Joey Miskulin
1. Riding the Winds of the West (Douglas B. Green)
2. The Texas Polka (Oakley Halderman–Vic Knight–Lew Porter)
3. Take Me Back to My Boots and Saddle (Teddy Powell–Walter
      Samuels–Leonard Whitcup)
4. After You've Gone (Henry Creamer–Turner Layton)
5. The Trail Tip Song (Fred LaBour)
6. Desert Serenade (Douglas B. Green)
7. Rawhide (Dimitri Tiomkin–Ned Washington)
8. The Whispering Wind (Douglas B. Green)
9. The First Cowboy Song (Douglas B. Green–Gary McMahan)
10. Idaho (Frank Basso)
11. The Running Gun (Tompall Glaser–Jim Glaser)
12. The Cattle Call (Tex Owens)

Public Cowboy #1: The Music of Gene Autry
(Rounder 0410, 1996)

Producer: Joey Miskulin
Studio: Brent Truitt Studio
Engineer: Brent Truitt
Mixing Engineers: Brent Truitt, Kurt Storey, and Joey Miskulin
Ranger Doug: Guitar, vocals
Too Slim: Bunkhouse bass, vocals
Woody Paul: Fiddle, vocals
String arrangements: Kris Wilkinson and Joey Miskulin
Additional musicians:
Accordion: Joey Miskulin
Trumpet: George Tidwell
Trombone: Louis Brown
Viola: Kris Wilkinson
Violin: Pamela Sixfin, David Davidson
Lab steel guitar: Robby Turner
1. Back in the Saddle Again (Gene Autry–Ray Whitley)
2. Sioux City Sue (Ray Freedland–Dick Thomas)
3. Mexicali Rose (Jack Tenney–Helen Stone)
4. You Are My Sunshine (Jimmie Davis)
5. Have I Told You Lately That I Love You? (Scott Wiseman)
6. Can't Shake the Sands of Texas from My Shoes (D. Johnson–
      Gene Autry–K. Pitts)
7. That Silver-Haired Daddy of Mine (Gene Autry–Jimmy Long)
8. Be Honest with Me (Fred Rose–Gene Autry)
9. Blue Canadian Rockies (Cindy Walker–Gene Autry)
10. Lonely River (Fred Rose–Gene Autry–Ray Whitley)
11. South of the Border (Jimmy Carr–Michael Kennedy)
12. Ridin' Down the Canyon (Gene Autry–Smiley Burnette)

Ranger Doug: Songs of the Sage
(Warner Western 9 46497–2, 1997)

Producer: Joey Miskulin
Studio: Brent Truitt Music and Musicwagon Studio
Engineers: Brent Truitt and Joey Miskulin
Mixing Engineers: Dan Rudin and Joey Miskulin
Additional Musicians:
Guitar: Ronnie Brooks, Jimmy Capps, Jeff King, Mark Howard
Fiddle: Barbara Lamb
Accordion, Keyboards: Joey Miskulin
Acoustic Bass: Freddy LaBour
Trumpet: George Tidwell
Clarinet: Denis Solee
Violin: Carl Gorodetzky, Pamela Sixfen
Viola: James Grosjean
Cello: Robert Mason
Background vocals: Carol Lee Cooper, Dennis McCall, Sally
    Green, and Joey Miskulin
String Arrangements: Larry Cansler and Joey Miskulin
1. Singing in the Saddle (Douglas B. Green)
2. Hurry Sunrise (Douglas B. Green)
3. Riding on the Rio (Douglas B. Green)
4. Virgen Maria (Why Are You Weeping?) (Douglas B. Green)
5. Amber Eyes (Douglas B. Green)
6. Night-Riding Song (Douglas B. Green)
7. Welcome to the West (Douglas B. Green)
8. Jesse (Douglas B. Green–Madeline Stone)
9. River of Mystery (Douglas B. Green)
10. Bells (Douglas B. Green)
11. Idaho Moon (Douglas B. Green)
12. Where the Wild Winds Blow (Douglas B. Green)

A Great Big Western Howdy! from Riders In The Sky
(Rounder 0430, 1998)

Producer: Joey Miskulin
Studio: B. Truitt Music, Musicwagon, and Mark Howard Studio, Nashville, Tenn.
Engineers: Brent Truitt, Joey Miskulin, and Mark Howard
Mixing Engineer: Dan Rudin
Joey the Cowpolka King: Accordion, vocals
Ranger Doug: Guitar, vocals
Too Slim: Bunkhouse bass, vocals
Woody Paul: Fiddle, vocals
Additional musicians:
Guitar: Mark Casstevens, Richard O'Brien, Mark Howard
Drums, percussion: Bob Mater
Trumpet: George Tidwell
Mandolin, Danelectro guitar: Brent Truitt
Violin, viola: Kris Wilkinson
Violin: David Davidson
Irish folk flute: Reilly McFeeney
Special Guest: Marty Stuart
1. Wah-Hoo (Cliff Friend)
2. A Hundred and Sixty Acres (David Kapp)
3. Cherokee (Ray Noble)
4. Autumn on the Trail (Don Robertson–Hal Blair)
5. The Ballad of Palindrome/Palindrome: The Scene with Johnny Western (Johnny Western–Richard Boone–Sam Rolfe–Fred LaBour)
6. Cowboy Camp Meetin' (Tim Spencer)
7. The Arms of My Love (Woody Paul)
8. Cimarron Moon (Douglas B. Green)
9. The Sidekick Jig (Douglas B. Green)
10. A Border Romance (Douglas B. Green)
11. One More Ride (with Marty Stuart) (Bob Nolan)
12. He Walks with the Wild and the Lonely (Bob Nolan)

Christmas the Cowboy Way
(Rounder 0445, 1999)

Producer: Joey Miskulin
Studio: B. Truitt Music and Musicwagon Studio
Engineers: Brent Truitt and Joey Miskulin
Mixing Engineer: Dan Rudin
Ranger Doug: Guitar, vocals
Too Slim: Bunkhouse bass, vocals
Woody Paul: Fiddle, vocals
Additional musicians:
Accordion, vocals, keyboards: Joey the Cowpolka King
Guitar: Richard O'Brien, David Hungate
Drums, percussion: Bob Mater
Violin: Jonathan Yudkin
Tenor sax: Jay Patten
Percussion: Bob Warren

1. Corn, Water, and Wood (Carol Ashford Elliot–Wendy Waldman)
2. Let It Snow/The Last Christmas Medley You'll Ever Need to Hear (Sammy Cahn–Julie Styne–Paul Chrisman)
3. The Christmas Yodel (Douglas B. Green)
4. Sidemeat's Christmas Stew (Douglas B. Green)
5. The Prairie Dog Christmas Ball (Douglas B. Green)
6. The Friendly Beasts (Charlie Louvin–Ira Louvin)
7. Virgen Maria (Why Are You Weeping?) (Douglas B. Green)
8. I'll Be Home for Christmas (Kim Gannon–Kent Walter–Buck Ram)
9. An Old-Fashioned Christmas Polka (Joey Miskulin)
10. The Twelve Days of Cowboy Christmas (Fred LaBour)
11. Just Put a Ribbon in Your Hair (Donald C. Huber Jr.–Robert Charles Burns)
12. O Come, O Come Emmanuel (P.D.: arr: Riders In The Sky)

Woody's Roundup Featuring Riders In The Sky
(Disney 60676, 2000)

Producer: Joey Miskulin
Executive Producer: Jay Landers
Studios: B. Truitt Music and Musicwagon
Engineers: Brent Truitt and Joey Miskulin
Mixing Engineers: Dan Rudin and Joey Miskulin
Ranger Doug: Guitar, vocals
Too Slim: Bunkhouse Bass, guitar, vocals, sound effects
Woody Paul: Fiddle, vocals
Joey the Cowpolka King: Accordion, vocals, keyboard,
    percussion, sound effects
Special Guest: Devon Dawson (vocal on "Jessie, the Yodelin'
    Cowgirl" and "How Does She Yodel")
Additional musicians:
Guitar: Richard O'Brien
Fiddle: Jonathan Yudkin
Drums, percussion: Bob Mater
Squeaky Toy: George LaBour
Children background singers: Casey Chrisman, Katherine
    Chrisman, Rebecca Chrisman, Grace Green, Alice LaBour,
    and Katie Miskulin
1. Woody's Roundup (Randy Newman)
2. Act Naturally (Johnny Russell–Voni Morrison)
3. Jessie, the Yodelin' Cowgirl (Douglas B. Green)
4. The Ballad of Bullseye (Fred LaBour)
5. You've Got a Friend in Me (Randy Newman)
6. Hey Howdy Hey (Michael Kostroff–Bruce Healey)
7. My Favorite Toys (Fred LaBour)
8. How Does She Yodel (Douglas B. Green)
9. Prospector Polka (Joey Miskulin)
10. You've Got a Friend in Me (instrumental) (Randy Newman)
11. "One, Two, Three," Said the Prospector" (Douglas B. Green)
12. Home on the Range (P.D. arr: Riders In The Sky)
13. To Infinity and Beyond (Fred LaBour)

Riders In The Sky Present A Pair of Kings
(Oh Boy OBR 022, 2001)

Producer: Joey Miskulin
Studio: B. Truitt Studio and Musicwagon Studio, Nashville, Tenn.
Engineers: Brent Truitt and Joey Miskulin
Mixing Engineer: Dan Rudin
Ranger Doug: Guitar, vocals
Too Slim, Bunkhouse bass, vocals
Woody Paul: Fiddle, vocals
Joey the Cowpolka King: Accordion, percussion, vocals
Additional musicians:
Mandolin: Jake Chrisman
Duet on "Don't Sweetheart Me": "Pops"
1. We're Burnin' Moonlight (Joey Miskulin)
2. Clarinet Polka (arr: Woody Paul–Joey Miskulin)
3. You Stole My Wife You Horsethief (Paul Reif–Harry Sims)
4. How High the Moon (Nancy Hamilton–William Lewis Jr.)
5. Texas Sand (arr: Woody Paul–Joey Miskulin–Fred LaBour–Douglas B. Green)
6. Celtic Medley (Annie Laurie/Scotland the Brave/Haste to the Wedding) (arr: Woody Paul)
7. I'm an Old Cowhand (Johnny Mercer)
8. Jessie Polka (arr: Woody Paul–Joey Miskulin)
9. Never Go to Church on Sunday (Woody Paul)
10. The Bunkhouse Race (Dizzy Fingers) (arr: Woody Paul–Joey Miskulin)
11. Don't Sweetheart Me (Cliff Friend–Charles Tobias)
12. Katherine's Waltz (Woody Paul)

Ridin' the Tweetsie Railroad
(Riders In The Sky, 2002)

Producer: Joey Miskulin
Studios: B. Truitt Music and Musicwagon
Engineers: Brent Truitt, Joey Miskulin, and Tim Roberts
Mixed by Keith Compton
Ranger Doug: Guitar, vocals
Too Slim: Bunkhouse bass, vocals
Woody Paul: Fiddle, vocals
Joey the Cowpolka King: Accordion, sound FX, vocals
Additional musicians:
Guitar: Richard O'Brien
Percussion: John Gardner
1. Tweetsie Railroad Line (Douglas B. Green)
2. New River Train (Carson Robison)
3. Casey Jones (P.D. arr. Riders In The Sky)
4. Great Northern (Douglas B. Green)
5. Rock Island Line (P.D. arr. Riders In The Sky)
6. I've Been Working on the Railroad (P.D. arr. Riders In The Sky)
7. Here Comes the Santa Fe (Douglas B. Green)
8. Railroad Corral (P.D. arr. Riders In The Sky)
9. Tweetsie Junction (Joey Miskulin)
10. Orange Blossom Special (Ervin T. Rouse)
11. Ghost Train (Fred LaBour)
12. Way Out There (Bob Nolan)
13. Wabash Cannonball (P.D. arr. Riders In The Sky)

Monsters Inc. Scream Factory Favorites
(Disney 60789, 2002)

Producer: Joey Miskulin
Executive Producer: Jay Landers
Recording at Musicwagon Studio and B. Truitt
Engineers: Joey Miskulin, Brent Truitt, and Tim Roberts
Mixed by Dan Rudin
Ranger Doug: Guitar, vocals
Too Slim: Bunkhouse bass, vocals
Woody Paul: Fiddle, vocals
Joey the Cowpolka King: Accordion, piano, banjo, sound FX,
     synthesizer, vocals
Additional musicians:
Drums, percussion: John Gardener
Guitar, ukulele: Chris Leuzinger
Violin: Jonathan Yudkin
Trumpet: George Tidwell
Synthesizer: David Hoffner
Drums: Bob Mater
Guitar: Jimmy Capps
Steel guitar: Stu Basore
Vocal: Harry Stinson
1. If I Didn't Have You (Randy Newman)
2. Doo-Wah Diddy Diddy (Mike's Song) (J. Barry–E. Greenwich)
3. I Only Have Eye For You (Douglas B. Green)
4. Monsters Inc. March (Fred LaBour)
5. Monster ABCs (Fred LaBour)
6. Lullaby for Boo (with Sonya Isaacs) (Paul Chrisman–Fred
     LaBour)
7. If I Didn't Have You (Instrumental) (Randy Newman)
8. It's Our Job (Joey Miskulin)
9. Paperwork (Roz's Song) (Douglas B. Green)
10. Monsters' Jubilee (Paul Chrisman–Douglas B. Green)
11. Under the Bed (Douglas B. Green)
12. The Perfect Roar (Sulley's Song) (Paul Chrisman–Archibalt
     Seiffer)
13. Big High Wire Hop (Instrumental) (Douglas B. Green–Fred
     LaBour–Paul Chrisman–Joey Miskulin)

Sessionography

Note: These dates and studios include only recording
basic tracks, not overdubs or mixing.

Nashville, Tenn.
Audio-Media Studios
November 26, 1979
Skyball Paint (Bob Nolan)
Three on the Trail (Douglas B. Green)
(Ghost) Riders In The Sky (Stan Jones)

Nashville, Tenn.
Audio-Media Studios
December 3, 1979
Blue Montana Skies (Douglas B. Green)
Riding Alone (Douglas B. Green)

Nashville, Tenn.
Audio-Media Studios
December 5, 1979
Cielito Lindo (P.D.)
Don't Fence Me In (Cole Porter)
When Payday Rolls Around (Bob Nolan)
So Long, Saddle Pals (Woody Paul)
That's How the Yodel Was Born (Douglas B. Green)
The Cowboy Song (Woody Paul)
Blue Bonnet Lady (Woody Paul)
Here Comes the Santa Fe (Douglas B. Green)

Nashville, Tenn.
Creative Workshop
December 17, 1980
Back in the Saddle Again (Ray Whitley–Gene Autry)
Cowboy Jubilee (Woody Paul–Fred LaBour)

Nashville, Tenn.
Creative Workshop
December 19, 1980
At the End of the Rainbow Trail (Douglas B. Green)
On the Rhythm Range (Bob Nolan)
Compadres in the Old Sierra Madres (Woody Paul)
Soon as the Roundup's Through (Woody Paul)
The Desperado Trail (Woody Paul)

Nashville, Tenn.
Creative Workshop
December 23, 1980
Ol' Cowpoke (Gary McMahan)
Red River Valley (P.D.)
Ride with the Wind (Douglas B. Green)
Riding Alone (Douglas B. Green)

Nashville, Tenn.
Creative Workshop
January 5, 1981
Ojo Caliente (Thomas Goldsmith)

Nashville, Tenn.
Creative Workshop
October 23, 1981
Christmas at the Triple X Ranch (Woody Paul–Karen Ritter)
Riding Home on Christmas Eve (Douglas B. Green)

Pittsburgh, Pa.
Audio Innovators
January 5, 1982
Bound to Hit the Trail (Woody Paul)
Cool Water (Bob Nolan)
Tumbling Tumbleweeds (Bob Nolan)
West Texas Cowboy (Woody Paul)

Pittsburgh, Pa.
Audio Innovators
January 6, 1982
La Cucaracha (P.D.)
Wasteland (Douglas B. Green)
Pecos Bill (Johnny Lange–Elliot Daniel)
That's How the Yodel Was Born (Douglas B. Green)
The Streets of Laredo (P.D.)
Singing a Song to the Sky (Douglas B. Green)

Nashville, Tenn.
Quadraphonic Studios
April 5, 1982
Blue Shadows on the Trail (Johnny Lange–Eliot Daniel)
Cowpoke (Stan Jones)
Home on the Range (P.D.)

Nashville, Tenn.
Quadraphonic Studios
April 6, 1982
Chasing the Sun (Douglas B. Green)
I Ride an Old Paint (P.D.)
Old El Paso (Douglas B. Green)
Pretty Prairie Princess (Woody Paul)
Prairie Serenade (Douglas B. Green)
Nevada (Woody Paul–Karen Ritter)
The Utah Trail (Woody Paul)
Jingle Jangle Jingle (Joseph J. Lilley–Frank Loesser)
Down the Trail to San Antone (Deuce Spriggins)

Alexandria, Va.
The Birchmere (live recording)
March 5–6, 1983
Cowboy Jubilee (Woody Paul–Fred LaBour)
The Yodel Blues (Johnny Mercer–Robert Emmet Dolan)
When the Bloom Is on the Sage (Nat Vincent–Fred Howard)
After You've Gone (Turner Layton–Henry Creamer)
The Cowboy Song (Woody Paul)
Varmint Dancing (arr.: Woody Paul)
Hold That Critter Down (Bob Nolan)

The Last Roundup (Billy Hill)
Cielito Lindo (P.D.)
Blue Bonnet Lady (Woody Paul)

Nashville, Tenn.
Studio 19
August 16, 1984
Get Along Little Dogies (P.D.)
The Biscuit Blues (Bob Nolan)

Nashville, Tenn.
Studio 19
August 21, 1984
The Old Chisholm Trail (P.D.)
There's a Great Big Candy Roundup (Lou Robino–Joe Estella–
    Dick Manning)

Nashville, Tenn.
Studio 19
August 22, 1984
I'm Going to Leave Old Texas Now (P.D.)
Betsy from Pike (P.D.)

Nashville, Tenn.
Audio Media
October 24, 1984
Slow Poke (Pee Wee King–Redd Stewart–Chilton Price)

Nashville, Tenn.
Studio 19
December 17, 1984
Clementine (P.D.)
"One, Two, Three," Said the Miner (Douglas B. Green)
The Cowboy's A-B-Cs (Douglas B. Green)
Down the Lullabye Trail (Douglas B. Green)
Fiddle Medley (arr.: Woody Paul)
Blue Bonnet Lady (Woody Paul)

Even Texas Isn't Big Enough Now (Kerry Chater–Patti
	Dahlstrom)
Nashville, Tenn.
Studio 19
January 9, 1985
Yippie Ki Yo and Away We Go (Woody Paul–Fred LaBour)

Nashville, Tenn.
Studio 19
April 8, 1985
Cimarron (Johnny Bond)
Soon As the Roundup's Through (Woody Paul)
Trail of Tears (Lee Domann–Pee Sebert–Ralph Whiteway)
Cowboy of the Highway (Woody Paul)

Nashville, Tenn.
Studio 19
June 10, 1985
I'm Satisfied with You (Fred Rose)
All Those Years (Douglas B. Green)

Nashville, Tenn.
Emerald Studios
February 14, 1987
Miss Molly (Cindy Walker)
Lonely Yukon Stars (Douglas B. Green)
Ride with Me, Gringo (Fred LaBour)
Faded Love (Bob Wills–John Wills)
Cherokee (Ray Noble)
Texas Plains (Stuart Hamblen)
Back in the Saddle Again (Ray Whitley–Gene Autry)
(Ghost) Riders in the Sky (Stan Jones)
Don't Fence Me In (Cole Porter)
The Salting of the Slug (Fred LaBour)
One More Ride (Bob Nolan)
The Call of the Canyon (Billy Hill)
Sidekick Heaven (Eddie Dean–Hal Blair–Fred LaBour)
Reincarnation (Wallace MacRae)
That's How the Yodel Was Born (Douglas B. Green)
The Wayward Wind (Herb Newman–Stanley Lebowsky)

My Oklahoma (Terrye Newkirk)
Stone's Rag (Oscar Stone)
Cimarron (Johnny Bond)
Riding down the Canyon (Smiley Burnette–Gene Autry)
Ride with the Wind (Douglas B. Green)
Cattle Call (Tex Owens)
Carry Me Back to the Lone Prairie (Carson J. Robison)
When Payday Rolls Around (Bob Nolan)
Happy Trails (To You) (Dale Evans)

Nashville, Tenn.
Emerald Studios
March 7, 1988
Riders Radio Theater Theme (Woody Paul–Fred LaBour)
Sundown Blues (Douglas B. Green)
Chant of the Wanderer (Bob Nolan)
So Long, Saddle Pals (Woody Paul)
Cattle Call (Tex Owens)

Nashville, Tenn.
Emerald Studios
March 8–9, 1988
Comedy bits and skits

Nashville, Tenn.
16th Avenue Recorders
March 13, 1989
Comedy bits and skits

Nashville, Tenn.
16th Avenue Recorders
March 14, 1989
Comedy bits and skits
There's a Blue Sky Way Out Yonder (Fred Hall–Bert Van Cleve–
    Arthur Fields)
Riding the Old Front Range (Douglas B. Green)
The Queen Elizabeth Trio (arr: Riders In The Sky)
No Rodeo Dough (John Jacob Loeb–Cy Coben–Lewis Harris)
Along the Navajo Trail (Larry Markes–Dick Charles–Eddie
    Delange)
Ride with Me, Gringo (Fred LaBour)

Nashville, Tenn.
16th Avenue Recorders
March 15, 1989
Comedy bits and skits

Nashville, Tenn.
16th Avenue Recorders
April 10, 1990
Ride, Cowboy, Ride (Rex Allen Jr.–Curtis Allen–Denny DeMarco)
Homecoming Yodel (Dougas B. Green)
The Call of the Canyon (Billy Hill)
The Arms of My Love (Woody Paul)
Sidekick Heaven (Eddie Dean–Hal Blair–Fred LaBour)

Nashville, Tenn.
16th Avenue Recorders
April 11, 1990
Someone's Got to Do It (Douglas B. Green)
Texas Echo (David Ball)
Maybe I'll Cry over You (Elton Britt)
The Line Rider (Douglas B. Green)
What Would I Do without You? (Woody Paul)
Living in a Mobile Home (Ronnie Scaife–Rory Michael Burke)

Nashville, Tenn.
Nightingale Studios May 13, 1991
Press along to the Big Corral (Romaine Lowdermilk)
Great Grand Dad (Frank Luther)
Ballad of Palindrome (Johnny Western–Richard Boone–Sam
    Rolfe–Fred LaBour)
Come and Get It (Tim Spencer–Glenn Spencer)
Cody of the Pony Express (Bob Nolan)
How Does He Yodel? (Douglas B. Green)
Face: The Music (Fred LaBour)

Nashville, Tenn.
Nightingale Studios May 14, 1991
Harmony Ranch (Woody Paul)
I Always Do (Douglas B. Green)
One Little Coyote (Douglas B. Green)

Prairie Lullaby (Woody Paul)
The Cowboy's A-B-Cs (Douglas B. Green)
Pecos Bill (Johnny Lange–Eliot Daniel)
Fiddle Medley (arr.: Woody Paul)

Nashville, Tenn.
Nightingale Studios
April 20, 1992
Riding Home on Christmas Eve (Douglas B. Green)
Sidemeat's Christmas Goose (Douglas B. Green)
Rudolph the Red-Nosed Reindeer (Johnny Marks)
Christmas at the Harmony Ranch (Woody Paul–Karen Ritter)
Navidad Y Año Nuevo (J.J. "Chucho" Navarro)
Jingle Bells (P.D.)
White Christmas (Irving Berlin)

Nashville, Tenn.
Nightingale Studios
April 21, 1992
Christmas Medley/The Greatest Gifts (arr.: Riders In The Sky/
    Douglas B. Green)
Here Comes Santa Claus (Oakley Haldeman–Gene Autry)
Silver Bells (Jay Livingston–Ray Evans)
Just Put a Ribbon in Your Hair (Donald C. Huber Jr.–Robert
    Charles Burns)
Christmastime's A-Coming (Tex Logan)

Nashville, Tenn.
Nightingale Studios
February 3, 1994
Early Autumn (Douglas B. Green)
The Yellow Rose of Texas (arr.: Douglas B. Green)
One Has My Name (The Other Has My Heart) (Eddie Dean–
    Dearest Dean)
La Malaguena (arr.: Douglas B. Green)
You're Wearing Out Your Welcome, Matt (David Kent–Joey
    Scott)

Nashville, Tenn.
Nightingale Studios
February 5, 1994
Along the Santa Fe Trail (Al Dubin–Edwina Coolidge–Will
    Grosz)
Farr Away Stomp (Karl Farr–Hugh Farr)

Austin, Tex.
Bismeaux Studios
February 16, 1994
Hang Your Head in Shame (Fred Rose–Ed Nelson–Steve Nelson)
I'm a Ding Dong Daddy (From Dumas) (Phil Baxter)

Nashville, Tenn.
Nightingale Studios
February 21, 1994
The Cowboy's in Love (Douglas B. Green)
Wimmen . . . Who Needs 'Em? (Douglas B. Green)
The Ballad of Palindrome (Johnny Western–Richard Boone–Sam
    Rolfe–Fred LaBour)
Sweet Señorita Teresa (Woody Paul)
The Running Gun (Jim Glaser)

Nashville, Tenn.
Mark Howard Studio
March 8, 1994
King of the River (Thomas Blackburn–George Bruns)
Heading for Texas (Douglas B. Green)
Old Betsy (George Bruns–Gil George)
The Ballad of Davy Crockett (George Bruns–Thomas Blackburn)

Nashville, Tenn.
Mark Howard Studio
March 9, 1994
Remember the Alamo (June Bowers)
Farewell (David Crockett–George Bruns)
Be Sure You're Right (And Then Go Ahead) (George Bruns–
    Thomas Blackburn)

Nashville, Tenn.
Mark Howard Studio
March 10, 1994
Colonel Crockett's Speech to Congress (Douglas B. Green)
The Grinning Tale (Jimmy Driftwood)

Nashville, Tenn.
Mark Howard Studio
March 6, 1995
Rawhide (Ned Washington–Dmitri Tiompkin)

Nashville, Tenn.
Mark Howard Studio
March 7, 1995
Desert Serenade (Douglas B. Green)
The Running Gun (Jim Glaser)
Cattle Call (Tex Owens)
Texas Polka (Oakley Haldeman–Vic Knight–Lew Porter)

Nashville, Tenn.
Mark Howard Studio
March 8, 1995
The First Cowboy Song (Douglas B Green–Gary McMahan)
The Wayward Wind (Herb Newman–Stanley Lebowsky)

Nashville, Tenn.
Mark Howard Studio
March 9, 1995
The Trail Tip Song (Fred LaBour)
I Still Do (Bob Nolan)
After You've Gone (Turner Layton–Henry Creamer)

Nashville, Tenn.
Mark Howard Studio
March 10, 1995
Boots and Saddles (Walter Samuels–Leonard Whitcup–Teddy
    Powell)
Riding the Winds of the West (Douglas B. Green)
Idaho (Frank Basso)
The Whispering Wind (Douglas B. Green)

Nashville, Tenn.
Brent Truitt Studio
June 17, 1996
Mexicali Rose (Jack Tenney–Helen Stone)
Lonely River (Ray Whitley–Fred Rose–Gene Autry)
Blue Canadian Rockies (Cindy Walker)

Nashville, Tenn.
Brent Truitt Studio
June 18, 1996
Be Honest with Me (Fred Rose–Gene Autry)
That Silver Haired Daddy of Mine (Gene Autry–Jimmy Long)
South of the Border (Jimmy Kennedy–Michael Carr)
Riding Down the Canyon (Smiley Burnette–Gene Autry)

Nashville, Tenn.
Brent Truitt Studio
June 19, 1996
You Are My Sunshine (Jimmy Davis–Charles Mitchell)
Have I Told You Lately That I Love You (Scotty Wiseman)

Nashville, Tenn.
Brent Truitt Studio
June 20, 1996
Back in the Saddle Again (Ray Whitley–Gene Autry)
Can't Shake the Sands of Texas from My Shoes (D. Johnson–K.
    Pitts–Gene Autry)
Sioux City Sue (Dick Thomas–Ray Freedland)

Nashville, Tenn.
Brent Truitt Studio
September 23, 1997
Wah Hoo (Cliff Friend)
Song of the Trail (Stan Jones)
Autumn on the Trail (Don Robertson–Hal Blair)
Cimarron Moon (Douglas B. Green)
A Border Romance (Douglas B. Green)
One More Ride (Bob Nolan)

Nashville, Tenn.
Brent Truitt Studio
September 24, 1997
The Sidekick Jig (Douglas B. Green)
A Hundred and Sixty Acres (David Kapp)
The Ballad of Palindrome (Johnny Western–Richard Boone–Sam
        Rolfe–Fred LaBour)
Trail Dust (Andy Parker)
The Arms of My Love (Woody Paul)

Nashville, Tenn.
Brent Truitt Studio
September 27, 1997
Cherokee (Ray Noble)

Nashville, Tenn.
Brent Truitt Studio
September 28, 1997
He Walks with the Wild and the Lonely (Bob Nolan)
Cowboy Camp Meetin' (Tim Spencer)

Nashville, Tenn.
Brent Truitt Studio
February 16, 1998
Corn, Water, and Wood (Wendy Waldman–Carol Elliot)
Let It Snow, Let It Snow, Let It Snow (Jule Styne–Sammy Cahn)
The Christmas Yodel (Douglas B. Green)
Sidemeat's Christmas Stew (Douglas B. Green)
The Prairie Dog's Christmas Ball (Douglas B. Green)

Nashville, Tenn.
Brent Truitt Studio
May 19, 1998
The Friendly Beasts (Ira Louvin–Charles Louvin)
Virgen Maria (Why Are You Weeping?) (Douglas B. Green)
I'll Be Home for Christmas (Walter Kent–Kim Gannon–Buck
        Ram)
Old-Fashioned Christmas Polka (Joey Miskulin)

Nashville, Tenn.
Brent Truitt Studio
May 20, 1998
The Twelve Days of Cowboy Christmas (Fred LaBour)
Just Put a Ribbon in Your Hair (Donald C. Huber Jr.–Robert
    Charles Burns)

Nashville, Tenn.
Brent Truitt Studio
January 7, 1999
O Come, Immanuel (P.D.)

Nashville, Tenn.
Brent Truitt Studio
April 13, 1999
Texas Sand (Buster Coward)
Dizzy Fingers (Edward E. Confrey)
Clarinet Polka (arr: Joey Miskulin–Woody Paul)
Medley: Annie Laurie/Scotland the Brave/Haste to the
    Wedding (arr: Joey Miskulin–Woody Paul)
Jesusita En Chihuahua (arr: Joey Miskulin–Woody Paul)

Nashville, Tenn.
Brent Truitt Studio
April 14, 1999
We're Burning Moonlight (Joey Miskulin)
Never Go to Church on Sunday (Woody Paul)
Katherine's Waltz (Woody Paul)
You Stole My Wife, You Horse Thief (Paul Reif–Harry Sims)
I'm an Old Cowhand (Johnny Mercer)

Nashville, Tenn.
Brent Truitt Studio
April 15, 1999
How High the Moon (Nancy Hamilton–Morgan Lewis)
Don't Sweetheart Me (Cliff Friend–Charles Tobias)

Burbank, Calif.
O'Henry Studio
August 24, 1999
Woody's Roundup (Randy Newman)

Nashville, Tenn.
Brent Truitt Studio
November 15, 1999
Woody's Roundup (Randy Newman)
Jessie, The Yodeling Cowgirl (Douglas B. Green)
How Does She Yodel? (Douglas B. Green)
The Ballad of Bullseye (Fred LaBour)
Act Naturally (Johnny Russell–Voni Morrison)

Nashville, Tenn.
Brent Truitt Studio
November 16, 1999
"One, Two, Three," Said the Prospector (Douglas B. Green)
You've Got a Friend in Me (Randy Newman)
The Prospector Polka (Joey Miskulin)
My Favorite Toys (Fred LaBour)
Two Roads (Douglas B. Green)

Nashville, Tenn.
Brent Truitt Studio
November 30, 1999
Home on the Range (P.D.)
Hey, Howdy, Hey (Michael Kostroff–Bruce Healey)

Nashville, Tenn.
Brent Truitt Studio
April 2, 2000
The Big High Wire Hop (Chrisman–Green–LaBour–Miskulin)

Nashville, Tenn.
War Memorial Auditorium
September 24, 2000
Billy the Kid (John Hartford)

Nashville, Tenn.
Brent Truitt Studio
September 28, 2001
There's a Star-Spangled Banner Waving Somewhere (Shelby
　　Darnell–Paul Roberts)

Nashville, Tenn.
Brent Truitt Studio
October 29, 2001
Here Comes the Santa Fe (Douglas B. Green)
Way Out There (Bob Nolan)
Woody's Roundup (Randy Newman)
How Does He Yodel (Douglas B. Green)

Nashville, Tenn.
Brent Truitt Studio
October 30, 2001
Texas Plains (Stuart Hamblen)
Cool Water (Bob Nolan)
That's How the Yodel Was Born (Douglas B. Green)
Blue Bonnet Lady (Woody Paul)
Ride, Cowboy, Ride (Rex Allen Jr.–Curtis Allen–Denny DeMarco)

Nashville, Tenn.
Brent Truitt Studio
October 31, 2001
Lonely Yukon Stars (Douglas B. Green)
The Line Rider (Douglas B. Green)
Ringo (Don Robertson–Hal Blair)
Reincarnation (Wallace MacRae)
Tumbling Tumbleweeds (Bob Nolan)
The Arms of My Love (Woody Paul)

Nashville, Tenn.
Brent Truitt Studio
November 15, 2001
Thomas Timberwolf (Douglas B. Green)
Riders in the Sky (Stan Jones)
My Oklahoma (Terrye Newkirk)
La Malaguena (arr: Douglas B. Green)

Nashville, Tenn.
Brent Truitt Studio
November 16, 2001
Sidekick Heaven (Eddie Dean–Hal Blair–Fred LaBour)
Phantom of the Chuckwagon (Fred LaBour)
Sundown in Santa Fe (Douglas B. Green)
Compadres in the Old Sierra Madres (Woody Paul)

Nashville, Tenn.
Brent Truitt Studio
January 29, 2002
Railroad Corral (Traditional)
The Great Northern (Douglas B. Green)

Nashville, Tenn.
Brent Truitt Studio
January 30, 2002
Tweetsie Railroad Line (Douglas B. Green)
Wabash Cannonball (A.P. Carter)
Orange Blossom Special (Rouse)

Nashville, Tenn.
Brent Truitt Studio
January 31, 2002
New River Train (Carson J. Robison)
Rock Island Line (P.D.)
I've Been Working on the Railroad (P.D.)

Nashville, Tenn.
Brent Truitt Studio
February 1, 2002
Casey Jones (P.D.)
Tweetsie Junction (Joey Miskulin)
Ghost Train (Fred LaBour)

Nashville, Tenn.
Musicwagon Studio
April 18, 2002
I Only Have Eye for You (Douglas B. Green)
The Perfect Roar (Woody Paul–Joshua Archibald–Seiffer)
Under the Bed (Douglas B. Green)

Nashville, Tenn.
Brent Truitt Studio
April 22, 2002
Monster, Inc. March (Fred LaBour)
Doo-Wah Diddy (Mike's Song) (J. Barry–E. Greenwich–F. LaBour)
Lullaby for Boo (Fred LaBour–Woody Paul)
Monster's A-B-Cs (Fred LaBour)
If I Didn't Have You (vocal version) (Randy Newman)
If I Didn't Have You (instrumental version) (Randy Newman)
It's Our Job (Joey Miskulin)
Paperwork (Roz's Song) (Douglas B. Green)
The Monsters' Jubilee (Woody Paul–Douglas B. Green)

Ranger Doug: Solo album sessions

Nashville, Tenn.
Brent Truitt Studio
July 29, 1996
Singing in the Saddle (Douglas B. Green)
Where the Wild Winds Blow (Douglas B. Green)
Riding on the Rio (Douglas B. Green)
Amber Eyes (Douglas B. Green)

Nashville, Tenn.
Brent Truitt Studios
July 30, 1996
Welcome to the West (Douglas B. Green)
River of Mystery (Douglas B. Green)
Bells (Douglas B. Green)
Virgen Maria (Why Are You Weeping?) (Douglas B. Green)
Night-riding Song (Douglas B. Green)

Nashville, Tenn.
Brent Truitt Studios
July 31, 1996
Shelter of the Wildwood (Douglas B. Green)
Jesse (Douglas B. Green–Madeline Stone)
Idaho Moon (Douglas B. Green)
Hurry Sunrise (Douglas B. Green)

Riders In The Sky: Recording Sessions with Others:

Nashville, Tenn.
American Studios
April 9, 1979
Larry Mahan: "Saying Goodbye to the West"

Nashville, Tenn.
American Studios
April 11, 1979
Larry Mahan: "The Old Double Diamond (Gary McMahan)
"Nashville Cowboy"

Aspen, Colo.
Aspen Sound Studios
January 11, 1980
John McEuen: "I've Been down That Road Before" (Hank
      Williams)

Los Angeles, Calif.
Sunset Studios
May 12, 1981
John McEuen: "I Am a Pilgrim" (P.D.)

Austin, Tex.
Wink Tyler Studios November 16, 1985
Al Dressen: "Down on the Rio Grande" (Al Dressen) "We're
Glad to See You" (Al Dressen)

Nashville, Tenn.
December 18, 1987
Gail Chazen: "High and Dry" (Gail Chazen)

Nashville, Tenn.
Jack's Tracks
January 12, 1989
Kathy Mattea: "Here's Hopin' (Bob Regan–Mark D. Sanders)

Nashville, Tenn.
Music Mill
October 10, 1990
Roy Rogers: "Happy Trails (To You)" (Dale Evans)

Nashville, Tenn.
Music Mill
February 5, 1991
Roy Rogers: "When Payday Rolls Around (Bob Nolan)
"Little Joe the Wrangler" (P.D.)

Nashville, Tenn.
Music Mill
February 6, 1991
Roy Rogers: "Tumbling Tumbleweeds" (Bob Nolan)
"Alive and Kicking" (Roy Rogers)

Nashville, Tenn.
Mark Howard Studio
September 13, 1994
Roy Rogers: "Whoopie Ti Yi Yo" (P.D.)
"Home on the Range" (P.D.)

Nashville, Tenn.
Mark Howard Studio
September 14, 1994
Roy Rogers:
"I Ride an Old Paint (P.D.)
"The Yellow Rose of Texas" (P.D.)
"The Streets of Laredo" (P.D.)
"The Old Chisholm Trail" (P.D.)

Nashville, Tenn.
Mark Howard Studio
September 15, 1994
Roy Rogers:
"Home on the Range" (P.D.)
"Happy Trails (To You)" (Dale Evans)
"The Buckaroo's Life" (Douglas B. Green)

Nashville, Tenn.
Mark Howard Studio
September 16, 1994
Roy Rogers: "Night-riding Song" (Douglas B. Green)

Nashville, Tenn.
Omni Studio
May 21, 1991
Michael Martin Murphey:
"Riding Home on Christmas Eve" (Douglas B. Green)
"Christmas Yodel" (Douglas B. Green)

Nashville, Tenn.
Omni Studio
June 7, 1991
Michael Martin Murphey:
"Good Night Ladies/Auld Lang Syne" (arr: Michael Martin
    Murphey)
"Riding Home on Christmas Eve" (Douglas B. Green)
"The Cowboy's Christmas Ball" (Larry Chittendon)

Austin, Tex.
Bismeaux Studios
January 27, 1993
Asleep at the Wheel:
"Dusty Skies" (Cindy Walker)

Nashville, Tenn.
Gene Breeden Studios
March 23, 1994
Stonewall Jackson: "Old Showboat (Marijohn Wilkin–Fred
    Burch)

Nashville, Tenn.
Jukebox Studios
June 8, 1995
Stephanie Davis:
"Salt River Valley" (Cindy Walker)
"River of No Return" (Ken Darby–Lionel Newman)
"Montana" (Lou Forbes–Bob Nolan)

Nashville, Tenn.
Jukebox Studios
June 9, 1995
Stephanie Davis:
"Prairie Lullaby" (Stephanie Davis)

Nashville, Tenn.
April 30, 1996
Stu Phillips:
"Colorado" (Dave Kirby)
"Blue Canadian Rockies" (Cindy Walker)
"Rangeland" (Stu Phillips)

Nashville, Tenn.
Creative Workshop
May 1, 1996
Marty Robbins:
"Rudolph the Red-Nosed Reindeer" (Johnny Marks)

Nashville, Tenn.
Musicwagon Studio
July 16, 1996
Frank Yankovic:
"Hoop Dee Doo" (Frank Loesser–Milton DeLugg)

Nashville, Tenn.
Robby Turner Studio
August 5, 1999
Luke Reed:
"Blue Mesa" (Luke Reed–Roger Brown)

Notes and Bibliography

I have known Douglas Green since around 1975, Fred LaBour from around 1977, and Woody Paul since 1978; as stated in this book, I was their first manager. We've kept in contact through the years, and this book evolved out of conversations Doug and I have had over the years about a variety of subjects. A couple of years ago I went on the road with them to do an article for *Country Music People,* a magazine based in London. At that time, Ken Griffis was working on the biography of the Riders; however, when Ken decided against moving forward with the project, Ranger Doug asked me if I was interested, and I said I was. This is the result of that decision.

Through the years I have written a number of books on country music, including a biography of Eddy Arnold, as well as an encyclopedia of cowboys *(Cowboys and the Wild West: An A to Z Guide from the Chisholm Trail to the Silver Screen).* I have written entries on the Riders for several encyclopedias, including the one compiled by the Country Music Foundation. I have also been involved in the Western Music Association and currently am editor of their quarterly publication, *The Western Way.* In addition, I am professor of Music Business at Belmont University, where I teach a "History of the Recording Industry" course as well as courses about the current music business.

I say all this to make a point: It is very difficult to do the traditional "notes on sources" that accompany most books published by an academic press. I've certainly compiled such lists in the past and could reprint them here. However, I have decided to give a much shorter bibliography, but one that is directly relevant to the writing of this book. Also, I've come to this work after years of being heavily involved in the subjects of Riders In The Sky and western music through years of conversations and visits with the

Riders, as well as research for a number of other projects. While that background has made writing this book enjoyable and relatively easy, trying to document all of it is like trying to straighten out a tangled fishing line.

During the time I've worked on this book, I've conducted a number of interviews with each of the Riders—from sitting down in their homes to backstage visits at the Grand Ole Opry to phone conversations to ask a question or clarify a point. I'd like to thank each one—Ranger Doug, Too Slim, Woody Paul, and Joey the Cowpolka King—for sharing their time, knowledge, and perspectives on a variety of topics. Not all of their revelations are included in this book.

One spring day I drove about a hundred miles to visit with Billy Maxwell as he shared his experiences with the Riders. That was one of the best days of research I ever spent, because Billy's contributions to this book are enormous as he reveals life on the road with a hard-traveling western singing group. I would also like to thank Ken Griffis, whose initial work made this project easy.

I've had a number of interviews and conversations with people whose input has helped in the writing of this book. These include Alan Sacks, Steve Arwood, Michael Mahaney, Bill Ivey, Bob Pinson, Paul Lohr, Lisa Harris, John Lasseter, John Sandidge, Mary Matthews, Sally Green, and Hal Cannon. Although David Skepner died before I had a chance to do a long interview with him about the Riders, I had known him for a number of years and talked with him about the Riders on numerous occasions.

I'd also like to thank the Riders' wives, Teresa Chrisman, Roberta Samet LaBour, Ann Marie Flores, and Patti Miskulin—each of whom I spoke with during the writing of this book.

Bibliography

Bane, Michael. "20 Questions with Ranger Doug." *Country Music Magazine*, January/February, 1992.

Bond, Johnny. *Reflections: The Autobiography of Johnny Bond*. Los Angeles, Calif.: The John Edwards Memorial Foundation, 1976.

Brooks, Tim and Earle Marsh. *The Complete Directory to Prime Time Network TV Shows 1946–Present*. New York: Ballantine Books, 1988.

Carey, Bill. *Fiddles, Fortunes and Fried Chicken: A Nashville Business History*. Franklin, Tenn.: Hillsboro Press, 2000.

Carr, Patrick. "Riders In The Sky: It's a Great Job and Someone Has to Do It." *Country Music*, May/June, 1989.

Country Music Magazine, eds. *The Comprehensive Country Music Encyclopedia*. New York: Times Books, 1994.

Cusic, Don. "Riders In The Sky: Doing it the Cowboy Way." *Country Music People*, May 2001.

———. *Cowboys and the Wild West: An A to Z Guide from the Chisholm Trail to the Silver Screen*. New York: Facts on File, 1994.

Dougherty, Steve, with Jane Sanderson. "Riders In The Sky Lasso Listeners by Poking Fun at Cowpokes While Singing Sweetly of the Prairie." *People*, February 27, 1989.

Green, Douglas B. *Country Roots*. New York: Hawthorne, 1976.

———. *Singing in the Saddle*. Nashville: Vanderbilt University Press and the Country Music Foundation, 2002.

Griffis, Ken. *Hear My Song: The Story of the Celebrated Sons of the Pioneers*. Northglenn, Colo.: Norken, 2000.

Hall, Wade. *Hell-Bent for Music: The Life of Pee Wee King*. Lexington: University Press of Kentucky, 1996.

Harrison, Nigel. *Songwriters: A Biographical Dictionary with Discographies*. Jefferson, N.C.: McFarland, 1998.

Hopper, Lawrence. *Bob Nolan: A Biographical Guide and Annotations to the Lyric Archive at the University of North Carolina, Chapel Hill*. Limited publication by Paul Lawrence Hopper, 2000.

Kingsbury, Paul, ed. *The Encyclopedia of Country Music*. New York: Oxford University Press, 1998.

Lomax, John A., and Alan Lomax. *Cowboy Songs and Other Frontier Ballads*. New York: Collier Books, 1986.

Malone, Bill, and Judith McCulloh, eds. *Stars of Country Music*. New York: Da Capo Press, 1975.

Malone, Bill C. *Singing Cowboys and Musical Mountaineers: Southern Culture and the Roots of Country Music*. Athens, Ga.: University of Georgia Press, 1993.

McCloud, Barry, ed. *Definitive Country: The Ultimate Encyclopedia of Country Music and Its Performers*. New York: Perigree, 1995.

O'Neal, Bill. *Ritter, Tex: America's Most Beloved Cowboy*. Austin, Texas: Eakin Press, 1998.

Oermann, Robert K. "The Ride of their Lives: Riders In The Sky Handle Success the Cowboy Way." *Nashville Tennessean*, October 14, 1995.

Pender, Linda. "Urban Cowboys: It's Happy Trails to You at the Emery Theater." *Cincinnati Magazine,* August 1990.

Phillips, Robert W. *Roy Rogers.* Jefferson, N.C.: McFarland, 1995.

Riders In The Sky (Too Slim, Ranger Doug, and Woody Paul) with Texas Bix Bender. *Riders In The Sky: The Book.* Salt Lake City: Gibbs Smith, Peregrine Smith Books, 1992.

Roland, Tom. "Santana's Supernatural Night Spices up a Grammy Show with Lots of Latin Sizzle." *Nashville Tennessean,* February 24, 2000.

Rothel, David. *The Gene Autry Book.* Madison, N.C.: Empire, 1988.

———. *The Roy Rogers Book.* Madison, N.C.: Empire, 1996.

Stambler, Irwin, and Grelun Landon. *Country Music: The Encyclopedia.* New York: St. Martin's Press, 1997.

Tinsley, Jim Bob. *For a Cowboy Has to Sing.* Orlando: University of Central Florida Press, 1991.

———. *He Was Singin' This Song.* Orlando: University of Central Florida Press, 1981.

Whitburn, Joel. *Top 40 Country Hits: 1944–Present.* New York: Billboard Books, 1996.

———. *Top Country Albums 1964–1997.* Menomonee Falls, Wisc.: Record Research, 1997.

———. *Top Country Singles 1944–1988.* Menomonee Falls, Wisc.: Record Research, 1989.

———. *Top Pop Singles: 1955–1990.* Menomonee Falls, Wisc. Record Research, 1991.

Zimmerman, David. "Hip Country Pops a Clever-Humor Cork." *USA Today,* January 17, 1989.